ON OUR WATCH
The Race to Save Australia's Environment

NICOLA MARKUS

MELBOURNE
UNIVERSITY
PRESS

MELBOURNE UNIVERSITY PRESS
An imprint of Melbourne University Publishing Limited
187 Grattan Street, Carlton, Victoria 3053, Australia
mup-info@unimelb.edu.au
www.mup.com.au

First published 2009
Text © Nicola Markus 2009
Design and typography © Melbourne University Publishing Ltd 2009

Photographs courtesy of WWF-Australia
Text design by Phil Campbell
Cover design by Nada Backovic Designs
Typeset by Sonya Murphy, TypeSkill
Printed by Griffin Press, SA

National Library of Australia Cataloguing-in-Publication entry

On our watch / Nicola Markus.

9780522855951 (pbk.)

    Includes index.
    Bibliography.

    Nature conservation—Political aspects—Australia.
    Plant conservation—Law and legislation—Australia.
    Wildlife conservation—Law and legislation—Australia.
    Endangered species—Government policy—Australia

333.720994

Mixed Sources
Product group from well-managed forests and other controlled sources
www.fsc.org Cert no. SGS-COC-005088
© 1996 Forest Stewardship Council

PURVES
ENVIRONMENTAL FUND

CONTENTS

PREFACE

The decision to write this book was drawn from conversations with people from a range of cultural and professional backgrounds and the realisation that the public's understanding of the conservation challenges Australia faces is often alarmingly poor. Many people are aware of issues such as land clearing, salinity and species loss, but only a few seem to have a sense of the scale and extent of those issues, their long-term implications and the effort needed to deal with them effectively. There is uncertainty about who is responsible for conserving our landscapes, and there is little sense of ownership of the impacts—direct and indirect—that our personal lifestyles have on this continent's unique and fragile landscapes. Yet understanding this connection has never been more important.

The first decade of the new millennium has presented us with a future far less comfortable and secure than the one we had anticipated. The rattling and hissing of the planet's pressure valves through drought, climate change, terrorism and an ever-increasing global population has become impossible to ignore. But while issues of terrorism and population growth are likely to remain in the domains of international politics and religion, the fate of the environment depends on the lifestyle choices of individuals and the message those choices send to our governments and industries. Although public awareness of the environment has never been higher, awareness is of no value if no action is taken.

Climate change is already taking its toll on Australia's environment: our alpine regions, coasts, savannas and the Great Barrier Reef are severely affected, and parts of these landscapes will be lost forever. But how many and how soon is as yet undecided—at this stage all may not yet be lost. Like the human body, our planet has its best chance of coping with major change if any additional stresses are minimised.

What we take for granted in this age of comfort and consumption comes at the expense of our natural environment. For me, a biologist with a lifelong passion for wildlife, plants and the breathtaking diversity of life, the rapid unravelling of the fabric of nature of which we are but one stubborn fibre is heartbreaking. The need to protect our landscapes becomes more urgent even as it slips further from our reach with each passing year. Extinction is forever. So what are we waiting for?

INTRODUCTION

A Day in the Year of the Dog

In 2006 the topic of climate change reached a global tipping point. In late October an independent report on the economics of climate change by the English economist Sir Nicholas Stern achieved what thousands of scientific reports until then had not: it drew the attention of politicians the world over. The review estimated that if no action was taken to deal with man-made contributions to climate change— that is, adhering to a business-as-usual approach—the consequences would equate to losing up to one-fifth of the global gross domestic product (GDP) each year, forever. But by reducing greenhouse gas emissions—the major cause of the current episode of climate change—the cost would be around only 1 per cent of the global GDP per year.[1] Given the faith placed in formal economic models by the world's capitalist economies, this presented the most convincing argument yet for the need for immediate action.

The Stern Report put the economic ramifications of climate change on the table. It was not, however, the only paper released that year that would have long-reaching consequences for the environment. Closer to home, barely a month later, there was other news. But rather than signalling action, it did something quite different, and its release was perhaps more under the table than on it.

Thursday 7 December 2006 was a dog day in the aptly named year in the Chinese astrological calendar for the many conservation professionals and volunteers (scientists, land managers, bureaucrats, NGOs, bushcare and landcare groups) committed to combating the alarming decline of Australia's iconic flora and fauna. On that day, the then federal Liberal government passed a bill to amend its *Environment Protection and Biodiversity Conservation Act 1999* (*EPBC Act*), one of the potentially strongest vices in Australia's political conservation toolbox.

The timing of this announcement was carefully chosen in the safe knowledge that, in the flurry of the usual pre-Christmas bustle, few people would take note of such an apparently minor event. As it turned out, this prediction proved to be true. But although the event slipped by all but unnoticed by the public, the media and most politicians, it was the day when hope for species protection under the Howard regime all but collapsed. Quietly and without fanfare, the primary legal foundation on which Australia's native landscapes and its many inhabitants depend had been injected with enough concrete cancer to guarantee it would crumble into useless fragments if pressure were applied. Never mind that such pressure was most likely to come as a response to the same factors that had warranted the drafting of the Act in the first place such as poor farming practices; unsuitable and thirsty crops; marginal pastoralism; relentless commercial development of sensitive ecosystems; and the destructive effects of myriad mining operations that, despite being comparatively contained in area, often destroy invaluable landscapes. With the passing of these amendments, the committed and active protection of Australia's large number of threatened species and landscapes— particularly those on land coveted by industry—had been ostensibly ruled out. This day provided confirmation that my decision to take time out from the conservation frontline was sensible, and the plan for this book began to take shape.

The weakened protection the Act now offered to the thousands of threatened Australian plants and animals was a stinging signal of the Howard government's diminishing commitment to the natural environment and its short-sighted support of big business in the form of mining and commercial development.

To the government's great advantage was the fact that environment law is often poorly understood by the people who would otherwise be well placed to lobby strongly in its defence. Many conservation professionals, scientists in particular, would rather leave the cumbersome tomes of law to the relevant legal experts while they continued to focus on practical conservation efforts. To anyone with an eye on the bigger picture, however, the importance of environment legislation cannot be overstated. Weak law equals poor protection, and this becomes all too apparent when its protective legal mechanisms are tested (such as applications to develop yet further precious coastal ecosystems) and fail to hold up against interests whose detrimental impacts on the environment they are supposed to guard against.

Environment legislation is critical to defend the many living systems that are fundamental to our survival and that of many other species. Although there are a number of species and nature-focused Acts that apply across different regions of this country, a federal Act is particularly important because it determines conservation priorities on a national scale and can provide the impetus to channel substantial resources towards them.

When the *EPBC Act* first came into effect in July 2000, it was hailed as a vast improvement on any previous environment legislation. Having identified threatened species and ecological communities as two of seven 'matters of national environmental significance', to its supporters it promised to deliver through maintaining functional landscapes and protecting Australia's natural heritage for the future.

The Act provided several avenues for guiding and regulating activities that could impact on the environment. Its most basic role was as a yardstick for the health of Australian landscapes, which used the conservation status of birds, mammals, reptiles, amphibians, invertebrates, fish and plants as indicators of their habitats' health. To fulfil this role, the Act listed species and ecological communities threatened with extinction *and* the factors that threaten them.

A second, and potentially highly powerful, avenue for species protection was that of identifying and listing habitat critical to the survival of those species under greatest threat. Once defined and clearly marked on accessible maps, 'critical habitat' would by definition warrant the highest level of protection. Given the considerable number of plants and animals that qualify as 'critically endangered' or 'endangered' nationally, a list of critical habitat would provide information that had been lacking as a clear focus for previous conservation efforts. With the proper administration (and therein lay the crux) this provision of the Act had real potential for regulating development and thereby preventing the extinction of species now dependent on specific patches of remnant habitat.

One of the most valuable features of the *EPBC Act* was a set of provisions to assess and thereafter accept, amend or reject, activities that could impact on the matters of environmental significance—world and national heritage locations, Ramsar wetlands, migratory species, Commonwealth marine areas and nuclear actions (including uranium mining). A range of activities could be included, though the emphasis would be on the careful assessment of activities most likely to affect the environment in commercial industries such as mining, forestry, agriculture, fisheries and urban development. The intent of the Act was to ensure that a healthy natural environment could exist alongside these industries, and so conservation professionals' expectations were high.

In 2005, however, a performance assessment of the Act conducted by the Australia Institute found that it had failed to produce 'any noticeable improvements in environmental outcomes'.[2] As it turned out, few potential powers of this legislation had been realised, and even the upkeep of its information features had been badly neglected. Lists of threatened species had not been well maintained, critical habitats had not been identified, and the assessments of activities most likely to impact detrimentally on the environment had yielded little to affect those activities. It soon became apparent that the listing of threatened species was influenced by the politics of the day, particularly where such listings could impact commercial interests.

When the commercially fished, highly valuable and demonstrably threatened southern blue-fin tuna failed to be listed under the Act in 2005[3], it had been common knowledge that the over-fishing of adults and juveniles had led to a dramatic decline—and the rapid reduction of fishing quotas—by the mid 1980s.[4] But despite acknowledging the radical decline of the tuna due to unsustainable fishing practices, the Howard government's unwillingness to curtail the operations of the southern blue-fin tuna fishery failed to protect the fish as well as the flagging fishery, which will soon be forced to focus on a different catch.

Another disappointment in the administration of the *EPBC Act* was its failure to list the many threatened ecological communities in need of active protection. Despite the government's own assessment and acknowledgment in 2002 that more than 2800 ecological communities—the associations of plants, wildlife and the natural processes they depend on—were threatened and in urgent need of listing[5], by July 2005 no more than ten plant and wildlife communities had been placed on the list. (In 2001, environment minister Senator Robert Hill had earmarked 500 communities for urgent listing. Five years later they had still not been included.)

The greatest disappointment, though, was the lack of recognition of habitat areas critical to the survival of threatened species. By July 2005 (and indeed as of September 2008), of the 150 animals and 585 plants federally recognised as threatened with extinction ('critically endangered' or 'endangered')[6], only *five* had had 'critical habitat' identified and listed; three of these were on offshore islands, areas unlikely to be contested by future activity proposals. Furthermore, it transpired that critical habitat could only legally be protected on Commonwealth lands, a situation that reduced incentives for pursuing critical habitat listings on land of any other tenure.

In light of this ignoble track record, independent organisations such as the Australian Network of Environmental Defenders Offices (ANEDO), the Australia Institute, WWF-Australia and the Humane Society International (HSI) were understandably apprehensive about the mooted 410-page amendments of 2007. Their suspicions were justified. With the passing of these amendments, the federal environment minister's powers of discretion would increase, while the transparency and public accountability of the government in matters of environmental decision-making would decrease. Perhaps the most alarming changes to the Act were those relating to the critically important assessment and approval processes of activities with the potential to harm the environment; the united view of conservation organisations was that the amendments would be 'knee-capping' the federal environmental law.[7] And in responding to a revealing government memorandum that stated one of several particular aims to be to 'reduce processing time and cost for development interests'[8], the Australian Network of Environmental Defenders Offices expressed concern that 'The attempt to cater for "development interests" must not be at the expense of accountability, public participation and full consideration of environmental impacts'.[9] In short, placing development interests before the protection of nature is not the role of environment law.

Some distance from Canberra, on Victoria's and New South Wales' High Plains, lives one of only two hibernating marsupials in the world. The mountain pygmy possum is a tiny marsupial with a dense coat of greyish fur and a long tail that lives in snow-covered alpine and sub-alpine regions. It is found in two separate subpopulations in Victoria and only one in New South Wales. The species' entire range is restricted to an area of less than six square kilometres above an altitude of 1400 metres.[10] As a specialist in this narrow environment, the diminutive forty-gram marsupial relies on the stability of its habitat and is therefore highly vulnerable to change. It particularly relies on a stable cover of winter snow, which acts as insulation and keeps it warm during hibernation, but in a country where snow is at a premium and winter sports are a popular pastime, this means that the mountain pygmy possum's small and restricted habitat is prime real estate for developers.

Needless to say, mountain pygmy possums and the alpine ski resorts at Falls Creek and Mounts Buller, Hotham[11], Blue Cow and Charlotte's Pass are uneasy bedfellows. For a small marsupial adapted to life among the shelter and crevices of heath-covered boulder slopes, the activities of commercial resort developments are bad news. The most obvious detrimental impact is the outright destruction of its habitat. Heavy machinery used to create infrastructure such as roads, car parks, buildings, pipes and ski trails inevitably causes massive damage, which is further compounded by the human traffic during the ski season. And other, subtler changes in the landscape affect the animal too. Once machinery has disturbed part of a scree slope or removed the native heath, feral animals and weeds move in, leaving the possums exposed to cats and foxes, and rock crevices to be invaded by noxious weeds such as blackberry and English broom. Where construction takes place upslope of possum habitat, run-off and sedimentation can clog the scree and further invade the habitat that is critical for the animal's shelter.

The full impacts of development are not always immediately obvious but can emerge over time. At Mount Buller in Victoria, the local population of pygmy possums declined from 300 breeding females when first monitored in 1996 to forty in 2004. The declines followed the construction of a large new chairlift in 1998. Found to have breached their proposal, the developers were forced to sign a conservation agreement and invest substantially in the rehabilitation of the damaged possum habitat. However, this investment came late in the piece. By 2005, only six breeding females remained in a subpopulation that was by then effectively 'extinct in the wild' and reliant on captive breeding to survive.[12]

At Mount Blue Cow in New South Wales, the census of mountain pygmy possums conducted annually between 1986 and 1999 had reliably found a population that revolved around twenty-nine breeding females. A sharp decline in this population was first noted in 2000, when only thirteen breeding females were found; by 2004, this number had plummeted to only two females. This sudden decline in numbers was attributed to a range of development-related factors that had resulted in an increase of feral cats.[13] After the rigorous control of cat numbers, the pygmy possums recovered to eleven breeding females by 2007; the survival of this subpopulation necessitates on-going cat management, but even that may not be enough when considering the additional pressures it confronts through low snow cover and fierce wildfires.

The ample evidence of the detrimental impacts of business development on flagship species such as the mountain pygmy possum makes it plain that *any* development within naturally restricted habitats must be stringently regulated and rigorously monitored if such vulnerable, iconic animals and all that share its habitat are to survive. Development assessments under relevant environment legislation need to consider the full scope of the likely impacts of the project. Considerations must include the status of the species, the past impacts of similar development, the extent and location of the proposed development and the development process itself, with the firm aim of ensuring that development will cause no further declines of this threatened species.

Victoria's last remaining stronghold of the mountain pygmy possum is at Mount Hotham, which still sustains a population of around 800 breeding females. Drawing on past experience, the critical management issue for this subpopulation and the species (as identified by Victoria's Department of Sustainability and Environment) is the conservation of the possums within the Mount Hotham Alpine Resort.[14] In 2006, the business group that owns this resort proposed a substantial redevelopment and expansion. Once completed, it was to include more than forty new luxury apartments, a large complex featuring a day spa, retail outlets, a cinema, restaurants and bars and 500 new car-parking spaces. Part of a revised plan for the redevelopment was the additional rerouting of the main road, but to enable this, the development would require an amendment of the relevant planning scheme.[15] Despite the sensitivity of the Mount Hotham area, the poor conservation record of other mountain pygmy possum populations and the deep concerns by scientists and conservation organisations on examining the proposal, the expansion of the resort (including the rerouting of the road) was approved in July 2006.[16] No comprehensive environmental impact study was undertaken and, despite the massive landscape alterations proposed, the developer's submission was considered to be sufficient assurance that the possum population would be fine.

The consequences of poorly administered or weak environment legislation are dire. Despite having been listed under four separate Acts—the *Environment Protection and Biodiversity Conservation Act 1999*, its predecessor the *Endangered Species Protection Act 1992*, Victoria's *Flora and Fauna Guarantee Act 1988*, New South Wales' *Threatened Species Conservation Act 1995*—none has prevented the mountain pygmy possum's rapid decline. And with the *EPBC Act*'s amendments announced on 7 December 2006, the possum's prospects had in no way improved.

The mountain pygmy possum's populations are already fragmented and depleted, but today this animal's precarious existence is even more at risk from the rising temperatures and declining snow cover brought on by climate change—something which even the most stringent environment laws cannot control. Studies have determined that an increase of one degree Celsius will be enough to drive it to extinction[17], which means this unique Australian alpine dweller is unlikely to survive my lifetime. And tragic as this loss will be, it is further amplified by the irony that the extensive tourist developments of the alpine regions that threaten the possum's survival are themselves vulnerable to the effects of climate change and will also suffer (economically) from declining snowfalls.

Part I

HOW WE GOT HERE

1

THE BIG DRY

There is no arguing that the reality of climate change has helped thrust environmental issues back into public debate after a long absence. And back home on the driest habitable continent on Earth, there has been a related and readily apparent environmental issue to consider: drought.

In 2006, after years of below average rainfall and the continued over-allocation of limited water supplies to agriculture, parts of southern Australia experienced their driest conditions on record.[1] For Australia's rural farming community extended periods of drought are a recurring challenge, predicated to a large degree by the patterns of the El Niño–La Niña weather cycle. But while it is farmers who generally bear the brunt of weather extremes, the profound absence of rain (clocked up to ten years in some parts of the country) had etched itself into the con-sciousness of *all* Australians; the lack of water in the catchments that supply the major cities ensured that nobody was left untouched.

Somewhat surprisingly, in terms of the size and number of existing dams and reservoirs around the country, Australians have the highest per capita water storage capacity in the world.[2] What we don't have is a reliable water supply to fill it.

In late 2001 dam levels in the Sydney region dropped from an average of around 80 per cent capacity to less than half that by November

2006. Warragamba Dam, 65 kilometres west of Sydney, is the city's main water supply and one of the world's largest domestic dams. When full, it contains four times the volume of water of Sydney Harbour and supplies around four-fifths of Sydney's water. By early 2007, the dam's water level had dropped to one-third of its capacity and debate raged about the future of water among politicians and their constituents.

While water levels in Sydney provided cause for serious concern, the situation in regions of Queensland was downright frightening. As rain had evaded the catchments for a number of years, water restrictions had become increasingly stringent. Wivenhoe Dam, with its catchment extending over 5554 square kilometres, is the largest of three dams supplying Brisbane and its surrounds in south-east Queensland. By October 2006, Wivenhoe's water level had dropped to a quarter of its capacity; in November 2007, it was around 20 per cent and Brisbane water restrictions reached an unprecedented Level 6.[3] Queensland's famously relaxed outdoor lifestyle was compromised as residents were forced to cut back on domestic water use by almost a third. Lawns and gardens could only be hand-hosed for one hour per week, and council permission to fill a new or renovated pool was only granted if the owners compensated by installing other water-saving measures in their households.[4]

Urban wildlife residents were also affected. Birds usually lively and active through the day such as noisy miners, lorikeets and grey butcher-birds now sheltered beneath shrubs, dishevelled, open-beaked and panting. Even common garden skinks, among the hardiest of native creatures, appeared on doorsteps seeking moisture from household pets' water bowls. As south-east Queensland residents anxiously followed media updates on the water crisis, many pondered the long-term implications to the fastest growing region of urban development in the country, which is expected to gain an extra one million residents over the next twenty years.[5]

On the other side of the continent, the water situation in urban Perth was just as serious. Unlike Queensland, which expects most rain in the summer months, Perth relies on substantial winter rain to fill its dams and recharge its aquifers. Approximately 60 per cent of Perth's water comes from underground aquifers (porous rock layers that store water), while the remainder comes from dams in the Darling Ranges and the south-west of the state.[6] While the population and water usage in and around Perth continues to increase (fed by the current mining boom), annual winter rainfall has declined by up to 20 per cent over the last thirty years, halving the run-off of water that feeds rivers, streams, dams and aquifers.[7] Between 2001 and 2004 the water supply dropped to such critical levels that radical solutions were considered. Among them was a plan to construct a 2500-kilometre pipeline to channel water from the Kimberley region in the north to Perth at a cost of $2 billion. While this idea appeared to be technically feasible, the project cost would have resulted in an astronomical increase in the cost of domestic water supply—by up to 400 per cent—and was therefore dismissed as uneconomical.

A year of average rainfall allowed for only a slight recovery in 2005, before 2006 became the driest year since Western Australian records began in 1876.[8] And by February 2007 dam levels had dropped to a combined average of less than 25 per cent.

★ ★ ★

The prolonged absence of rain has exacted a considerable toll across the entire Australian community. While restricted urban water supplies were (and remain) apparent in our major cities (Brisbane, Sydney, Canberra, Melbourne, Adelaide and Perth), rural production has been most severely affected across the Murray–Darling Basin and the Snowy River catchment in the east, and in the agricultural areas in the west of the country.

The Murray–Darling Basin spans more than one-eighth of the continent. It includes large parts of three eastern states, South Australia and the entire Australian Capital Territory[9]; it also includes Australia's three largest rivers—the Murray, the Darling and the Murrumbidgee—and their tributaries. This vast region accounts for more than 40 per cent (around $4.5 billion per annum) of the country's gross value of agricultural production, justifying its reputation as the nation's food basket.

Around 3 million people are directly dependent on its water[10], while many more around the country and internationally, through a number of export markets, rely on the fresh produce it yields.

The yields of the Basin, however, come at a huge cost. Irrigation in this region alone consumes a staggering 75 per cent of the water used in Australia. A number of water-intensive industries such as cotton, rice, horticulture and dairy help account for this extraordinary figure and pits them squarely against the interests of the natural environment. In September 2008, this conflict was reflected in the federal and New South Wales governments' purchase of Toorale Station in the north-west of the state. Located at the junction of the Darling and Warrego rivers, the 91 000-hectare station holds 20 billion litres of water and was permitted to extract 14 billion litres each year. The Rudd government's decision to act decisively and buy this station differed markedly from the position of the Liberal Party, which remained more concerned with the socio-economic impacts of such farm closures than with the environmental imperative to return water to the dying landscape.[11]

Drought has had a marked impact on this region, but the Murray–Darling Basin's value in agricultural and economic terms is easily matched and exceeded by its natural values. The Basin contains a wide range of different ecosystems that incorporate temperate and semi-arid grasslands, acacia and eucalypt woodlands, dense eucalypt forests and even alpine regions, and it is home to many unique plants and animals. The species that are among the most threatened live in the deltaic (low-lying) semi-permanent wetlands—of which the Basin is home to 30 000—that normally spring to life when rivers and creeks burst their banks following ample rains in the catchments. Before the damming of the rivers for agriculture, the water regimes of the Basin were extremely variable. The flow of its rivers, which originate mainly from run-off from the western slopes of the Great Dividing Range, could fluctuate from almost ten times their average one year to less than 5 per cent of that average in another.[12]

In addition to the many resident waterbirds such as egrets, herons, spoonbills, ducks and brolgas, these wetlands are vital habitats for birds that travel thousands of kilometres each year from Siberia, northern China and Alaska to escape the harsh northern winter. Frequent visitors include red-necked stints, sharp-tailed and curlewed sandpipers as well as resident stilts, avocets, plovers, pelicans, many species of duck and the rare fairy tern. The Basin's rich biodiversity and its role in supporting the waterbirds has resulted in twelve of the Basin's wetlands—including the Narran Lake and Macquarie Marshes nature reserves, and the Gwydir and Coorong wetlands—being recognised under the Ramsar Convention's List of Wetlands of International Importance.[13] This international treaty, with 158 signatory parties including Australia, promotes the wise use of wetlands and their resources as critical factors in the sustainability of development.

The Murray–Darling Basin has always been a sumptuous haven on this otherwise dry continent. Once richly populated by almost half of the country's birds, a quarter of its mammals and a fifth of its reptiles, extensive changes to the Basin since European settlement have cost it its wildlife.[14] Twenty of the Basin's mammals are now extinct, with scores more heading towards the same fate.

★ ★ ★

Water is essential for all forms of life. On the driest habitable continent on Earth, much of Australia's flora and fauna has evolved to cope with the high temperatures and limited or unpredictable rainfall that have been the norm across three-quarters of the continent. But not all native species are so resilient. In a country where drought and natural water shortages are the order of the day, the conservation of the natural environment relies on water policy that sets the price of water to reflect the needs of the landscapes ahead of those of industry. Water use and water allocation are discussed later, but before agricultural practices are investigated it is necessary to consider how the presence or absence of water is, and will continue to be, the most defining force in shaping Australia's living landscapes.

2

A SNAPSHOT OF AUSTRALIA

When Captain James Cook first set foot on Australian shores at Botany Bay in April 1770, the coastal stretches of land he saw made a favourable impression. He noted that 'The woods are free from undergrowth of every kind and the trees are at such a distance from one another that the whole country or at least a great part of it might be cultivated'.[1]

This early perception determined not only the location of the first convict settlement but also set high expectations of the continent's suitability for settlement and agriculture. What Cook could not have known was that his impression was not representative of the whole; that Australia's geological history had left most of the country with ancient and tired soils lacking the rich nutrients fundamental to much of Europe's agriculture.

Over thousands of millions of years the rifting and stretching of Gondwana—through cycles of rising and receding sea levels and emerging and eroding mountain chains—shaped the landmass that, around 45 million years ago, broke away to become its own continent. While at first the land was still swathed in rainforest, the continent's fluctuating climates gradually became drier. Over time, rainforest gave way to drier forests, woodlands and grasslands, and wildlife was forced to adapt to these new and demanding environments. As seasonal aridity and reduced rainfall favoured open and drier vegetation, this in turn provided fuel for ferocious lightning-caused fires that swept across the land. Fire soon became a major force in shaping Australia's landscapes, and plants had to develop ingenious strategies for fire tolerance and greater resilience—the evolution of a larger variety of hardy eucalypts is one such example.

Good quality soils are the result of past volcanic activity, and unfortunately Australia has experienced little of this. An exception is the Great Dividing Range, where basalt-enriched volcanic soils formed the foundation for the rich forest ecosystems that Cook had encountered. Had he had been aware of how deceptive his first impressions really were, would he still have recommended Australia as a suitable place for a penal colony?

The reality is that Cook's advice was taken and 220 years have passed since British settlement—barely a blip in the history of the planet but plenty of time to alter the natural fabric of a continent. Enough time, for instance, for the population to increase from around 750 000 to 20.7 million—and for the numbers of indigenous Australians to fall from 100 per cent to around 2.5 per cent.[2] More than enough time to establish major industries, cultivate the limited arable land and populate the habitable coast. Enough time, too, to clear vast tracts of the landscape, trigger significant soil erosion, salinity and acidification, degrade wetlands and waterways, introduce foreign plants and animals and cause the extinction of more than one hundred plant and wildlife species. Enough time, therefore, to leave an indelible footprint on an ancient and fragile continent.

★ ★ ★

In the past fifty years, Australia's population has more than doubled, and by 2050 it is expected to reach around 28 million people.[3] Given the continent's considerable size of 7.6 million square kilometres, this figure might seem modest when compared with the populations of other countries. Excluding Alaska, the mainland United States, for example, is comparable in size and accommodates 297 million inhabitants, more than ten times as many as Australia. India, with a landmass of only 2.9 million square kilometres is home to over one billion people and grows 1.38 per cent per year.[4] Even the United Kingdom, one-thirtieth the size of Australia, has more than twice as many inhabitants (60.6 million). And yet the impact of the comparatively small number of resident Australians now exceeds what the environment can provide or absorb.

An 'ecological footprint' is the measure commonly used to assess and compare levels of consumption. It includes the area of productive land and water needed to provide all the resources we use and absorb the waste we produce. The resources each of us consumes include plant- and animal-derived foods as well as fibres, timber, minerals, coal, oil and fossil-fuel derived products such as plastics; our waste comprises everything we discard that is not reused or recycled.

In 2003, it was estimated that the total capacity of the world's productive areas could accommodate a footprint of 1.8 global hectares per person.[5] The actual levels of consumption across the planet, however, vary greatly from this recommended maximum. Per capita, the footprint produced by India's more than one billion people was less than 1 global hectare per person. Not so in the developed countries. The USA came in at a staggering 9.6 global hectares per head, while the UK had a less hefty 5.6 global hectares per person.[6] Australia, shamefully, had an average footprint of 6.6 global hectares per person.[7] What this statistic meant is that we are consuming more than three and a half times what the world's resources can supply and we had the sixth largest ecological footprint among the 150 countries assessed.

In 2002 the Commonwealth Scientific and Industrial Research Organisation (CSIRO) modelled the impacts of three domestic population growth scenarios by 2050. The potential options included low growth (maintaining the current population levels of around 20 million people), medium growth (25 million) and high growth (32 million), and the scenarios factored in implications for finite resources such as fish stocks, freshwater, oil and air quality in major cities.[8] Under the low population scenario advocated by many environmental groups, issues of environmental quality (air, household water use) stabilise, but the pressures on health care and pension systems from an ageing population would necessitate structural changes to maintain economic growth. Under the medium growth scenario, which approximates the current immigration rates and assumes a stable population after 2050, resource use and environmental pressures continue to grow. Here, 'aggressive and positive action' is needed to address failing marine fisheries, declining biodiversity and land and water degradation, as well as to restrict urban expansion in capital cities, lower carbon transport and energy options, and redirect short-term economic gains from gas and oil resources into environmentally sustainable options. The third scenario, one promoted by many business leaders, politicians and economic analysts, projected a growth of 32 million by 2050 (and 50 million people by 2100). The key challenge here is to prevent triggering a condition termed 'hyper-materiality', which is a continuously growing loop of construction and consumption. In a press release one of the report's authors, Barney Foran, identified infrastructure, lifestyle, energy use and international trade and technology as areas in need of review to reduce the energy and materials consumed by Australians.[9] In other words, almost every aspect of our everyday lives needed to be re-evaluated.

The WWF's Living Planet Report uses a number of indicators to measure an ecological footprint (per person/per country):

- proportion of built-up land
- amount of nuclear energy consumed
- amount of carbon emissions released by burning fossil fuels (often referred to as our 'carbon footprint')
- area of croplands, grazing lands, forests and fishing grounds required to supply the food
- quantity of fibre and timber consumed.[10]

Many consumable goods are imported, so a country's footprint has to factor in the areas needed to produce these, wherever they occur on the planet.[11]

The fossil fuels that supply our electricity and our transport systems comprise the largest part of the footprint of Australians. Coal-fired electricity and the carbon emissions from cars, trucks and planes are a key driver of climate change. A large proportion of these emissions is generated by the daily long-distance transport of food from remote rural regions or rangelands to cities' dining tables, often located thousands of kilometres away.

Apart from carbon emissions, our ecological footprint is also defined by the land and living resources needed to produce the many things we consume. More than three-quarters of Australia's water is used by the agricultural–pastoral sectors and, as consumers of the products this water yields (plus household water), Australians are the thirteenth-highest water consumers in the world!

And our record gets worse. Approximately one-third of our combined footprint comes from eating meat, in particular beef. Meat requires vast amounts of water and land to produce it, and is transported over large distance to end up on our tables.[12] Of higher impact still, the large amount of water needed to produce pasture and crops for dairy cows makes milk, butter, yoghurt and cheese extremely expensive in environmental terms. According to the Australian Conservation Foundation's estimates in 2000, the dairy industry used a quarter of all water consumed in Australia in that year.[13] Who would have thought that the humble cow could exact such a toll from the environment?

Everything we buy, whether manufactured or grown, has an impact on the natural environment. Clothes, toys, cars, whitegoods, power tools and electrical and electronic appliances, furniture and decorative knick-knacks all require land, water, materials and electricity to be produced.

The clothing industry, for example, has a large footprint due to the amount of land, water and energy needed to make new clothes, and the impact of chemicals used to produce fibres such as cotton, which then leach into the natural landscape. Estimates of the water used to produce the clothing bought annually by an average Australian household run to around 150 000 litres—without ever turning on a tap.[14] Far from being linked only to the purchase of luxury items, our individual footprint grows quite inadvertently as we go about our daily lives.

At the other end of all this consumption is the waste that our (bad) habits produce. Hazardous waste, whitegoods, oil, plastics and packaging, and all the other items we acquire and then throw away. According to the Australian government, more than a million computers and 2.5 million major appliances are discarded each year and most of them end up in landfill.[15] Each Australian produces more than 1.6 tonnes of solid waste each year, over half of which ends up in landfill.[16] Australians are among the highest waste producers in the world, despite adopting recycling practices in recent years. On Clean Up Australia Day in 2007, more than 8000 tonnes of rubbish were retrieved from rivers, creeks, bays, beaches, parks and other public spaces around the country.[17] It's time to change these thoughtless habits. Considering the multiple environmental costs of producing raw materials, using them to manufacture goods and then discarding them, the merits of repairing, recycling and reusing objects whenever possible are obvious.

★ ★ ★

The clearing of native forests, woodlands and grasslands for agriculture and residential development, and the resulting fragmentation of the remaining vegetation into isolated pockets, continues to be the main threat to Australia's biodiversity. Since European settlement, around one-third of the natural landscape has been cleared or modified in the intensively used regions of the country.[18]

Most of Australia's population is concentrated into cities and towns and the majority of Australians live within 50 kilometres of the coast.[19] The highest densities of people are found in and around our coastal cities and with the growing trend to 'sea-change' living, pressures on the coastal environment are immense, especially where residential development competes with agriculture for arable land.

On the east coast development pressures from urban expansion are concentrated in two main regions: the greater Sydney region between

Wollongong and Newcastle, and the Queensland–New South Wales border region, ranging from Byron Bay north to Hervey Bay.[20] Sydney's Pittwater Spotted Gum Forest is an example of an ecological community threatened by a steady urban creep. The community once occupied stretches of open forest on the Barrenjoey Peninsula and the western Pittwater foreshores that now house some of Sydney's most exclusive waterfront suburbs. Growing on well-drained, shale-derived soils, the forest consisted of tall spotted gums, grey ironbarks, smooth and rough-barked apples (*Angophoras*) and other trees and shrubs that were rich sources of nectar and pollen and habitat for an abundance of wildlife. Possums, gliders, koalas, wombats and wallabies roamed as freely here as skinks, snakes and goannas, and fruit- and insect-eating bats and birds, including delicate honeyeaters and raucous cockatoos. Today, only sparse patches of woodland remain, carefully protected within a national park.

The causes of the spotted gum forest's decline are typical of those of other coastal ecosystems: clearing for residential development results in soil erosion from stormwater run-off, which leaves any undeveloped patches in poor condition. The invasion of weeds such as lantana and morning glory soon follows and any remaining remnants of bush become isolated and degraded. Additionally, the build-up of dead and dry vegetation in remnant bushland can fuel destructive wildfires (or fires lit by arsonists) that are hotter and/or more frequent than native vegetation communities can withstand. And the illegal dumping of rubbish and the mowing and grazing of bush areas also makes it harder for the native plants to recover. Bit by bit, the native forest is either lost or reduced to motley patches among the expanding suburbs; populations of native wildlife are separated and their vulnerability to hazards like fire and traffic or predation by cats, dogs and foxes is increased.

Along the coasts of northern New South Wales and south-east Queensland, the climate is mild and the rainfall was traditionally reliable. In this region, endangered ecosystems include freshwater wetlands and coastal floodplains, littoral rainforest, lowland rainforest and subtropical coastal floodplain forest. All have been extensively cleared, and the floodplains have been drained and filled in and the land developed for holidaymakers and sea-changers; only 10 per cent of the wetlands remains.[21] The once extensive paperbark ti-tree forests that are vital for communities of nectar-feeders have suffered, as have the wallum heath wetlands, home to the remarkable 'acid frog', specially adapted to its acidic water habitat. No fewer than 169 native species in this area are recognised to be under threat of extinction under New South Wales legislation with additional species in Queensland. The birds include the barking owl, brolga, Albert's lyrebird and the broad-billed sandpiper with many species of insectivorous and nectar-feeding bats, and other tree- and ground-dwelling mammals such as the koala, the long-nosed potoroo, the rufous bettong, the squirrel glider and the yellow-bellied glider. The numbers of frogs, skinks and fish are also declining, as are those of many unique plants including the brown fairy-chain orchid, Davidson's plum, the fine-leaved tuckeroo and the giant fern.[22]

Just north of this border, in the hinterlands of the Gold and Sunshine coasts, expanses of majestic subtropical rainforest that once featured gigantic strangler figs, the exquisite Coxen's fig parrot, the giant barred frog and the stunning Richmond birdwing butterfly have been replaced with treeless pastures and expanding settlements that stretch right down to the ocean.

Habitat loss and fragmentation have caused the death and displacement of many millions of animals and have played major roles in species extinctions. In 2002, the first systematic attempt to identify the conservation status of Australia's terrestrial ecosystems found 2891 native ecosystems to be threatened with extinction, and 'vegetation clearing' and 'habitat fragmentation' topped the list of threatening processes.[23] Some ecological communities like the bluegrass on the Darling Downs and the temperate grasslands in southern Australia have been reduced to less than 1 per cent of their original range.[24] Despite the long recognised impacts of removing native vegetation, in Queensland the legal commitment to end broad-scale clearing was not made until 2003 (and deferred until 2006), and in the years 2000–04, around 1.5 million hectares of native and non-native forests were cleared nationally, mostly in that state.[25]

Despite the profound nutrient deficiency of the soils in most of the country, agriculture remains Australia's main land use and 61 per cent of land is subject to primary production, which includes grazing and dryland and irrigated agriculture such as cropping, dairy farming and fruit growing.[26] In addition to the local consumption of goods derived from agriculture and pastoralism, extra pressure is placed on our natural resources through Australia's food and fibre export industries. Subsidised by the country's natural ecological capital, beef, wheat and wool combined to make up around 6.6 per cent of Australia's total export income in 2005–06.[27] But our biggest export resource is, of course, coal.

★ ★ ★

Compared with agriculture, the mining industry—often considered to be highly damaging to the environment—occupies only 0.02 per cent of land and impacts on a far smaller scale.[28] This is not to say, however, that the impact of mining is insignificant. Liquid petroleum, coal, gas, iron ore and other minerals are major export industries for Australia and leave their marks on the land during extraction and in the atmosphere during consumption.

The economic incentive to mine coal at the expense of the environment remains enormous. Recently, a new coal mining project was approved at Anvil Hill in New South Wales' Hunter Valley. As a major agricultural region, the Hunter Valley has already undergone extensive land clearing for the dairy and wine-growing industries as well as for coal mining and urban settlement. The small areas of native vegetation that remain in this region are now critical to hundreds of plants and animals that have nowhere else to go. The new open-cut coal mine is to be located in the largest intact stand of remnant vegetation on the Hunter Valley floor—more than 2200 of the 3700 hectares of this precious woodland will be cleared or disturbed by the mine.[29] According to the state's conservation council, the woodland contains around five hundred species of plants and one hundred and eighty species of wildlife, including the koala, the squirrel glider, three species of owl, the brush-tailed rock wallaby and birds such as the square-tailed kite and glossy black cockatoo.[30] In addition to the mine's direct environmental impacts (habitat loss and likely waterway pollution), the impacts of the *burning* of the coal should also be considered. Extraction of the mine's predicted 150 million tonnes of coal will release around 170 000 tonnes of carbon dioxide into the atmosphere annually, but the much greater emissions impact will be felt through the burning of the coal, most of which will be exported overseas. More than 27 million tonnes of carbon dioxide will be released annually from the coal produced from this mine, an amount that will comprise 0.1 per cent of total global carbon emissions each year![31] The Land and Environment Court ordered that NSW planning minister Frank Sartor take into account the greater public interest in this case; regardless, the mine was approved in June 2007.[32]

A joint venture partnership between ChevronTexaco, Shell and ExxonMobil known as the Gorgon Project was also recently approved. It proposes to mine natural gas from gas fields off the Pilbara coast of Western Australia and to establish a gas processing complex on the internationally recognised Barrow Island Nature Reserve. Barrow Island is host to an amazing twenty-four species found nowhere else on Earth.[33] In large part because it's an island, there are no invasive or domestic species such as cats, rats, foxes or stock to affect its flora and fauna. The gas complex will occupy up to 300 hectares of the island and its development will include a 3-kilometre jetty and sea terminal, a dredged shipping channel, an off-loading causeway (nearly 1 kilometre long) and a carbon dioxide waste treatment plant. There is also an option to add additional gas plants and connect a pipeline to the mainland. Admittedly Barrow Island, despite its nature reserve status, has been the site of a producing oil field since 1964 and currently has several hundred active wells. But to date, the wells have been carefully managed and the small, fly-in–fly-out workforce has had a limited impact on the island. The proposed development poses many risks, not least that the exclusion of invasive species and diseases will be all but impossible because of increased shipping traffic and a much larger workforce—3300 people at peak construction times. The invasion of foreign species would have devastating results; Dirk Hartog Island lost ten of its fifteen species after the introduction of cats, rodents, and the grazing of sheep and goats.[34] But the Gorgon Project is the largest and most lucrative ever proposed in Australia, and once again environmental considerations have lost out to economic drivers. On green-lighting this project the Australian government alone will benefit to the tune of $17 billion in taxes and royalties.[35]

★ ★ ★

The combined environmental impacts of Australia's agricultural and extractive industries, and the high-impact lifestyles of its growing population are persistently altering this country at its peril. To date, 104 Australian plants and animals have become extinct in just on 220 years of European settlement. Under the federal *Environment Protection and Biodiversity Conservation Act 1999*, eighty-eight species are currently critically endangered and on the imminent verge of disappearing, while a further 1502 meet the criteria for endangered, vulnerable or conservation dependent. The extinction of so many species in such a short time frame is both a shocking track record and a tragic indictment of ignorance and poor stewardship. And given the highly complex network of ecosystems, *no one* can be quite sure how these cumulative losses will affect the environment's ability to function.

Overseas, an illuminating example of unexpected consequences of species loss on a natural ecosystem was observed in Wyoming's Yellowstone National Park. In the 1920s, the eradication of wolves to protect the previously over-hunted elk left a large gap in the park's ecosystem where wolves had been the top-order predators. The subsequent explosion in the elk population affected the availability of their food sources, among them the groves of aspen trees that were native to a section of the park. Aspen groves, popular with the elk, had also provided important habitat for myriad bird species and understorey plants typical to this ecosystem. As the numbers of elk increased, the aspen trees were browsed so heavily that saplings were unable to grow. The subsequent lack of mature trees then took its toll on the dam-building capabilities of the local beavers, which were unable to find timber. As beaver numbers decreased, the construction of fewer beaver dams resulted in less flooding, which in turn reduced the habitat preferred by the aspen trees. Only when the wolves were reintroduced to the park, reducing the number of elk and enabling the aspen groves to recover somewhat, did beavers return to Yellowstone and some natural equilibrium was restored.[36]

The highly monitored environment of a national park enabled scientists to track what effects removing the wolves had over a considerable period, and to compensate for this failed management strategy. In much of Australia's vast landscapes, we are not able to correct our mistakes as easily. Nevertheless, it is clear that species within ecosystems have complex relationships, and every effort must be made across our continent to avoid further species loss, especially at a time when major changes in climate will reduce the ability of natural systems to adapt and survive.

3

ONE HUNDRED FOOTBALL FIELDS AN HOUR

Land Clearing

The defining activity that marked the transition of humans from a nomadic hunter–gatherer lifestyle to a settled culture of pastoralism and agriculture was the clearing of land. Where our early nomadic ancestors moved in harmony with seasonally available food and mild climates, settled cultures changed the natural environment to suit their personal needs year-round. The shift from one lifestyle to the other reveals a fundamental shift in attitudes towards nature: the first adapts to any limitations and lives *with* nature; the second challenges nature and motivates people to manipulate the environment to their own ends, often far beyond its capacity.

When Australia was first settled by Europeans in the late eighteenth century, the new arrivals were surprised to find an indigenous population that had remained contentedly nomadic. The Europeans considered Australia's Aborigines primitive and uncultured because of their lack of clothing, permanent settlements and domesticated stock; they failed to identify the profound suitability of this ancient way of life in an equally ancient and complex continent. The Aboriginal ethos—of living by the seasonal yields of the land, carefully reading any signs of change, and hunting and collecting food within their tribal lands—was to belong to the landscape, to 'look after country' and to respect it. And although the extinction of Australia's megafauna some 45 000 years ago has been attributed by some to Aboriginal hunting[1], no resource in recent millennia appears to have been exploited beyond its capacity to regenerate. When Aboriginal people manipulated parts of the landscape by lighting fires—harvesting first the dead or fleeing wildlife then, later, some of the fresh growth of plants—the burnings were conducted with an intimate understanding of how the landscape would respond. Where, when and how extensive the area was to be lit were all integral factors in this land-management practice.

It is estimated that for tens of thousands of years this nomadic lifestyle sustained populations of between 250 000 and 750 000—until the foreign colonists' arrival in 1788. Barely off the ships and alarmed by the unrestrained wildness of the place, the mainly British settlers wasted no time and began large-scale clearing almost immediately.

★ ★ ★

The term 'land clearing' is often thought to mean forest logging or clear felling and conjures up images of roaring chainsaws, sweat-glazed workers and crashing stands of timber. Strictly speaking, however, logging and clear felling are terms applied only to the removal of trees, while land clearing refers to the complete removal of *all* vegetation.[2] Forests, open woodlands, expansive heath and mixed shrubland, vegetation alongside rivers and streams (riparian vegetation), coastal mangroves, paperbark swamps and native grasslands are all natural landscapes that have been extensively cleared since European settlement. More than 60 per cent of original vegetation has been cleared or modified in New South Wales, Victoria and South Australia, and around 25 per cent in the more mountainous but much wetter state of Tasmania.[3]

In several recent reports—the Australia: State of the Environment Report 1996 and 2001 and the Australian Terrestrial Biodiversity Assessment 2002 among them—the ongoing clearing of mature native vegetation was formally identified as the single biggest threat to native biodiversity.[4]

Land clearing has been listed as a key threatening process under national and New South Wales legislation, though it still occurs in that state. (It is not listed in South Australia, Victoria and Western Australia—states where most land has already been cleared.) Extensive clearing continues in Tasmania and the Northern Territory, and Queensland is also yet to demonstrate the power of its stronger clearing controls.[5] In south-west Western Australia, around 90 per cent of native vegetation has been lost in the agricultural, climatically marginal wheatbelt region of the south-west, much of which is now suffering from increasing expanses of rising salt. By the time clearing was banned there in 1995, the state had lost about one-third of its vegetation.[6]

From the earliest days of the Australian colony, the motivation to clear land of native vegetation far exceeded any latent desire to preserve it. Land was needed for housing and farms, and there was food to be grown, roads (and later railways) to be built and prosperity to be pursued. Clearing first commenced along coastal areas and ports so that stock could be grazed and crops grown for the hard-working settlers. By the 1850s, clearing for the wheatbelts in the east and west of the country had commenced, and in the 1880s the stump-jump plough and stripper replaced axes and saws while the extension of the transport and rail systems improved access. At around the same time, the budding dairy industry began to clear the more heavily forested country situated on fertile volcanic soils. Before long, the Strzelecki and Otway ranges in Victoria, the Illawarra and New England Tablelands in New South Wales, and Queensland's Blackall Ranges, Lamington region and the Atherton Tableland, as well as parts of Tasmania, were home to mobs of dairy cattle that fed on new pasture. The 1880s also saw the cultivation of crops like sugarcane in Queensland and New South Wales, and of irrigated crops (fruit, vegetables, pasture) along the River Murray and other river systems.

As early as 1895, the rampant loss of mature forests, the poor management of clearing operations and inadequate laws to protect forests were brought to the attention of the public. A report commissioned by the Victorian government found that the management of government-owned state forest was 'in an extraordinarily backward state' and the amount of revenue it returned to be 'ridiculously small'.[7] The report triggered a royal commission and led to the introduction of better legislation in 1908 and a general improvement in forest management thereafter. But in spite of this, clearing was about to explode.

The most senseless and misguided periods of land clearing in Australia were triggered by the return of Australian servicemen from the two world wars, in particular after World War I. In an effort to stimulate the economy and provide a fresh start for the returning soldiers, the Commonwealth and state governments established schemes that provided cheap land for anyone willing to clear and cultivate it. As most of the fertile patches had already been appropriated, this push led to the clearing of vegetation on much poorer soils in the south-east and south-west of the country. Many ex-soldiers who took up this offer had little or no previous experience as land managers and did not question the suitability of the land for cultivation, nor were they willing to refuse such an opportunity.

Following World War I further large areas of forest were cleared, including Victoria's Strzelecki Ranges, which had already been harvested for timber. Tragically, the unsuitability of much of this region for agriculture was only discovered *after* the land had been cleared, and the people who had removed its natural ecosystems were soon forced to abandon it. By the 1930s reforestation programs commenced to recover the abandoned land for commercial eucalypt and pine plantations, which provided some—if temporary—habitat for native wildlife.

A more recent episode of out-of-control clearing began in Queensland in the 1960s—more land was cleared in this state in the second half of the twentieth century than in the 150 years before.[8] Using bulldozers and huge metal chains strung between tractors to drag down enormous swathes of bush, around 3 million hectares of native bushland disappeared. This was called the Brigalow Scheme, a joint federal and state government initiative, so named because of the abundance of brigalow, a silver-leafed wattle of the region that extends from inland and eastern Queensland to northern New South Wales. Areas once unprofitable to clear by hand now became profitable with the use of large machinery, and so even the heavy soils of the Brigalow Belt became available for cropping.

The Brigalow Scheme precipitated the first expressions of concern about the impacts of land clearing in Queensland, but it wasn't until the late 1990s, and more recently, that the full impact became known. A report commissioned by WWF-Australia outlined that Queensland's clearing rate between 1997 and 1999 was estimated at around 446 000 hectares per year, a rate equivalent to *one hundred football fields every hour*! The 'panic clearing' of brigalow, gidgee and eucalypt open forest and woodland before stricter clearing regulations came into force in late 2004 is estimated to have caused the deaths of about 100 million native mammals, birds and reptiles each year.[9] For the Brigalow region alone, conservative estimates of the wildlife toll of the clearing of 112 million trees per year have included the combined annual deaths of more than 1 million koalas, kangaroos, wallabies, echidnas, possums, gliders, bandicoots and smaller marsupials such as dunnarts and antechinuses. The clearing also accounted for the killing of more than 5 million woodland birds such as bellbirds, honeyeaters, robins, finches, parrots and wrens, and around 52 million reptiles including goannas, geckoes, skinks and snakes.[10] The open woodlands of the southern Brigalow Belt are home to populations of almost half of all bird species found in Australia. Broad-scale clearing of these woodlands has removed around 60 per cent of the original extent of the wildlife habitat and occupants of this region. One hundred football fields every hour.

As in the east and south-east of the country, the majority of land clearing in Western Australia also occurred in the second half of the twentieth century. Large tracts of public land in the south-west—secretly considered to be 'unproductive scrub wasteland'—were opened up and promoted as the cheapest land in Australia.[11] In a now familiar pattern, individuals were allocated farms under one condition: that the land be cleared for agriculture. Any landholder who defied this condition risked losing his land allocation and faced an uncertain future. During each year of the 1960s, a staggering 1 million acres (404,686 hectares) of marginal bushland was released to agriculture and most of the hardy native bush was replaced with fields of wheat. Today, an estimated 18 million hectares (87 per cent) of Western Australia's south-west agricultural region, as well as 93 per cent of the adjoining wheatbelt, have been cleared of native vegetation.[12] Despite definitive evidence of dryland salinity and declining species as early as the 1920s, broad-scale clearing in Western Australia only stopped in the 1990s, when farmers were no longer able to ignore the increasingly salt-contaminated land and decreasing rainfall patterns.[13]

On an international scale, the rate of land clearing in Australia in the recent past has been on a par with the worst in the developing world. This list is topped by Brazil, which in 2000–05 logged 3.1 million hectares per year, followed by Indonesia with 1 million hectares per year, Sudan (587 000 ha/yr), Burma (465 000 ha/yr) and Zambia (445 000 ha/yr).[14] Clearing rates in Queensland alone towards the end of the last decade were comparable to those in fourth (Burma) and fifth (Zambia) place. For a wealthy, developed country in an infinitely better position to make rational choices about the environment this is an unforgivable result.

The destruction caused by massive vegetation loss is usually felt in stages—some impacts emerge only after weeks, months, years, and sometimes many decades. The consequences can be felt on vastly different scales and may come about with the loss of only a few isolated trees. In short order, however, clearing damages complex communities of plants, animals, invertebrates, moulds, fungi and soil bacteria that occur among grasses, leaf litter and fallen logs, in shrubby understorey, in the hollows of old trees and among the branches and leaves of the canopy. Depending on the type, location and extent of the vegetation being cleared, the removal of deep-rooted plants may also raise water tables and salt levels or cause the erosion of the fragile layers of valuable soil. Without the appropriate vegetation to anchor it, nutrient-laden soil can wash into waterways, reduce the water quality and in turn affect species such as fish, frogs, platypus, waterbirds and myriad invertebrates.

One ecological community whose incremental removal has affected a range of native species is found in Victoria. Buloke is a type of casuarina that grows with other woodland species on the fertile sandy-clay soils sought after for pasture and cropping. It is also an important late summer and autumn food source for the endangered south-eastern red-tailed black cockatoo, a highly specialised feeder that relies on the fruit of only three native tree species.[15] The survival of this magnificent bird—of which no more than a thousand individuals remain—depends on the protection of its food trees as well as on the presence of mature eucalypts like river red gums that have taken one hundred years or more to form hollows large enough for the birds to nest and breed in. Unfortunately for the cockatoos and the many other members of this community, many individual buloke trees are now found on private farming land where they often obstruct centre-pivot irrigation equipment that can only operate in entirely cleared areas. The continuing loss of individual bulokes is leading to the gradual 'death by a thousand cuts' of the tree community and its dependent wildlife. A 2004 survey conducted by the Threatened Species Network found that landholders in this area often confused the red-tailed black cockatoo with the yellow-tailed black cockatoo, which is known to be more common and less in need of protection. The landholders were simply not aware that the future of the mascot of the 2006 Commonwealth Games is largely in their hands.

The consequences of clearing large sections of prominent ecological communities—such as the Brigalow Belt, the Cumberland Plain Woodland near Sydney or the Jarrah forests of Western Australia—in the first instance are visually dramatic, but how the long-term impacts play out depends on many factors: the type of vegetation cleared, its location, the species and diversity of plants and wildlife it supports, how much of it has been cleared already, what condition the remaining vegetation is in and how fragmented it is. Immediately, of course, there is the destruction of the vegetation itself, which means a lost source of food and shelter for native wildlife. Nesting and fledgling birds, tree- and ground-dwelling mammals, slow-moving reptiles and invertebrates are either killed by the clearing itself, or starve to death or, suddenly without shelter, fall victim to predators or vehicular traffic. Some birds and mobile mammals may seek food and shelter elsewhere, but other remnant habitats are inherently problematic, and the survival rates of the refugees are likely to be low. Besides that, many mammals are highly attached to the location of their habitat and refuse to leave the site even after its destruction. The poignant image of a koala sitting in a lone eucalypt on the nature strip of a busy road is a fitting example. Faithful to its territory and at a loss to deal with the sudden changes to its environment, its options are extremely limited.

American science writer David Quammen uses an evocative analogy to illustrate just how diminished remnant habitats are. In his book *The Song of the Dodo* he writes:

> Let's start by imagining a fine Persian carpet and a hunting knife. The carpet is twelve feet by eighteen, say. That gives us 216 square feet of continuous woven material ... We set about cutting the carpet into thirty-six equal pieces, each one a rectangle, two feet by three. Never mind the hardwood floor. The severing fibers release small tweaky noises, like the muted yelps of outraged Persian weavers. Never mind the weavers. When we're finished cutting, we measure the individual pieces, total them up, and find that, lo, there's still nearly 216 square feet of recognizably carpet-like stuff. But what does it amount to? Have we got thirty-six nice Persian throw rugs? No. All we're left with is three dozen ragged fragments, each one worthless and commencing to come apart ... An ecosystem is a tapestry of species and relationships. Chop away a section, isolate that section, and there arises the problem of unraveling.[16]

No salvage project, no matter how complex, is able to restore this Persian carpet to a comparably valuable whole. And the same applies to the environment. The forced displacement of wildlife into comparatively small remnants has consequences that may take decades to be realised. Initially, a sudden influx of new animals can lead to the increased degradation of habitat as food and shelter are stretched beyond their limits. More gradually, fierce competition between resident wildlife and the new arrivals leads to the death or displacement of individuals until populations adjust to what the habitat can sustain. For some species the new conditions will not be suitable for breeding: appropriate nesting sites may be absent or occupied, an excess of predators may eat the eggs or kill the young, and disputes over limited breeding territories may end in death. With no recruitment from outside the isolated remnant, the population becomes extinct when the last of the individuals die.

The quality of remnant habitat is usually further reduced by the invasion of weeds and feral animals—weeds can smother or replace native plants and destroy important shelter or food sources, while feral animals compete for limited food or prey on native species. The habitat's borders may adjoin busy urban areas, thereby exposing species to roads and traffic; where roads and highways have been built through the area, even higher risks are created for the wildlife.

Because of the limited size of remnant habit, the wildlife is particularly vulnerable to catastrophic events such as fire. Fires can wipe out entire remnant patches, causing instant population extinctions, and sometimes it is impossible for the wildlife to return. This was the case in the Royal National Park near Sydney in 1994, when a large wildfire that swept through the tall forest habitat of a well-known population of greater gliders led to its extinction. Although there were three nearby habitat patches from which the gliders could have recolonised this area once the bush had recovered, this had not occurred even ten years after the event— the absence of corridors between these patches prevented migration.[17] Genetic isolation in remnant populations is another problem: as the gene pool becomes smaller, inbreeding further increases the vulnerability of the isolated population to diseases or changing conditions.

One native mammal that has suffered continuous displacement from land clearing is the flying fox. All four species of this large fruit bat are at home among the coastal eucalypt forests, mangroves and melaleuca wetlands most coveted for development. Once able to pursue seasonal nectar, fruit and pollen by travelling through vast forest and woodland expanses, populations of flying foxes and their daycamps are now often located in or near urban areas. Up to three species of flying fox may share a camp at certain times, and the combined impact of thousands of roosting flying foxes, each weighing between 500 and 1000 grams, on a limited number of trees can be severe. Broken and denuded branches often recover, but some trees cannot withstand the damage and die. As flying foxes tend to remain loyal to a number of permanent local campsites and move between them, the clearing of any permanent camps increases the pressure on others or results in the establishment of new camps at often inconvenient sites nearby. Unwittingly, the bats become both the displaced victims of clearing and, elsewhere, much-maligned contributors to habitat decline.

On a seemingly smaller scale than fragmentation, though no less threatening to remnant habitats, is the collection of firewood for domestic use. In many regional areas, fallen timber is still collected and dead trees cut down to fuel stoves and fireplaces as they have been for centuries. This might not seem harmful, but collectively this practice removes 4.4–5.5 million tonnes of wildlife habitat and shelter from the natural landscape each year.[18] For many native animals, dead and fallen timber is vitally important habitat. The hollows high above the ground are particularly prized as they can reduce predator access and house nests for species like gliders, small insect-eating bats, and a range of threatened birds like the south-eastern red-tailed black cockatoo, south-west Western Australia's Carnaby's cockatoo, the swift parrot and the Tasmanian and northern masked owls. On the ground, dead and decaying timber supports mosses, lichens and fungi that provide rich pickings for invertebrates and food and shelter for close to three hundred species of frogs, reptiles, birds and mammals.[19] And on a more fundamental scale, the loss of decaying timber deprives forests and woodlands of nutrients essential for maintaining the ecological processes of decay and renewal. In 2001, all states and territories and the federal government adopted a national approach to firewood collection to increase the public profile of this issue, enforce a national code of practice among commercial firewood merchants and reduce illegal collection.[20] What happens on private properties, however, remains in the hands of the landholders. It is their responsibility to ensure that dead and fallen timber in all stages of decay stays in the landscape.

★ ★ ★

The delayed death of species or local populations of plants or animals as a result of the long and complex chain of consequences of clearing is known as the 'extinction debt'. To the natural environment, the extinction debt is the long-term price it pays for the clearing of habitats in the past. Over time, a series of local extinctions in different habitat remnants may result in the loss of a species at a regional level, and unless decisive action is taken to halt its decline, it will disappear altogether. Currently, more than 1500 individual plants and animals and close to 3000 ecological communities are threatened with extinction due to inappropriate land-management practices and other processes that began with the broad-scale clearing of native vegetation.

One last consequence of land clearing that still needs to be mentioned is soil erosion. The formation and quality of Australia's soils are determined by factors such as the geology and shape of the land, its plant cover, climate and rainfall, and the degree of weathering that has taken place over time. As outlined earlier, volcanic activity leaves behind basalt-enriched soils that form a fertile basis for complex vegetation communities such as forests. Left to be governed by natural processes, soils are held in place by the roots of trees, shrubs and ground-cover such as forbs, sedges and grasses, and in the arid rangelands of Australia, a thin but vital layer of lichen that forms a duracrust. The cover of vegetation ensures that the soil is protected and held in place and not washed away by rain or blown away by wind. The continual process of the death and decay of organic matter ensures that it is constantly replenished. Most importantly, however, the plants that grow in different ecosystems are adapted to the soils that support them, and conversely, the quality of the soil indicates the type of vegetation it can readily support. But what if, through land clearing and farming, little or no vegetation is left?

A recent State of the Environment Report found that the rate of soil erosion in pasturelands is twice that of natural erosion, and that there has been a fivefold increase in the artificial improvement of pastures with fertilisers[21], indicating that soils are struggling to support pastoral expectations. Erosion can take several forms—soil can be blown away by winds in dust storms or, loosened by rain, it can wash down the slopes of hilly areas or along gullies into waterways. The pollution of natural waterways such as rivers and creeks from loosened soil can have a severe impact on the health of these waterways.[22]

The platypus is found in rivers along the Great Dividing Range from the tropics to Tasmania. It is at home in clear streams where it feeds on small benthic invertebrates such as insect larvae that live in the water and in the sediment along the bottom of the streams. While platypuses are still considered common throughout their range, they have been found to avoid streams that have become turbid from sand or silt dislodged by erosion. In the greater Melbourne area, a study demonstrated that breeding sites chosen by platypuses had much lower levels of dissolved nutrients such as phosphorous and organic nitrogen as well as significantly lower levels of cadmium, lead and zinc than comparable reaches in the same river systems not chosen for breeding.[23] The research also suggested that the algal outbreaks caused by high levels of dissolved nutrients could interfere with the animal's ability to detect food.[24] Just as fish don't belong in a forest, soils—however precious on land—do not belong in waterways.

★ ★ ★

In 2008, while some land clearing is still occurring and regulations continue to be tightened, its prominence as a primary cause of the loss of plants, animals and ecological communities is now largely retrospective. The fallout from *past* clearing, however, is in full swing. In May 2004, the Queensland government passed a new law to phase out broad-scale land clearing of mature remnant bushland on freehold and leasehold land. Close to 20 million hectares of native bushland that would otherwise have been open to clearing could now be protected. This law was seen by conservation groups such as The Wilderness Society as a proactive move because it set out to halt broad-scale clearing *before* widespread land degradation became established in that state.[25]

With the exception of the Northern Territory and Tasmania, all states now have laws that make large-scale land clearing illegal. The federal *EPBC Act* 1999 recognised land clearing as a key threat to species and ecosystems, and any proposed clearing with a potentially significant impact on nationally threatened species or ecological communities has to be referred to the Australian government. But while the devastating impact of clearing is now common knowledge, an abatement plan is yet to be drafted and any ongoing clearing issues have been largely left to the states. How willing and able they are both to enforce their clearing laws and to invest in the broad-scale regeneration of lost ecosystems where possible remains to be seen.

4

THIRSTY WORK

Pastoralism and Agriculture

The image of the man on the land, Akubra pulled low and a face set with the determination to take on the elements and win, is traditionally and quintessentially Australian. It takes tough men and women to farm this country, and toughness is what this country prides itself on.

Modern Australia owes its beginnings to those who coaxed food from the ground, forged sheep and cattle runs from the foreign bush, cleared the ground for crops and pasture and tackled the challenges of heat, drought and poor soils in the best way they knew how. Even if this 'how' came from cultures that considered nature to be unquestionably at the service of people and whose experiences were of verdant pastures grown in temperate climates on rich soils with regular rain.

Soon after their arrival in January 1788, the settlers of the First Fleet were in for a rude shock in respect to their new home's agricultural potential. Captain James Cook's earlier expedition had returned to England with glowing accounts of Australia's fertility, and expectations on Captain Phillip's ships were high, even if the settlers' land management skills were low. The first shipment of domestic stock included 'seven horses, six cattle, twenty-nine sheep, twelve pigs, and a few goats' and many more were to follow.[1] Unbeknownst to Phillip, the stock on his ships featured the first sets of hard hooves to make their mark on Australia. Two hundred years on, three of those species—horses, pigs and goats—now occur in feral populations that cost millions of dollars to try to control, and all five contribute to large-scale environmental degradation across the continent.

★ ★ ★

The immense fragility of Australia's ancient and weathered rangelands has meant that the pastoral practices of sheep and cattle grazing have left a large and detrimental legacy in these extensive land-use regions. Covering almost three-quarters of the continent, the ecosystems of the rangelands reflect the immense aridity of this country. Extensive woodlands of eucalypts, eucalypt mallees and acacias with grassy understorey in the northern regions of the rangelands morph into shrublands of casuarinas and acacias (mallee and mulga) in central and central-western regions, which in turn give way to native grasslands of spinifex, tussock and other grasses as well as salt and drought-tolerant chenopods such as bluebush and saltbush in the southernmost parts.[2] The tropical savanna woodlands, which occur in a narrow band of seasonal high rainfall north of the Tropic of Capricorn, make up a fourth and more diverse ecosystem.

The rangelands provide habitats for an amazing two-thirds of Australia's reptiles, almost two-thirds of its birds, half of its frogs and a third of its mammals.[3] All of these animals have evolved to be at home in these unpredictable and often hazardous landscapes. The rangelands are characterised by poor soils and low and unpredictable rainfall and the plant life has adapted accordingly—the less rain, the tougher and hardier the vegetation. A common feature is specialised foliage that minimises evaporation allowing the plants to conserve water. Casuarinas and acacias such as mulga and brigalow have stick-like and waxy leaflets with a minimal surface area, while hummock grasses like spinifex have dense clumps of matted stems and stiff, pointed leaves. Bluegrass, samphire and saltbush can be completely leafless and also feature salt-excreting pores.

Many plants in the driest parts of the rangelands provide fibre and roughage but little of the nutrition needed for good pasture (although plants like Mitchell grass flourish after rain and young grasses provide a welcome boost to grazing animals).

Despite the tough conditions, rangelands across half of the continent are being extensively stocked at great cost to the natural landscapes. Attempts to increase plant foliage for sheep and cattle by avoiding traditional Aboriginal patch-burning regimes, creating artificial watering points and introducing foreign pasture plants have made pastoralism an active driver of the rapid decline of native plants and wildlife and the degradation of ecosystems across this vast region.

This is not an issue confined only to Australia. Around the world overstocked rangelands are typical indicators of land unsuitable for crop production in regions where few alternative livelihoods exist. Cattle, introduced for their ability to process even the toughest plants and produce milk and meat for human consumption, have damaged vast regions of Africa, the Middle East, Central Asia, India, Mongolia and northern China and turned many native rangelands into deserts.[4]

The impact that only two centuries of grazing cattle, sheep and other hoofstock have had on Australia's landscapes is ample evidence of how unsuited these introduced grazers are when compared with our native mammals. Two obvious differences are size and weight. While many mammals—and birds and reptiles—found in the rangelands are small to medium in size, have soft feet and weigh less than 5.5 kilograms, adult beef cattle average around 450–500 kilograms in weight, are hard-hooved and leave a very different imprint on the landscape. Not much about a large steer is subtle or delicate, least of all its appetite. A steer may consume around 3 per cent of its bodyweight in natural vegetation per day (around twelve kilograms of plant matter for a 400 kilogram steer), laying waste to any available grasses, shrubs and hardy chenopods in the process. Even with low stocking rates environmental damage is inevitable. A single steer may be up to one hundred times larger than a brushtail possum, a species that, though common and adaptable elsewhere, is now endangered in the Northern Territory and rare throughout Central Australia. The decline in possum numbers is attributable to competition for food plants from introduced herbivores like cattle, predation by feral animals such as cats and foxes and habitat changes that have resulted from altered fire regimes.[5]

The weight of a steer carried on its hard hooves—a characteristic shared by other introduced plant-eaters such as horses, donkeys, buffalo, goats and sheep—has its own destructive capabilities. As the legs of a solid oak dining table leave permanent imprints in the carpet it stands on, small feet with hard hooves amplify the considerable weight they carry and annihilate whatever they step on: delicate grasses and other flowering plants, birds nests, eggs and chicks and, most critically, the thin permanent duracrust that holds the soil in place where vegetation is absent. Even where stocking rates are low, pronounced degradation occurs where the animals congregate near open water. Hoofstock physically damages riparian zones and stream banks, waterholes and delicate wetlands and further pollutes them with its dung.

Between the 1960s and 1980s large populations of buffalo caused havoc to the wetlands and floodplains of northern Australia. In addition to the disturbance caused by buffalo trails and wallows and the decimation of plants and water pollution from dung, the buffalo created deep channels between saltwater and freshwater habitats, and many freshwater-dependent plants, fish, frogs and waterbirds died from the brackish conditions. Efforts to cull the buffalo through shooting and some commercial harvesting have significantly reduced their numbers from a peak of around 350 000 in the 1980s. In 1996, fewer than 250 remained in Kakadu National Park where they are herded and eaten by Aboriginal communities.[6] However, in the absence of a reliable commercial market for buffalo these days, their numbers in the wild are once again increasing and on the Arnhem Plateau had reached more than 80 000 by early 2008.[7] Once more, scientists are calling for their culling.

★ ★ ★

Australia's tropical savanna landscapes are characterised by extensive grasslands that can also feature a few scattered trees or even quite dense woodlands, but always with a grassy understorey. Fire plays a major role in the landscape ecology of the savannas, which feature mainly drought-adapted plants. Whether that role is beneficial or detrimental for an ecosystem depends on a range of factors: the seasons in which the fires occur, what part of the landscape they affect (the grassy understorey, the canopy or the entire ecosystem), how frequently they occur and how intensely they burn.[8] Fires are generally triggered by lightning strikes or lit by people. Over tens of thousands of years, Aboriginal people have deliberately burned Australia's landscapes. This usually occurred in the cooler and moister early dry season and took into consideration natural firebreaks such as creeks and rock formations to prevent the fire's random spread. This considered use of fire served to flush out wildlife, prevent destructive wildfires and promote new plant growth.

Today, pastoralists and land managers are increasingly coming to appreciate the merits of traditional Aboriginal burning practices. The cultivation of a landscape 'mosaic' containing plants and habitats in different stages of maturity, as well as the reduction of fuel and woody weeds to prevent uncontrollable wildfires would, it turns out, benefit domestic stock as much as it does native wildlife and ecosystems. But a lack of knowledge about how to do this at the right scale, and a reluctance to deal with the short-term loss of stock feed where a recent burn has taken place, are slowing the uptake of this land management method. So far, the failure to fully understand the highly localised knowledge that underpinned traditional burning, and the avoidance of deliberate burning altogether, have made destructive wildfires one of the main threats to plant and animal species, particularly in northern Australia.[9]

Changed fire regimes are known to have played a role in the decline of nineteen plant species and may well have brought about the extinction of others.[10] As a result of their impacts on plants and vegetation structure, changed fire regimes are also considered to have affected a staggering 43 per cent of Australia's mainland bird species including the glorious Gouldian finch, the dainty striated grasswren, the pale-pastel princess parrot and the quirky, mound-building mallee-fowl, all of which are now threatened with extinction.[11] Many of these birds depend on fire to release seeds for food or to generate new shoots for nesting material.

Of the many factors that threaten rangelands—overgrazing, poor fire management, weeds and feral animals like rabbits, cats and foxes—it's usually a combination that leads to large scale environmental degradation; and to make matters worse, some threat factors exacerbate the impacts of others. Exotic pasture grasses introduced to supplement the yields of native grasses and better support herds of beef cattle are a case in point. The importation of many of these has resulted in several negative consequences. Some exotic grasses like buffel, couch, gamba and para grass have become weeds that have invaded the wider landscape and have out-competed native grasses. This has changed the natural vegetation structure and consequently the habitats of native wildlife. And in their prolific spreading, dense grasses such as buffel (first introduced to control erosion and only later used as pasture) have added to the natural fuel in the landscape. Buffel burns at higher temperatures than native grass species and has the inadvertent impact of exacerbating the intensity of wildfires when they do occur.

The lifecycles of the grasslands' occupants are carefully attuned to the characteristics of their vegetation, and native grasses come in a variety of shapes, sizes and densities. Wallaby and spear grasses are fine-leaved grasses that tend to grow in separate bushels; hummock grasses grow in dense clusters that can reach 2–3 metres in diameter. Species of both these groups can grow to more than 2 metres in height.

Grasses are used as nests or nesting material, shelter from predators, direct sources of foliage and seeds, and habitat for skinks, snakes and invertebrates that are in turn prey for birds, mammals and larger reptiles. Many rangeland birds such as delicate grasswrens, communal finches and the quirky-looking plains wanderer are declining in number as their grassy habitats and food sources have suffered. Small mammals like the long-tailed dunnart, the native plains rat, the kowari, the bilby and the rufous hare–wallaby (mala) have suffered from the combination of altered fire regimes, competition and habitat degradation from rabbits, predation by stealthy cats and foxes and are now threatened or near-threatened with extinction.[12]

Attempting to restore balance in the rangelands is a momentous task and one further complicated by the changing climate. If the predicted increase in rain in the north stimulates plant growth during some parts of the year, and increasing temperatures produce a drier climate during others, fires are likely to increase in frequency and severity. Never has it been timelier for land managers to consider the merits of proactive and careful fire management.

★ ★ ★

Of the many changes to the rangelands brought about to support pastoralism, one of the most dramatic is the impact of artificial watering points. Tapped from underground aquifers like the ancient Great Artesian Basin, watering points like dams, open drains and artificial wetlands have been installed widely across the rangelands to supply water for wandering livestock. The native wildlife of arid and semi–arid Australia, however, is specially adapted to the absence of water for much of the year and depends on these periods to regulate its populations to sustainable levels. Under natural conditions, the drying up of waterholes during dry times leads to the reduction of these native grazers by death or migration, leaving the native vegetation in the vicinity of the waterhole to recover. This has not been the case for some time.

The introduction of artificial watering points by the mid twentieth century was intended to quench the thirst of domestic cattle and sheep, but the availability of fresh water also drew in native herbivores and birds as well as feral mammals and has resulted in a string of changes to the landscape. At first glance some changes appeared to be positive: the creation of artificial wetland habitats for flora and fauna, larger distribution ranges for birds that rely on open water sources and the possible expansion of breeding ranges of water-dependent invertebrates. The negative impacts, however, soon became apparent. As with natural water sources, the congregation of large numbers of cows and sheep caused severe damage. And stock was not the only culprit—feral horses, donkeys, goats and, in some regions, pigs, took advantage of the water and contributed to the degradation of these sites. Populations of native herbivores like kangaroos also increased near the water, placing more pressure on an already overgrazed landscape. Not surprisingly, foxes and cats thrived near these water sources and made the most of the opportunity to prey on the wildlife at these sites. One study found that destruction zones of up to 500 metres around watering points were common.[13] And given their relatively dense distribution—watering points are spaced no more than 10 kilometres apart—*vast* areas of the landscape were degraded in this way.[14]

The impact of artificial watering points and modified pastoral lands on birds has been closely studied and managed by Birds Australia on Gluepot Reserve, located in the semi-arid mallee riverland of South Australia. A haven for waterbirds, birds of prey, parrots, as well as owls, kingfishers, wrens and honeyeaters, the plethora of wildlife on the reserve today belies its pastoral history.

Before its acquisition by Birds Australia (formerly the Royal Australasian Ornithologists Union) in 1997, Gluepot had been a working pastoral lease stocked with sheep for more than 120 years and it carried the scars to prove it. To support its stock, the property's 54 000 hectares had been amply supplied with eighteen dams that were freely accessible to the sheep and all other animals on the property, including feral goats, foxes and kangaroos. The extensive damage to the natural environment surrounding the dams was evident in the decimation of native vegetation, soil erosion and infestations of weeds like the lavender-like and unpalatable bushy horehound. For some species, this decline in habitat quality had further complex consequences. The degraded habitat around the watering points opened the way for the invasion of the yellow-throated miner into what was previously the undisturbed mallee habitat of the black-eared miner. The incursion of the yellow-throated miner led to interbreeding between the two species and, together with the loss of its habitat, propelled the black-eared miner onto the national list of 'critically endangered' species.

The new management regimes of Gluepot were founded on intense research into the impact of watering points on this mallee reserve, which does not naturally feature any permanent water. A PhD study looked at the impact of dams on the native vegetation and bird fauna at various distances from the dams.[15] It found that while some water-dependent species such as the red wattlebird were more abundant closer to the water, ground-foraging birds of conservation concern like the striated grasswren, southern scrub robin and shy heathwren were less abundant because the compacted and trampled soil near watering points had inhibited the low-growing shrubs important to them.

In response to these findings Birds Australia commenced a staged program of dam closure on the property in 1999. In addition to closing sixteen dams over three years and fencing the remaining two to exclude herbivores, active weed removal commenced alongside a revegetation program initiated with seeds collected and propagated on the reserve. According to property manager Duncan McKenzie, however, the removal of grazers (sheep, most feral goats, and kangaroos) and weeds proved so successful that the revegetation program was unnecessary— the plants recovered naturally. Free of constant grazing and invasive plants, the vegetation around some of the dams recovered so well that within a few years it was impossible to see that a dam had ever existed.[16]

A fire management plan was also put in place to address the large areas of mallee that had not been burned for a long time, which if destroyed from wildfire would impact further on threatened birds like the black-eared miner and the malleefowl. One by one, each threat was tackled and brought under control.

The highly successful restoration of Gluepot via the management of the identified threats of stock, weeds, feral animals, dams and fire was a sensible, long-term strategy. And it was good news too for the threatened black-eared miner. With water availability drastically reduced, numbers of the yellow-throated miner also decreased and the pressure on the black-eared miners eased. Gluepot Reserve is now home to more than a hundred bird species, including eighteen that are nationally threatened with extinction. The lessons learned and implemented from the research conducted on the property have earned Birds Australia more than thirty well-deserved environmental awards.

It would, however, be foolish to assume that simply closing all artificial watering points could fix what has become a complex issue. In some regions, artificial wetlands, such as those around bores, have replaced natural ones and now play a significant role in sustaining wildlife. In Western Australia, the Port Hedland Saltworks provide such a wetland in a profoundly arid region, and similarly important artificial sites can be found in South Australia, New South Wales and Victoria.[17] In these areas, wildlife has become adapted to the greater availability of water, and fauna now depends on its reliable presence. A detailed understanding of the beneficial versus the detrimental impacts of individual bores, dams and open drains on local wildlife is essential when deciding on the best management strategy for any given site.

★ ★ ★

While pastoralists in the driest parts of the country have relied on artificial watering points to support their livelihoods, farmers in regions where water has been more easily available have fared no better in managing this essential resource. The many decades of persistent over-allocation of Australia's available fresh water to the more intensive agricultural industries have left larger areas of the natural environment high and achingly dry.

Around half of Australia's agricultural production comes from the Murray–Darling Basin and is built around the water drawn from its extensive river systems. Irrigated agriculture in the Basin includes dairy, cotton, rice, cereals, grapes and other fruit and vegetables as well as pasture for sheep and beef cattle.[18] The remaining agriculture is concentrated on the small patches of fertile coastal soils in the eastern, south-eastern and south-western parts of the country.[19] About one-third consists of production and plantation forestry, half of grazing on modified pastures, and the remainder of the water-costly practices of irrigating pastures, cropping and horticulture.[20]

But the problems with the thirstiness of specific agricultural crops cannot be explained without once again considering the soils they grow in. One of the many ironies of Australia's agricultural experience is that in some regions the clearing of forests for pasture and crops is leading to the rise of underground salt levels which poison the ground and make traditional agriculture impossible. Salinity now affects large areas of Western Australia, increasing parts of the Murray–Darling Basin and is rising in most rivers in southern Australia.[21] Most of the salt in our landscapes was deposited in small amounts over tens of thousands of years, carried from the ocean by winds to be captured and bedded down into the subsoils by a combination of rain and dust.[22] Traditionally, the moisture needs of deep-rooted native vegetation such as eucalypts kept the water table low; land clearing brought the salts to the surface. In Western Australia's wheatbelt, the once uniformly planted wheatfields are now a patchwork of still-arable land interspersed with salty-white zones devoid of vegetation.

More than 5 per cent of Australia's cultivated land is already affected by dryland salinity. In 2001, estimates of the area likely to be affected by rising salt stood at 5.7 million hectares and was expected to increase to 17 million hectares by 2050.[23] Many communities in low-lying catchment areas that include wetlands, woodlands, river systems, lakes, and hundreds of plant species and invertebrates are at risk. And salt will increasingly affect drinking water and damage infrastructure—roads, railway lines, buildings, farm dams—and entire townships in areas where little or no deep-rooted vegetation remains. Three initiatives focused on rehabilitating soil poisoned by salt and in preventing future salinisation have identified a number of activities to slow rising salt by keeping the water table low.[24] They include the farming of perennial pastures such as lucerne (or rotating lucerne and wheat); agroforestry systems comprising blocks of, or even individual, trees dispersed throughout paddocks (contradicting the trend of clearing such trees for centre-pivot irrigation); and plantation forestry in cleared areas.[25] To farmers in nine catchments of the Murray–Darling Basin alone, the costs of impact and preventative measures amount to close to 12 million dollars annually.[26]

In addition to the problems of salinity and soil erosion, limited fertility affects the land's ability to yield food and fibre. The most common way for farmers to boost this is through the application of fertilisers and pesticides. Australia is generally considered to use fewer polluting chemicals than other developed countries, and broad-spectrum and persistent chemicals have been largely phased out, but pesticide use in the production of rice, cotton, sugarcane, fruits, vegetables, grains and oilseed crops such as peanuts and sunflowers is still considerable. Around one billion dollars is spent on the annual application of herbicides, fungicides and insecticides that make their way into the wider landscape and affect unintended species.[27] Cotton crops use large quantities of pesticides and the expansion of cotton farming in catchments in north-western New South Wales has led to an increase in chemical levels at water monitoring sites. One commonly used insecticide, Endosulfan, is highly toxic to fish even at low concentrations and its use can have detrimental consequences especially after heavy rains and irrigation.[28]

Australian soils are particularly prone to acidification through millennia of extensive weathering. Increased acidity occurs most commonly through ammonium-based nitrogen fertilisers, the leaching of nitrate from pasture and legumes such as clover, and the constant removal of alkaline plant and animal waste which withdraws these pH-buffering components from the landscape. Acidification is most likely to occur on light sandy or loamy soils in areas of good rainfall. The consequences of acidification include the loss of microorganisms that help with the recycling of nutrients and the release of aluminium—an element that is toxic to plants and microorganisms.[29] Close to two-thirds of Australia's south-west agricultural region and many other areas are at risk of acid-ification and lost productivity from reduced plant growth.[30]

★ ★ ★

All things considered, most of Australia's soils are anything but suited to agriculture, let alone to the types of agriculture that depend on ample water for their yield. But competing for the natural resources of the Murray–Darling Basin are some of the world's thirstiest crops: pasture, lucerne, grapes, citrus, olives and forage crops as well as cotton and rice. Of these, pasture and crops to feed livestock use more than twice as much water as cotton and rice put together, reflecting the immense extent of the dairy, beef and wool industries.[31] The practice of intensive irrigated agriculture in an area such as this, where water availability is variable, has relied on the regulation of the flow of rivers and the construction of large dams to capture these flows. Once contained, water is allocated to industry and the natural environment in accordance with a carefully negotiated management plan. Irrigators purchase five-yearly water licences, assigning them rights to a specified volume of water that con-verts to an annual allocation that may vary depending on the year's river inflows and dam levels. While the environment is also a stakeholder in this equation, it receives only a proportion of the water not used by industry. Needless to say, this is far less than it requires. And adding insult to injury is the fact that much of the water siphoned off for agriculture never makes it to its intended destination. Despite the massive Murray–Darling infrastructure, staggering amounts of water continue to be lost through evaporation and leakage. A recent report on the Darling catchment found that inefficient water storage is responsible for the annual loss of 2 million megalitres of water—equivalent to four times the volume of Sydney Harbour.[32]

Irrigation for livestock, pasture and crops has a long history in the Basin, but irrigation for cotton only dates from the mid 1960s. In recent years, controversy surrounding the cotton industry has stemmed from the monopoly that cotton farms in south-western Queensland have on the water supply of an entire river system. Just north of the New South Wales–Queensland border on the Condamine–Balonne system is Cubbie Station, the largest of those farms. It occupies a strategic location high up on a river that supplies large areas of floodplain with water downstream of the property. The farm has effectively cut off the supply of water to grazed floodplains and reserves downstream. Privately owned, Cubbie Station channels the river's water into giant storage dams (these hold a volume equal to Sydney Harbour) to irrigate more than 20 000 hectares of cotton. The company that owns Cubbie Station claims the operation to be an 'economic and ecological model for sustainable development in Australia'.[33] The reality is that the farm's vast water demands and other irrigators' allocations upstream deny water to downstream ecosystems in Queensland, New South Wales and the Darling River.

Dams constructed to regulate water flow and ensure supply in dry years have manipulated river flows so much that they no longer resemble their natural flow regimes. Instead of the irregular floodings that are vital for the natural ecosystems, irrigation requires consistent summer flows to boost plant crop and pasture growth. Thousands of dams now prevent natural flow regimes throughout the intensively farmed regions of Australia, leaving the amount of water left to nature in the hands, and at the mercy, of irrigators and politicians.

Burrendong Dam near Wellington in New South Wales was constructed in 1967 to provide flood mitigation and controlled flows for the region. The dam captures the waters of the Macquarie and Cudgegong rivers for the local irrigators, and natural flows occur only if tributaries below the dam carry enough water or if the dam overflows. As a result, floodplains and freshwater ecosystems like the beautiful Macquarie marshes in central New South Wales have had almost no flooding since 2000, preventing birds from breeding, fish from migrating and causing riparian plants to die and toxic algal blooms to flourish in the stagnant remnant pools. In a year of good flooding under natural conditions, the muddy riverbanks of the Macquarie break to cover more than 200 000 hectares of the marshes' floodplains with more than 500 million cubic metres of water.[34] The flooded wetlands are a magnet to migrant birds and to threatened species such as the graceful brolgas, blue-billed and freckled ducks and the painted snipe. For some of these birds, the marshes are a vital breeding ground; however, waterbirds that breed in colonies such as ibis, egrets, herons, cormorants and spoonbills will not do so if flooding is inadequate.[35] Under the water-sharing plan for the marshes, its *full* allocation is only 160 000 megalitres (for years when full allocation is possible), and less in years of poor rains and low dam levels when competition with industry is greatest.[36] Early in 2003 some rain fell in the catchments supplying the Macquarie marshes. All of it was caught by the Burrendong dam—none reached the wetlands.

In late 2005, in acknowledging the vulnerability of the Macquarie marshes, the relevant governments, irrigators and graziers agreed to release some 30 000 megalitres from Burrendong Dam. This, combined with some rainfall, initiated the breeding of a few waterbirds such as straw-necked, glossy and white ibis, spoonbills and magpie geese. Sadly, the inadequate amount of water and its bounty of food receded too quickly and the breeding failed, leaving chicks to die and the water-birds' populations unreplenished.[37]

The only way to resolve this dilemma is to incorporate the environmental cost of diverting water from the natural landscapes into the bills paid by those who use it—industries and consumers. Inevitably, this will mean a reassessment of the viability of particular agricultural sectors and a long overdue restructure. The agriculture industry has long been subsidised by government, and water continues to be vastly under-valued; the price paid for water by irrigators does not cover the cost of the major infrastructure such as dams and delivery, let alone the real value of water.

The amount of water required by water-thirsty industries is aston-ishing. Up to 29 000 litres of water are needed to produce just one kilo-gram of irrigated cotton, enough to make one T-shirt and one pair of jeans.[38] Vast amounts of water are also required to grow rice and pasture for beef cattle. Growing just one kilogram of rice takes between 3000 and 5000 litres of water; and producing one kilogram of beef, including the irrigation of pasture and the processing of cattle carcasses, consumes up to 3700 litres of water.[39] Economically, however, the returns of cotton are considerably higher than those of irrigated grazing and cropping.

In 2004–05, rice and pasture were the lowest value crops per mega-litre of water consumed, while vegetables and fruit produced the highest return for water invested. Overall, the gross value of irrigated agricultural production in Australia in 2004–05 was around 25 per cent of all agricultural commodities produced during that period.[40] While this figure can be considerably higher during non-drought periods—in 1996–97 irrigated agriculture accounted for 38 per cent of the total gross value of agriculture—it makes a relatively small contribution to the economy when compared with its enormous cost to the environment.

In a country where drought and natural water shortages are now the norm, a revised water policy that sets the price of water to reflect the needs of the landscapes ahead of those of industry is essential. Water prices that are commensurate with environmental value will favour higher-value industries over those of low value. Such water pricing schemes should put a stop to the cultivation of irrigated rice, drastically reduce the production of pasture and curb the irrigated sectors of the beef industry to concentrate instead on fruit and vegetable crops in areas where water is more readily available.

If policies fail to reflect the real value of water and continue to support its unsustainable use, freshwater ecosystems that are of immense natural value will disappear. Many unexploited rivers still exist in the north of Australia, and pressure to expand agricultural production in that part of the country is growing; it is imperative that the hard-won lessons learned about water over-allocation in the east are not senselessly repeated.

In 2003 the issues of water over-allocation and the distribution of water licences became the drivers of the Living Murray Agreement between all states covered by the Murray–Darling Basin and, the following year, led to the founding of the National Water Initiative. These initiatives seek to identify over-allocated river systems and to restore a semblance of balance through improved efficiencies, water planning and 'clarity around the assignment of risk arising from future changes in water availability' for rural industries and urban areas.[41]

Sufficient water allocation for the environment must be made a non-negotiable priority—especially in times of drought—because any intermittent rains may simply come too late to save our invaluable fresh-water ecosystems.

5

THE BAD AND THE UGLY

Weeds and Feral Animals

Many people on being quizzed about weeds and feral animals in Australia are likely to list a familiar few—sprawling bushes of lantana and morning glory, gangs of Indian mynahs in their gardens, the neighbour's predatory cat, rabbits and foxes, and those crafty cane toads that hitch rides in the chassis of cars. Some may also remember the much-publicised discoveries of fire ant colonies in Queensland in 2001, or the threats from the crown-of-thorn starfish on the Great Barrier Reef.

Biased by their familiarity, people are unlikely to consider their own beloved dog and cat companions, or their camellia, rose and magnolia-adorned gardens as dangerously foreign. Instead, foreign plants and animals are generally accepted as a fact of life and their control in the environment is largely considered the job of volunteer bushcare groups and scientists.

Invasive species are a commonly underrated threat to native land-scapes and ecosystems, and to the multitudes of plants and animals that are smothered, choked, poisoned, starved, trampled, harassed, evicted or killed and eaten by them. Many of Australia's now highly problematic species did not arrive here as unwelcome invaders but were deliberately introduced for a variety of reasons: as ornamental plants for gardens;

pasture grasses to feed domestic stock; exotic fruit for horticultural purposes; and animals for pastoralism, hunting and fishing, to control pests, and as human companions.

Outside of their native African, South American, Asian or European environments and the natural controls of their native ecosystems, many hundreds of introduced species have wandered far beyond the specific landscapes and uses for which they were imported. Today the war against foreign landscape invaders is being fought on many fronts. In both agricultural and environmental contexts, it comes at an enormous cost. The management of weeds and major feral pests, and the cost of agricultural production lost to these two factors (let alone the costs to the natural environment) add up to more than $4.7 billion annually.[1] A 2004 senate inquiry into invasive species found that 'the scale of the problem is enormous and the challenges daunting'.[2] And that is an understatement.

★ ★ ★

The Hilda Brabben-inspired 1950s English television program *Bill and Ben: Flower Pot Men*, set among a pile of gardening utensils, portrayed the character of Little Weed as a pretty, harmless and friendly flower, protective of its shy potted friends and happily tolerated by the unsuspecting gardener. But 'harmless' is not a description suited to most weeds and, on a continent far removed from this small English garden, Australians would eventually learn that the Little Weed of their childhood has some very nasty cousins.

Since Europeans first set foot on Australian soil more than 28 000 plants have been introduced to, or have accidentally arrived on, these shores.[3] Of that number, 10 per cent (2800 plants) are now considered to be weeds that are harming the environment. The defining characteristics of weeds are that they occur *outside* their natural ecosystems, are able to spread rapidly and harm the environment. Often the spread of an introduced plant is helped by the production of large amounts of seeds, which are dispersed by wind, water, or by birds and mammals that consume then deposit them via their droppings in other parts of the natural landscape, sometimes many kilometres from their source. Wildlife-dispersed weeds include fruiting trees, palms and shrubs, and some of the most common are Chinese elm, cocos palm, blackberry, lantana, wild tobacco and asparagus fern, all of which produce smallish fruits eaten by birds, fruit bats, brushtail and ringtail possums and other animals.

Some introduced plants can also spread quickly by producing runners that allow new plants to shoot from underground stems or rhizomes (*Sansevieria* aka mother-in-law's tongue, horsetail and alligator weed), or by sprouting new shoots directly where drooping branches touch the ground (cat's claw, blackberry and willows).

Along the freshwater habitats of rivers, creeks, ponds and lakes, aquatic weeds are easily spread when they get caught in boat trailers, fishing gear and heavy equipment such as trucks or excavators, and are then inadvertently transported to another waterbody. Many weeds are also carried on the feet of waterbirds such as ducks and geese. After being deposited in a new creek or dam, the plants multiply rapidly and can threaten the environment in a number of ways: they can pollute drinking water, reduce the lake or dam's capacity to store water and trap wildlife in the dense masses of choking leaves, roots and filaments.[4] The small, floating salvinia fern reproduces so quickly that a small infestation of only a few plants can double in size every two to three days until the entire water surface is covered with a dense mat, making the creek or dam uninhabitable for wildlife, including fish.[5]

Not all introduced plants become weeds, however, and not all weeds are introduced. Grown outside of their natural ecosystems, some native plants have the potential to become invasive and impact on the landscape. Understanding that 'native' plants are native only within their natural habitats and distribution ranges and not to the entire country explains the very nature of a weed.

Like introduced plants, the spread of native vegetation beyond its natural range is often actively promoted. Acacias are hardy and attractive plants with showy flowers, and the Cootamundra wattle and the Queensland silver wattle have been planted extensively on farms and along roadsides outside of their natural ranges. From there, their seeds are naturally carried by strong wind, ants, or spread by human activity (as mud or soil containing seeds is carried in the tyres of cars or farm machinery). Wattles' seeds can remain viable for years as they are protected in a seed pod. Seeds can lie dormant until an event like a fire, where heat triggers the explosion of the seeds' pods, or disturbance caused by groundworks precipitates their germination.[6] Where lots of seeds germinate, wattles can grow in dense stands and out-compete native plants by absorbing most of the limited soil moisture and nutrients.

Coastal ti tree, sweet pittosporum and species of melaleuca and hakea are popular garden plants that can also become invasive, as they have in parts of Victoria.[7] Along the east coast tropical trees such as cadaghi, a eucalypt that grows south to Rockhampton, and the fast-growing umbrella tree, found naturally north of the Tropic of Capricorn, are also popular garden plants whose spread is aided by wildlife. Both have reached weed status in many urban and near-urban areas. Even within Queensland, its state of origin, the umbrella tree is recognised as a weed for its copious seed production and subsequent ability to spread to native bushland, national parks and reserves where it out-competes and displaces local plants and disturbs the balance of ecosystems.[8]

★ ★ ★

Many thousands of weeds occur in Australia—more than 350 have been declared 'noxious'[9] and twenty so far have been labelled as Weeds of National Significance (WoNS). This label recognises the widespread environmental damage that these plants have already caused and the dangers they present in spreading further across the country. An inkling of the scale of the weed problem is gleaned from the diverse ecosystems affected by these twenty species. They include rainforest (rubber vine and pond apple), rangelands (athel pine and mesquite), floodplains and wetlands (prickly acacia, olive hymenachne, parkinsonia and mimosa), coastal dunes (bitou bush and boneseed), bushland (blackberry and bridal creeper), grasslands (Chilean needlegrass and serrated tussock), watercourses (alligator weed, cambomba and salvinia), riverbanks (athel pine, prickly acacia, and gorse) and highly disturbed areas such as road-sides, fencelines and pastures (blackberry, gorse and lantana). Sandy, cracking or clay soils; fresh, brackish and salt water; tropical, temperate, arid or alpine climates—weeds have infiltrated every environmental niche with devastating impacts.

In Queensland in the late 1860s, rubber vine was first planted to decorate the gardens of northern mining towns. By the early twentieth century this climbing shrub, with many stems native to Madagascar, had become recognised as a weed and it now threatens woodlands, rare vine thickets, rainforest and waterways including large areas of the Wet Tropics World Heritage area. Its spread is helped by profuse seed production and their ready transportation along rivers and creeks. The Cooperative Research Centre for Weed Management (CRC Weed Management) estimates that a hectare of rubber vine can produce millions of seeds per year.[10] Where rubber vine has run amok, the once healthy native landscape is reduced to the eerie skeletons of dead trees draped in masses of the plant that killed them. As well as producing seeds, rubber vine also spreads by extending long, whip-like branches across to neighbouring vegetation and 'climbing' onto its next plant victim. And rubber vine is not selective about where it grows—it also smothers pasture and cultivated grasses, and its damage to the beef industry in 1995 alone was estimated at around $18 million.[11] In 2003 rubber vine infestation in Queensland was estimated at 35 million hectares—one-fifth of the state.[12] The majestic gallery forests of northern Queensland are particularly at risk as the invasion of rubber vine has already caused the disappearance of the rufous owl and now threatens the local populations of the greater glider and squirrel glider whose forest habitats it steadily invades and destroys.[13]

The consequences of weed invasions are many and varied. Of great concern is that many native species are disappearing largely unnoticed by all but the scientists who monitor them. This is particularly the case with native plants that occur in localised habitats. The pink pimelea or rice flower, a small shrub adorned with clusters of elegant, pale pink flowers, is found only in the endangered Cumberland Plain woodland of western Sydney.[14] While the woodland once extended across 125 000 hectares, extensive clearing for the development of Sydney's western suburbs and agricultural regions has reduced it to less than 9 per cent of its original extent. What little remains of the once imposing woodland of tall red gums, spotted gums, grey box, narrow-leafed ironbark, acacias and its understorey of herbs and grasses is now highly vulnerable to threats such as weeds from the developed urban areas nearby. The delicate pink pimelea's future is now jeopardised by the highly invasive bridal creeper. Introduced as a garden plant, bridal creeper (like rubber vine) literally smothers the landscapes it invades. Its masses of climbing branches and foliage cover all plant life below and block out the sun, while its mat of tuber roots crowds out other root systems and prevents the establishment of new plant seedlings. The pink pimelea is, however, by no means the only plant at risk; in South Australia and south-west Western Australia bridal creeper is considered the most important weed threat to biodiversity.[15]

★ ★ ★

As weeds take over, wildlife too finds its habitats destroyed and shelter exposed to predators, whether by innocuous-looking flowering plants like the bright pink, dune-covering pigsface, by climbing vines, foreign palms or deciduous African, Indian and European trees. In some cases, animals find their familiar native food plants replaced with similar-looking exotic plants that reveal themselves to be toxic when eaten.

One of Australia's largest and most beautiful butterflies is the Richmond birdwing. With a 15-centimetre wingspan, a red body and bright yellow abdomen, and an iridescent green pattern adorning the black-and-yellow hindwings of the male, this member of the spectacular birdwing family captures the attention of anyone lucky enough to glimpse it. Sadly, the introduction of a South American ornamental vine, the Dutchman's pipe (*Aristolochia elegans*), has made it one of Australia's most threatened invertebrates. Dutchman's pipe is extremely similar in appearance to one of the two native birdwing vines (*Pararistolochia praevenosa*) on which the butterfly traditionally lays its eggs and whose leaves are the sole food of its growing caterpillars. Attracted by the deceptive similarities, the female butterfly lays its eggs on the young leaves of the exotic vine, unaware that the plant is toxic and will kill its caterpillars as soon as they hatch and feed. The sight of a Richmond birdwing cruising through rainforest from northern New South Wales to northern Queensland was once a cheerful sign of summer.[16] Extensive land clearing resulting in the loss of the native birdwing vine, followed by the spread of the exotic Dutchman's pipe have reduced the Richmond birdwing's status to 'vulnerable to extinction' and it now occurs only in a few small pockets of its former range.

Wildlife inhabitants of swamps, wetlands and waterways have suffered considerably from invasive plants. Over thirty aquatic and semi-aquatic weeds have been recognised as 'noxious', with seven being Weeds of National Significance.[17] Some, like the South American alligator weed, are thought to have arrived in the ballast waters of foreign ships that were emptied into local harbours on their arrival in Australia. This tenacious weed pollutes the water by forming suffocating mats across its surface, which reduces the oxygen exchange and degrades the water quality for fish and invertebrates. Cabomba, a fast-growing weed that now clogs up creeks, streams and dams in four states, was initially introduced as a decorative aquarium or fishpond plant. Like many aquatic weeds, this submerged plant can take over the entire waterbody in which it grows, reducing its ability to store water and crowding out wildlife such as platypus from their natural habitats.[18] Hymenachne, a semi-aquatic grass that grows to more than 2.5 metres in height, was deliberately introduced into northern Queensland and the Northern Territory as a ponded fodder plant. Within only ten years of being approved for release in 1988, it had infested dozens of sites in the Wet Tropics and now threatens vast areas of wetlands throughout tropical Australia, including Kakadu and other national parks. Thick stands of this tall weed (which often grows alongside the equally invasive para grass) crowd out lagoons and leave no room for wading birds such as the graceful black-necked stork (jabiru) to trawl through the shallows in search of small fish and frogs, forcing them to abandon these sites and seek food elsewhere.

★ ★ ★

Another major route for invasive weeds into Australia has been the introduction of foreign pasture plants, a move originally intended to improve the quality of food for the livestock (cattle and sheep) that roam the rangelands. Between 1947 and 1985, 460 species of pasture grasses and legumes were brought into the country and trialled for their suitability in northern Australian conditions. Of those that passed the test, a staggering sixty became weeds and are now wreaking environmental havoc. Only four out of the total number tested fulfilled their intended purpose as stock feed without also invading the wider environment.[19]

Once weeds are released into the landscape their control can consume endless resources. On a local scale some weeds can be cut and pasted with weed killer or pulled up by hand, sometimes a back-breaking effort. On a landscape scale, the removal of larger weeds may involve the use of heavy machinery, the spraying of toxic herbicides or the use of biological means like predatory beetles or destructive fungi. And, ironically, the vectors that helped spread them, such as fire and grazing stock, can sometimes control weeds. Cattle grazing on African lovegrass prevent the grass from seeding and therefore help contain its further spread. The removal of established weeds almost always requires concerted, ongoing effort; short-term bursts of funding may enable the temporary control of a weed on a local scale but are insufficient to prevent its permanent removal, ultimately wasting all previous efforts.

Without question the most effective way of controlling a weed is to prevent its introduction in the first place. A preventive policy requires the full support of the agricultural and horticultural industries as well as sound quarantine laws and their stringent enforcement. Australia's quarantine laws were strengthened in 2006, but the quarantine network continues to be hampered by a hotchpotch of mismatched state laws.

The result is that many high-risk invasive plants banned for sale in one state are freely available in another. Of course, this greatly increases the risk of weeds spreading from a region or state where they are non-invasive to one where they have the potential to become invasive and cost the environment (and the agricultural industry) dearly. 'Until major weed pathways, such as the legal movement of high risk garden plants are closed,' says former WWF-Australia campaigner Andreas Glanznig, 'Australia's national weed defence system will continue to resemble a car spluttering along on three cylinders.'[20]

★ ★ ★

When Europeans began exploring the arid central and western interior of Australia in the mid nineteenth century, suitable domestic animals were needed to carry supplies and people through the blistering desert conditions. Nothing fit the bill better than the camel, and several thousand were promptly imported from India, Pakistan and the Middle East. Camels accompanied such famed adventurers as Burke and Wills on their ill-fated expedition from Melbourne to the Gulf of Carpentaria in 1860–61. Camels also carried material for the construction of the overland telegraph line and extensive fencelines, and for the building of the cross-continental railway tracks. With the advent of railways and cars in the 1930s, however, the services of the trusty 'desert ships' were no longer needed. Many of the thousands of unwanted camels were shot while others were simply abandoned. Left to their own devices, these hardy animals made themselves at home in the ecological niche of tall vegetation browsers and proceeded to breed. And the breeding continues to this day—populations in some areas double about every eight years, and recent estimates tip camel populations at one million animals and rising.[21]

The early impact of individual camels on the delicate desert landscape was considerably less destructive than that of sheep and cattle. Their soft feet protect the soil crust, and their ability to survive for extended periods without water made the colonisation of the arid interior comparatively easy. At high densities, however, camels these days consume more than 80 per cent of available plants and can damage them beyond their ability to recover. And despite their ability to survive for periods without water, thirsty camels can destroy fences (and outhouses) to get to it and foul important water sources with their copious droppings. As watering holes provide crucial refuges for a large range of native wildlife in dry times, the degradation of these life-giving oases affect many species and may bring about local extinctions of threatened marsupials. In parts of the Simpson Desert, camels, along with other introduced herbivores and predators, are a threat to the survival of the ampurta, an arid-adapted marsupial that lives in mature spinifex grassland and cane grass on sand dunes.[22] The herbivores overgraze and degrade this habitat, increasing the marsupials' exposure to predators.

Hundreds of animals introduced or accidentally imported over the last two hundred years have happily adapted to their new surrounds and taken up roles as predators and competitors among the native fauna. Rats, mice, buffalo, deer, pigs, cane toads, and species of ants, fish, flies, bees, wasps, spiders, snails, earthworms, shellfish, crayfish, crabs and geckoes are only a small sample menu of the diversity of foreign fauna currently found in Australia. Feral animals can impact on the environment in a number of ways including by over-consuming food, water and shelter at the expense of native species (competition), killing and consuming native wildlife, often beyond sustainable limits (predation), destroying delicate environments such as watering holes or soil crusts, or producing toxins that kill native predators.

As with exotic weeds, most animals now feral were deliberately introduced with specific uses in mind. Horses, donkeys and camels served early settlers, explorers and industry, while cattle, sheep, goats and pigs were the founding stock of traditional European farming practices. Sport hunters and fishers set their sights on traditional target species, and rabbits, foxes, deer and trout were placed alongside native species. And despite the bounty of tropical fish found along the east coast, ponds and fish tanks were stocked with exotic species such as carp, mosquito fish and tilapia. Cats and dogs, trusted companions the world over, were brought to Australia and found the native fauna, in particular the many small birds and mammals, conveniently meal-sized and easy to catch.

★ ★ ★

Species that arrived in Australia without invitation—as stowaways in import cargo, aboard ships and in their ballast waters—have increased significantly with growing maritime traffic.[23] The northern Pacific seastar is one of more than one hundred exotic marine species in Australian waters and was first discovered in the Derwent River estuary near Hobart, Tasmania, in 1986. The yellow and purple seastar, native to the coasts of China, Korea, Russia and Japan is a voracious predator that feeds on mussels, scallops, clams and crabs, and threatens marine ecosystems as well as the shellfish seafood industry.[24] A report by the Australian Biosecurity Group highlights that a large female seastar can lay an astonishing 19 million eggs, and that Australia now has 100 million hungry starfish that are devouring native shellfish.[25] The seastars' rapid colonisation of Tasmanian waters and subsequent arrival in Victoria's Port Phillip Bay in 1995 prompted the initiation of a national control plan for the starfish in 2000 and, in anticipation of its continued spread, it has been made a research priority for the CSIRO's Centre for Research on Introduced Marine Pests.[26]

★ ★ ★

To date thirty-four exotic fish have taken up residence in Australian waters, accidentally or deliberately freed from the confines of ponds and aquaria.[27] Of the larger, land-based species introduced to Australia's mainland, twenty-five mammals, twenty birds and four reptiles have established wild (feral) populations.[28] So far, seven of them—goats, rabbits, rats, cats, foxes, pigs and cane toads—have been listed as key threats to native species under the *EPBC Act*, while wild populations of camels, horses, donkeys and water buffalo have been earmarked as species of 'significant concern' by the federal government.[29] And yet the impacts of the vast numbers of introduced cattle and sheep that graze more than two-thirds of the country are far more significant than those of all feral hoofstock put together.

★ ★ ★

One of Australia's longest running sagas in battling to control a feral pest has to do with rabbits. Domestic rabbits are said to have arrived in Australia with the First Fleet, and about seventy years later a dozen were released into the environment by a property owner near Geelong, Victoria.[30] Less than thirty years later rabbits had reached the Queensland–New South Wales border, and by 1910 had covered much of the continent.

The animal's extraordinary success is in no small part to do with its reproduction. Female rabbits mature at only four months of age, which means they can have more than five litters a year. Each litter yields four or five young, which in turn will be able to breed another four months down the track, enabling populations to soar when conditions are suitable. Rabbits are also resilient and highly adaptable plant-eaters, and their habits of feeding on plant foliage above ground and digging to forage for roots and build warrens below means little if any vegetation is left intact.

The combined impacts of competition and land degradation by rabbits and predation by foxes are thought to have caused the extinction of the burrowing bettong in central Australia in the 1940s.[31] With the digging work already done for them, rabbits evicted the bettongs, colonised their burrows and competed for their food, leaving them exposed and vulnerable to preying foxes. Burrowing bettongs now remain only on a few offshore islands and in a number of carefully managed colonies in Western Australia.[32]

Attempts to control rabbit populations have become part of Australian folklore. The early 1900s saw the construction of two rabbit-proof fences that traversed Western Australia and measured 1834 and

1166 kilometres, respectively.[33] Built in desperate attempts to keep rabbits from destroying crops and pasture as they had in the eastern states, the first fence bisected the state from the north-west coast to the south. But both fences were doomed to failure—even before their completion, a number of rabbits had made it through and invaded the west.

In 1950, disease was used to control rabbit numbers. The release of the myxoma virus killed more than 90 per cent of the rabbits that developed myxomatosis, but as individuals developed a resistance to the virus it became less effective, particularly in wetter regions of the country. The subsequent introduction of calicivirus in the mid 1990s compensated somewhat for the increasing resistance in the wetter parts and together both diseases have kept populations of rabbits reasonably managable. But the devastation caused by rabbits when its populations explode should never be underestimated.

Macquarie Island, located south-east of Tasmania, is a World Heritage-listed breeding site for penguin, seal and seabird populations, in particular the magnificent but threatened wandering and grey-headed albatrosses. In 2006, the distinctive tussock grasses of the island's coastal slopes, which are nesting and roosting grounds for thousands of birds, were found to have been obliterated by rabbits. The complete removal of groundcover from overgrazing, and the construction of burrows by a population of around 100 000 rabbits, had left most of the island a virtual wasteland. Where tussock grasses once provided nesting material and shelter, the birds were now left exposed, and soil slopes were eroding at an alarming rate. Landslides had become such a serious problem that they physically threatened wildlife at the base of the slopes. In September 2006, a slide of about 500 square metres of soil mass-buried parts of a king penguin colony that included both adults and chicks.[34] Hundreds of birds were killed, and this event brought to light a political stand-off between the federal government and the Tasmanian government over responsibility for the conservation and management of the reserve.[35] Only once the country's attention had been directed to this situation through the media did the two governments agree to share the cost of eradicating the remaining feral species from the island.

While rabbits have been present on Macquarie Island since the 1870s, their overall numbers had been kept in check by introduced cats; where rabbits are present, they constitute the main prey of cats and thereby ease the pressure on native species.[36] But cats (and rats) also preyed on the seabirds and their eggs and chicks. In 2002 the cats were eradicated, an act that was vital to protect the nearly four million seabirds that come to the island to breed. The eradication of the cats, however, coupled with an increased resistance to myxamatosis and warmer winters enabled rabbits to produce an additional litter of young and catapulted rabbit numbers into orbit. An eradication plan to remove rabbits, rats and mice has now been developed and funded and provides hope for the restoration of this seabird haven.

Macquarie Island is not the only island to suffer from a rabbit scourge. In the Norfolk group of islands, Phillip Island was completely ravaged by rabbits, pigs and goats which were introduced during its time as a penal colony and caused the local extinction of at least two plant species. Tellingly, the island's remaining vegetation recovered remarkably once the rabbits had been eradicated.

★ ★ ★

Cats and foxes have had a profoundly detrimental impact on our native wildlife and controlling their numbers on the mainland is an immense challenge. Foxes occur across 80–90 per cent of the continent, avoiding only the northernmost tropical regions and some offshore islands.[37] Cats, however, have surpassed even this expansive range and are now found across the entire continent as well as on many offshore islands.[38] Traditional pest control methods of shooting, poisoning, fencing and trapping have helped control these two stealthy predators' numbers, but their eradication is an as yet unattainable goal.

Cats arrived in Australia with the First Fleet and possibly even earlier. By the middle of the nineteenth century, a number of domestic moggies had cut loose and feral populations had become established in the wild. Around the same time the numbers of introduced rats, mice and rabbits, natural prey species of cats, were causing concern to farmers. In an ill-conceived effort to control the smaller pest species, additional cats were released and further boosted feral cat numbers.[39] In the 1870s, one hundred years after the introduction of cats, foxes were released for recreational hunting in Victoria and spread rapidly, closely shadowing the distribution of rabbits.[40] Within a few decades, the combination of cats and foxes had triggered a wave of species extinctions across the country and left indelible voids in its biodiversity. But as the presence of cats did not lead to the extinction of *all* prey species wherever they occurred, it is likely that the exotic felines were not solely to blame. Instead it seems that their impact was more pronounced in areas where major habitat changes had taken place through land clearing and altered fire regimes. While many native populations might have survived the threat of cats in isolation, the combination of cats, habitat degradation and altered fire regimes was simply too much.

In the arid zones, cats and foxes prey on many ground-dwelling birds and small- to medium-sized mammals typical of the rangeland fauna. They have been implicated in the decline in numbers of central Australia's threatened long-tailed dunnart, the dusky hopping-mouse, the mulgara and ampurta, the kowari, the brushtail possum, the night parrot and the great desert skink. Between them, the two exotic predators have played major parts in the regional extinctions of the short-tailed and long-tailed hopping mouse and the Alice Springs mouse in the early 1900s, the lesser stick-nest rat in the 1930s, the numbat, central hare-wallaby, pig-footed bandicoot, brush-tailed bettong (woylie), burrowing bettong and red-tailed phascogale around the 1950s, and the western quoll, lesser bilby, crescent nail-tailed wallaby and desert bandicoot in the 1960s.[41] In the Northern Territory native animals such as the northern quoll, Carpentarian rock rat, bilby, golden bandicoot and the dusky hopping-mouse, the malleefowl and the night parrot remain under threat of extinction, with cats and/or foxes partly responsible for their demise.

The most convincing evidence of the impact of feral predators is provided by projects where predator removal has led directly to the recovery of native wildlife populations. In Western Australia the Western Shield Project was initiated in 1996 and continues to be the largest project of its kind. In that state, where fauna and flora are isolated from the east and therefore particularly vulnerable, cats and foxes have been held responsible for the extinction of twelve species of mammals and the decline of many others.

By using poisoned baits across almost 3.5 million hectares in the south-west, the Western Shield project has aimed to retrieve species from the brink of extinction. Interestingly, the local wildlife had a natural advantage. The 1080-poison used for the baits is naturally found in the 'poison pea' plant (*Gastrolobium*) that is native to Western Australia. Having evolved alongside this plant, the local wildlife is immune to the poison and not at risk of death from consuming the bait.

An independent review of the project in 2003 found that in the seven-year period since its commencement, the successful control of feral predators had led to such improvements in the populations of brush-tailed bettongs, tammar wallabies and quendas that they were removed from the state's threatened species list. Many other species— the chuditch (western quoll), numbat, bilby, malleefowl and western swamp tortoise—also fared better, with new populations re-established in regions where they had previously disappeared.

This project has demonstrated without any doubt that the control of feral predators on a suitably large scale was a fundamental step in enabling the recovery of species threatened by predation. The use of 1080-poison in other parts of the country is a more controversial issue, as the native wildlife is more susceptible to the toxin and may be killed inadvertently. To reduce this risk, more target-specific baiting methods continue to be developed.

The ongoing control and, wherever possible, eradication of introduced plants and animals that threaten Australia's landscapes and ecosystems requires unwavering commitment and considerable resources. The cost of ignoring weeds and feral pests at the peril of Australia's natural capital is, on the other hand, unimaginable.

6

STEALTHY THREATS

Diseases

Of all the bizarre and fantastically evolved creatures that call Australia home, one that impresses with pretend-ferocity, big teeth and woeful table manners is the Tasmanian devil. The size of a smallish dog, with a solid, stocky build, a large head and even larger teeth, the nocturnal devil roams Tasmania's coastal heath, open forests and rainforests on the look-out for food, sleeping in dens or among dense vegetation during the day. At night it searches for dead animals (carrion) to scavenge on and often devours carcasses bones and all. With its awesome groaning howl, the devils' nightly feeding never fails to scare the bejesus out of unsuspecting campers, but their lingering impression of this animal as an aggressive bully potentially dangerous to humans is utterly inaccurate.

For all its cantankerous posturing, the devil is the landscapes' garbageman and it occupies this ecological niche with gusto, often disappearing entirely inside the carcass of a large dead cow or kangaroo as it feeds on its innards. Despite battle-scarred faces that only a mother or biologist could love, the Tassie devils are synonymous with the state they call home, having been out-competed by dingoes on the mainland long before the first European settlers pulled into Botany Bay. And after losing the magnificent Tasmanian tiger forever in 1936, where would the apple isle be without its remaining wildlife icon?

Sadly, this question now occupies the minds of scientists and conservationists alike. In only ten short years the possibility of losing the devil has become all too real. In 1996, a number of devils photographed in Tasmania's north-east displayed facial sores and growths that had never been seen before. Some animals had huge tumours that obscured parts of the face and neck, covered eyes or grew from the mouth or jaw and made feeding all but impossible. The devils were grossly disfigured and many were weak and emaciated as the disease had prevented them from feeding. Initial investigations found that the cancerous tumours would lead to death within three to eight months of the first visible symptoms[1]; by May 2007, devils in over half of the state had been affected by the disease. Sightings of the animals across the state had dropped by more than 50 per cent, and in the area where tumour-affected devils had first been observed that figure was as high as 90 per cent.[2] The Tasmanian devil was in serious trouble.

The sudden appearance of this new disease—named Devil Facial Tumour Disease (DFTD)—sent shock waves through Australia's wildlife research community. Where had the disease come from, and why now? Was it somehow a reflection of a damaged environment that had left wildlife unhealthy and more susceptible to illness? What would this mean for the future of the devil? To date, the origins of DFTD remain unknown, but research has shown that the cancer appears to spread from contact between individual animals. Contrary to expectation, it can affect perfectly healthy animals with well-functioning immune systems as easily as older or weaker individuals.

The rapid decline of devil populations has resulted in it being listed as 'vulnerable to extinction' under Tasmania's environment legislation, although the rapid rate of its decline already qualifies it for the higher listing of 'endangered'. Urgent research continues and healthy individuals are being evacuated to zoos and sanctuaries for captive breeding while the cancer continues to spread across Tasmania. The immediate future of the devil in the wild looks bleak, and some researchers estimate that it may be gone in as little as twenty years.[3]

The extinction of the Tasmanian devil would be a truly tragic loss to Australia's and the world's biodiversity, and its disappearance from Tasmanian ecosystems could have further long-term consequences. As one of only a few native mammal predators in the state, the loss of the devil, and even its decline, may lead to an increase in the number of feral cats and foxes which will prey on carrion as well as on small native fauna. Cats have long been a major threat to Tasmania's bird, skink, frog and small mammal populations. With fewer devils to tidy up the carcasses in the landscape, cat populations will be boosted by the additional food. And they are not alone.

Although cats have been present since European arrival, Tasmania had remained free of foxes until, to the stunned disbelief of conservation agencies and organisations, it was deliberately introduced as a target species by hunters in 2001. A growing log of reported sightings since then indicates that fox numbers are increasing.[4] Almost eighty vertebrate species in Tasmania are at risk from fox predation, including geographically restricted species like the eastern quoll and pademelon. The declining populations of Tasmanian devils may make it easier for foxes to take hold and expand their populations at the expense of wildlife and to the devils themselves. Should the incidence of disease in devils ever decline, the larger fox populations may out-compete them and prevent them from recovering.[5]

★ ★ ★

As is the case with weeds and feral animal pests, diseases can also threaten populations, individual species or entire landscapes and almost inevitably have consequences for the wider environment. 'New' diseases like DFTD are completely unpredictable and can strike out of the blue with devastating results. Without knowing their origins, causes or their impacts in the longer term, it is all but impossible to manage outbreaks effectively. On occasion, however, foreign diseases and pathogens may be introduced deliberately to help control populations of feral animals—as with the myxoma virus and calicivirus, brought in to reduce the populations of feral rabbits. Other new diseases arrive accidentally and are discovered only once they have taken hold somewhere in the environment.

Phytophthora cinnamomi is a tiny soil-borne water mould thought to have been attached to orange trees that were imported from Asia to establish our citrus industry. Phytophthora dieback, often called root rot, is a disease that affects large numbers of native plants (as well as crops and horticultural plants) and occurs predominantly in coastal forests and heathlands. The mould's spores live in the soil and are spread by water and a range of other mechanical means. Any activity that moves infected soil helps to increase its distribution—bushwalking, road construction, timber harvesting, mining and the movement of large animals are just a few examples. Once introduced to the soil, the spores wait for warm and moist conditions to germinate and infect new plants.[6] Phytophthora invades then destroys the root system of plants, preventing the uptake of water and nutrients and essentially starving them. Across millions of hectares of Australia's coastal and near-coastal vegetation like Western Australia's Stirling National Park, Sydney's Eastern Suburbs Banksia Scrub or Queensland's subtropical Eungella Plateau, it affects plant communities featuring eucalypts, banksias, grevilleas, grass trees, heath, ferns, cycads, grasses and native peas among others. Not surprisingly, it is also a threat to suburban gardens and to soil-based industries. The mould is invisible so it's extremely difficult to map exactly where it occurs and how much vegetation has been affected until the plants start to die. To date, only the chemical phosphite is able to slow the onset and impact of the disease, but it can do so only with repeated and expensive application and is therefore not considered to be a viable solution to fighting the pathogen in the long term.[7]

Infection with phytophthora can have wide-ranging impacts on plant communities and habitats. A large proportion of south-west Western Australia makes up a region recognised as one of only twenty-five global 'hotspots' of particularly rich and unique biodiversity. The South West Botanical Province features more than 5700 plant species and is characterised by the diverse vegetation found in its eucalypt woodlands, mallee shrublands and kwongan heaths.[8] More than 50 per cent of these plants are endemic to this region so it comes as no surprise that here, phytophthora has been likened to a 'biological bulldozer'.[9] At least 40 per cent of native plants and their dependent fauna are under threat in the South West Botanical Province and include already highly threatened species of banksia, dryandra and lambertia.[10]

The yellow-footed antechinus (or mardo) is a small, insectivorous marsupial that lives, feeds and breeds on the forest floor in the south-western corner of the continent as well as along and near the east coast.[11] The Western Australian mardo has declined noticeably in sections of jarrah forest affected by phytophthora dieback compared with those that are disease-free. As nesting sites, refuges and food resources become more scarce, mammals such as the mardo are pushed into remaining healthy areas. But as the fungus naturally creeps forward by about one metre a year—faster if moved by people or machines, healthy habitat is steadily decreasing. Phytophthora-damaged ecosystems may also affect the Gilbert's potoroo, Australia's most critically endangered mammal. With only around fifty individuals remaining and under pressure from fox and cat predation, phytophthora dieback constitutes an additional threat to the species' survival. Degradation of undergrowth and shelter, and a decline in the native truffles that are the potoroo's only food source and that are vulnerable to attack by the introduced water mould could easily drive it to extinction. In addition to the ground-dweller, phytophthora dieback also impacts on the nectar feeders that roam through the tops of flowering trees and shrubs such as the tiny honey possum. This exquisite little mammal, which weighs less than ten grams, relies on a suite of flowering banksias and other plants to provide a diet of nectar throughout the year. While extracting the nectar with its delicately pointed snout and long tongue, the possum collects pollen and plays an important role in the pollination of the food sources across its range. Unfortunately, banksias are highly vulnerable to phytophthora dieback. As banksia–dominated woodlands and kwongan are being killed or degraded by the disease, populations of the honey possum are also declining.

Given the ease of the spread of phytophthora dieback and the enormous value of coastal ecosystems to biodiversity and industries such as forestry, horticulture and tourism, conquering this biological bull-dozer is of critical importance to Australia. The economic losses from phytophthora dieback to these industries are currently estimated at around $160 million per year.[12] *Phytophthora cinnamomi* has been recog-nised as a key threatening process under the *EPBC Act 1999*. The only real hope for containing the ever-expanding destruction brought by this disease is to adopt a united approach to containing this pathogen across all levels of government, supported by a well-informed commu-nity actively involved in minimising its spread.

★ ★ ★

In many parts of the world, the mention of the amphibian disease chytridiomycosis (by those who can pronounce it) can plunge frog lovers into despair. Also known as amphibian chytrid fungus, this dis-ease is one of the biggest known threats to frogs, toads, newts and salamanders worldwide and has already caused the extinctions of frog populations in Australia and Panama and recorded declines in Venezuela, Ecuador, New Zealand and Spain.[13] In Australia, chytrid fungus is thought to have been present in local frog populations since the late 1970s although it was only discovered in 1993.[14] There is some evidence that the disease originated in Africa and spread to other coun-tries with the burgeoning trade in a particular African frog species in the 1930s.[15] As with phytophthora dieback, the introduction of amphib-ian chytrid fungus appears to have been unintentional and attributable to poor trade and quarantine practices.

Amphibian chytrid fungus is spread from frog to frog or by water containing spores shed by diseased frogs. The ability of the spores to survive in water makes the transmission of the disease all too easy.

Once infected, the spores attack regions of the frog's skin that contain keratin. Frogs breathe through their skin (as well as using their simple lungs) and rely on it for water balance and protection from toxins and pollutants; infection with chytrid fungus may compromise these protective skin functions and affect the frog's water and electrolyte balance and its respiration. Some of the symptoms in frogs include reduced movement as the skin becomes infected and damaged, odd postures due to damage to the nervous system, and weight loss. It is also possible that the fungus produces toxins that slowly poison the frogs.[16] The mechanism that causes these deaths is yet to be established but there is no disputing the now wide distribution of chytridiomycosis. Individuals of fifty Australian frog species, almost a quarter of all known Australian frogs, have been found to be infected with the fungus so far[17], and in Queensland, entire populations of the great barred frog and the northern tinker frog have already been wiped out by the fungus.[18] Chytrid fungus is a suspected threat to nine of the fourteen most critically endangered frogs in Australia, including the yellow-spotted frog, the baw baw frog, the southern corroboree frog and remaining populations of the northern tinker frog.[19]

The epidemiology of diseases in other species indicates that it is possible that frog populations already stressed by environmental changes such as chemical pollutants, introduced predatory fish, changing climate or degraded habitat are more susceptible to infection than those that live in a healthy environment. Frog extinctions are often speculatively attributed to a combination of factors, but sometimes there is little evidence to support such speculations. Two of Australia's most remarkable frogs whose extinction was a heartbreaking loss to this country's biodiversity were the gastric brooding frogs, once found in different stream systems of Queensland. In a fantastic feat of evolution, the females of these two aquatic species swallowed their tiny tadpoles after fertilisation and brooded them internally. What made this possible was the females' ability to stop the production of their stomach acid periodically so that it would not attack the growing young. Seven to eight weeks later, the females regurgitated their young once they had developed into froglets.[20]

Despite this amazing method of protecting their young, the southern gastric brooding frog disappeared from its south-east Queensland stream habitats of the Conondale and Blackall ranges and was last seen there in September 1981.[21] The extinction of the second species, the northern gastric brooding frog, from its small range in Eungella National Park followed only a few years later.[22] Herpetologist Keith McDonald was a witness to both of these historical extinctions as well as that of the southern day frog, not seen since 1979. When McDonald first noticed the disappearance of the southern day frog and southern gastric brooding frog from Queensland's south-east he was deeply perplexed by the lack of clues to explain their sudden declines. According to McDonald, the frogs' habitats were isolated and in excellent condition, and there was no evidence of water pollution or predatory fish in the areas. When populations of the northern gastric brooding frog also began to disappear eighteen months later, confusion turned to despair. Hoping for a miracle, McDonald continued to monitor these sites for four more years before coming to the conclusion that he had been the last person ever to see these truly remarkable animals alive. Twenty years after the initial declines of the gastric brooding frogs, researchers suggested that the cause for the extinctions was a newly discovered fungus that also affected several species of stream-dwelling frogs in the Wet Tropics. Chytrid fungus had been discovered

Our large number of frog species makes Australia an international hotspot of amphibian diversity and it is a source of pride for amateur and professional herpetologists.[23] One species survives only in tiny pools of water in Australia's alpine heathlands, one burrows into desert sands to re-emerge only when it rains, and another is confined to a single tropical peak in Far North Queensland. And who can resist a grin when lifting the lid of a tropical toilet to find the compact shape of a green tree frog tucked tightly into the rim of the cool, moist bowl? Or on hearing a male frog happily lodged in a downpipe, enjoying the marvellous amplification of his croak for all within earshot?

Frogs are also well recognised as natural indicators of environmental decline. The toll chytridiomycosis has inflicted on native frog populations is a sign that, in addition to other factors such as habitat degradation, pollution and climate change, the introduction of new diseases is pushing many amphibians beyond the limits of their resilience.

Phytophthora dieback and amphibian chytrid fungus are new diseases to this country, which gives them an advantage in that their plant and frog hosts have not evolved alongside them and so have not yet developed any resistance to them. The diseases' targets are, therefore, extremely vulnerable. Other diseases have been present in native populations for much longer, although they often do not produce any symptoms in otherwise healthy individuals. Once the individual's resistance is in some way lowered and the animals or plants become stressed, however, clinical symptoms of the diseases may become apparent.

A classic example of a disease whose symptoms are believed to be triggered by stress is a chlamydial disease that affects koalas. Chlamydophila is present in most koala populations, but infected koalas often show no symptoms and are ostensibly healthy. In some koalas, however, chlamydial infection can cause a variety of symptoms: the most obvious is conjunctivitis (inflamed eyes with a weepy discharge) which can lead to blindness, urinary tract infection (wet and dirty bottom), and disease of the reproductive organs that can cause female koalas to become infertile. A link between environmental disturbance and chlamydial disease of koalas has long been accepted, though it has been difficult to ascertain which specific aspects of disturbance are responsible. Potential culprits include territorial or energy stress due to fighting and increased foraging brought on by habitat destruction, inbreeding due to habitat fragmentation and the potential introduction of new chlamydial strains by livestock. In reality, a combination of these may be responsible.

One interesting hypothesis concerned habitat degradation and the role of nutrients and toxins in eucalypt foliage. The nutritional content of eucalypt leaves is affected by factors such as the amount of light and water the tree receives as well as the quality of the soil in which it grows.[24] Excessive amounts of light and changed water levels (caused by land clearing and forest fragmentation among other factors), and reduced soil quality (such as is caused by changed fire regimes or erosion), can reduce the nutritional content of eucalypt leaves and increase leaf toxin levels. It is therefore quite possible that there is a direct link between habitat degradation, clearing and changed burning practices leading to poor nutrition, ill health and the higher incidence of chlamydial disease in koalas. The link between this disease in koalas and the role of environmental factors is a subject of ongoing research.

★ ★ ★

On occasions, certain diseases can become transmissible ('spill over') from wild animals to domestic animals or directly to people. The means by which this can happen demonstrates that damaged and fragmented habitats for wildlife can also have direct consequences on human health. In the 1990s several cases of disease drew the attention of the public and the scientific community to rest on Australia's flying foxes.

In September 1994, a horse trainer, his stablehand and most of his horses in the Brisbane suburb of Hendra (after which the virus was named) suddenly fell ill with a mystery illness. Within several days both the trainer and fourteen of his horses had died while the stablehand slowly recovered. The diagnosis of the affected animals revealed that the disease was a new virus (a paramyxovirus) that had not been seen before in Australia or elsewhere. Its sudden appearance baffled both scientists from Queensland's Department of Primary Industries and from the CSIRO's Australian Animal Health Laboratory (AAHL) who investigated the deaths.[25] As the virus was entirely new, the search began to determine where it had come from. The most likely explanation was that there was a 'reservoir' or carrier species for the disease. Following considerable testing of a number of potential carrier species (possums, rats) without success, flying foxes showed positive results for antibodies of the disease in all four mainland species and were identified as natural hosts of Hendra virus.[26] Subsequent tests found the virus in frozen tissues of flying foxes long dead, and when experimental infection of bats with the virus produced no symptoms (as in the wild populations), the role of flying foxes as the reservoirs of the disease was confirmed.

But one question remained: how did the disease get from flying foxes to horses and humans? While the direct link between flying foxes and horses has never been proven, the most likely theory is that one or more flying foxes visited a fruiting or flowering tree in a horse paddock and deposited the virus via excreta (faeces or urine), saliva-laden fruit remnants spat out by the bats[27] or via aborted foetal tissues or fluids subsequently eaten by a grazing horse. From there, it was transmitted to other horses in the stable and to the trainer with fatal consequences. Further investigations found evidence that the virus could not be passed directly from bats to humans and that the trainer's death had resulted from contact with infected horses. The possibility of future direct transmission between flying foxes and people was therefore deemed unlikely. An important issue highlighted by the discovery of Hendra virus, however, was that flying foxes now live in close proximity to people and domestic animals and that this affects both bats and people. Three further human casualties from the Hendra virus (initially referred to as equine morbillivirus) followed in Mackay in 1995, in Cairns in 1999 and most recently in Brisbane in August 2008, and three horses, one in 2004 and two others in 2006 have also succumbed to the virus.[28]

While Hendra was still fresh in people's minds, a second flying fox-related disease was discovered in 1996. This second virus was found in flying foxes (and later in insectivorous bat species) in the course of wildlife surveys seeking to elaborate the frequency and distribution of Hendra virus. Later that year, this new virus was identified as the cause of death of a wildlife carer who had been bitten by a yellow-bellied sheathtail bat.[29] Following the bite, the site of the injury had become numb and within a few days the woman had fallen into a coma; she died five weeks later. To the alarm of all involved, the woman tested positive to a rabies-related virus subsequently named Australian Bat Lyssavirus (ABL or lyssavirus). This finding was particularly surprising as Australia had thus far been considered free of rabies and rabies-like diseases.[30] A second fatal case—that of a woman who had been bitten two years earlier by a flying fox without developing immediate symptoms—followed in 1998.

Unlike Hendra virus, ABL could also develop into full-blown disease in its host species, although they often appeared healthy and showed no symptoms in the early stages. The diseased bats typically had neurological symptoms: they displayed weakness in the legs and could become aggressive, which made bite injuries for people in close contact more likely. The possibility of contracting the disease from healthy-looking animals had clear implications on how wild bats would have to be handled in the future. Fortunately, the vaccine for the related rabies virus offered protection against ABL, and human immunoglobulin appears to be an effective (if painful and expensive) treatment option in case of a bat-related injury for an unvaccinated person. These, together with safe handling techniques, now allow for the continued responsible handling of orphaned and injured bats by wildlife carers, veterinarians and zoo staff.

Australia's flying foxes' public image was at an all-time low when they became linked to yet another new disease in 1997. This time the disease was first diagnosed in domestic pigs. Over a 4-month period, sows in a New South Wales piggery began to give birth to increasing numbers of stillborn, mummified or deformed piglets.[31] Antibodies for the disease were first found in the blood of flying foxes on the farm, and subsequently in flying foxes all over Australia. Investigators found that the disease was a new paramyxovirus (named Menangle virus) in the same family as Hendra. Two people who had worked with the pigs also displayed antibody levels in their blood and had been suffering from severe flu-like illnesses and rashes at the time of the outbreak in pigs, but both recovered. The most likely means of Menangle virus transmission from bats to pigs was through the flying foxes' droppings. The bats were known to fly over the piggery to and from their day camp and would occasionally drop faeces in flight. It was therefore probable that the pigs came into contact with the virus by walking through the faecal material and ingesting small amounts of it.

The three flying-fox-borne diseases illustrate that wildlife diseases are not necessarily confined to their host species but may affect the broader environment. Fifteen new paramyxoviruses have been discovered worldwide in the past forty-five years and four of them are found in Australia. They occur in animal hosts that range from dolphins and seals to rats, bats, snakes, horses and humans and continue to be a focus of research for their ability to affect humans, livestock and wild-life populations.[32]

Australia's four mainland species of flying foxes are critically important to the health of Australia's many forest ecosystems. As prolific consumers of seasonal fruit and nectar, flying foxes help pollinate the flowers of native trees and shrubs and disperse the seeds of the fruits they eat. In the process, the bats contribute to the regeneration of eucalypt woodlands, forests and rainforests along the east coast and across the northern half of the country.

The grey-headed and little red flying foxes are seasonal long-distance travellers that feed in areas where trees are in flower and then move on to new flowering sites elsewhere. Both species can cover hundreds or even thousands of kilometres each year in search of new sources of nectar. In the once intact forests of pre-European eastern Australia, flying foxes foraged across vast expanses of woody ecosystems and were assured of food year-round. This is no longer the case. The clearing of native trees and shrubs and the fragmentation of the bats' natural coastal habitat—often to accommodate expanding urban metropolises—has left large gaps in the bats' distribution ranges and in their seasonal menu. In search of reliable food, the bats have been forced to live in closer proximity to the human settlements that replaced their forest homes. In times of drought, often the only sources of food to be found are in suburban gardens and orchards. Unfortunately for bats and people, this forced proximity can lead to problems that would be unlikely to occur if the bats' habitat had not become a fractured patchwork of what it once was.

★ ★ ★

Diseases, weeds and feral animals are all threats affecting our landscapes already, yet safeguards must be put in place to protect our environment from any future biological invasions. Internationally, one of the most feared diseases is guava rust, a disease that originated in the Amazon rainforest but spread into eucalypt plantations in South America and killed thousands of young trees.[33] Similarly frightening is the potential spread of siam weed; it has already wrought havoc in the Asian tropics and, alarmingly, has been discovered in north Queensland.[34]

To date our quarantine laws continue to permit the importation of many plants and animals with the potential to become invasive. Complicated quarantine procedures—laws that differ greatly between the states, and the absence of an overarching federal law—along with gaps in the swift detection of invasives and poor protocols on what needs to be eradicated first and at whose cost, mean that the opportunities for new invasions are many. Considering the horrendous consequences that foreign species and diseases have already had on the environment (and the economy), there can be no excuse for not aligning the laws to provide a sound wall of protection for this vulnerable island continent.

7

MORE FRIGHTENING THAN A SCIENCE FICTION MOVIE

Climate Change

Changes in climate, even dramatic ones, are nothing unusual in the history of the planet. Regular ice ages, interspersed with warmer inter-glacial periods such as the one we are in at the moment, have come and gone for millions of years. What is of great concern about the current period of climate change is the rapid rate at which it is occurring. Not since the extinctions of the dinosaurs around 65 million years ago have mass extinctions seemed so likely. At that time, extraordinary changes to the Earth's atmosphere were attributed to the impact of a meteorite that caused dust particles to block out the sun, killing plants and depriving animals of food. This single event, and the centuries of change that followed it, caused the extinction of most life on Earth.[1]

The current period of climate change is due to the rapid, human-driven accumulation of greenhouse gases—carbon dioxide, methane and nitrous oxide—in the atmosphere. The natural carbon cycle of the planet used to ensure that carbon released into the atmosphere, primarily from burning or decaying plant matter, was reabsorbed by living plants, soils and the oceans, but today's levels of greenhouse gases far surpass the planet's ability to absorb them. Right now, climate change is the price we are paying for the 'sins' of the recent past. Sins that include phenomenal amounts of logging and land clearing, soil-damaging land management, and long-term and exponential rises in carbon emissions from cars, trucks, planes, coal-fired power stations and fossil-fuel driven industries have now made climate change the most significant environmental issue of our time.

★ ★ ★

Scientists have used computer modelling to predict future scenarios as a result of climate change, but the real extent of what is going to happen is not certain. What is clear, though, is that despite efforts to mitigate a potential catastrophe by reducing the use of fossil fuels, temperatures will continue to rise for the foreseeable future and many consequences are no longer preventable. Indeed, undeniable signs of rising temperatures already include melting polar icecaps, the receding of ancient glaciers, rising seas and expanding deserts. At the same time, crucial ocean currents that play a vital role in regulating the world's climate are under threat of slowing down or stopping altogether and, ironically, could plunge the world into another ice age. To Australians, our own changing rainfall patterns and more frequent wildfires, violent storms and floods illustrate that change has already arrived. How we will be affected personally and how much change the world will face, even in our own lifetimes, is yet to be determined.

Global governments and industries are now beginning to plan for this new reality. There is much to be done as each sector is forced to develop an almost entirely new view of its future role. Agricultural industries must take account of the changing temperature and rainfall patterns across the country and adjust the locations of crops and stock accordingly. Coastal cities and councils must prepare for the impacts of sea surges, storms and floods, reinforce infrastructure like buildings, roads and bridges, and ultimately plan to abandon coastal regions that were developed on low-lying swamps and floodplains. Insurance companies must devise premiums that will cover policyholders for damage to property and business losses as a result of catastrophic events, while lawyers must prepare to defend lawsuits brought against councils and companies that ignore the warnings of climate change and do not take adequate precautions to protect residents and clients. The fall-out from ignoring long-term implications became evident in outer Melbourne in September 2008. A housing estate built too close to a former landfill site had to be evacuated when potentially explosive levels of methane gas were detected. As the local council and the developer blamed each other, residents demanded compensation and prepared to sue.[2]

And those who are at the frontline, the public health and medical practitioners, must steel themselves for a triple whammy of events. There will be increases in extreme weather events requiring medical responses on a large scale (hurricanes, flash floods), increases in direct heat-related conditions such as heart attacks and heatstroke among vulnerable sectors of the population, and increases in insect-borne tropical diseases such as malaria, dengue fever and Ross River fever.

The ability to adapt to these changing times, whether by physically relocating or by drawing on a natural resilience to adjust to the new conditions, is as important to Australia's plants and animals and their ecosystems as it is to its human population. The enormous significance of these still early stages of climate change is that we must decide *right now* how this land and its priceless natural bounty will be managed. How much more of nature are we prepared to sacrifice? Hundreds of species? Thousands? How many ecosystems? Do we resign ourselves to our manmade fate or do we have a moral obligation to do everything we can to slow the juggernaut we've unleashed?

Since the seriousness of climate change was internationally acknowledged through the establishment of the Kyoto Protocol in 1997, the estimates of its impacts have changed exponentially. The Intergovernmental Panel on Climate Change (IPCC) was set up in 1990 to monitor and review emerging science on the changing climate. In its 1995 report it predicted that the rise in global temperatures could be contained between one and three degrees Celsius if drastic action was taken to reduce greenhouse gas emissions in the twenty-first century.[3] Today, as a result of action being hampered (and indeed deliberately undermined) by the resistance of the fossil-fuel driven global economies to reduce greenhouse gas emissions, the IPCC has amended its temperature estimates to a rise of 1.8–4°C by the end of this century.[4] The predicted environmental consequences to this increase are 'as frightening as a science fiction movie', according to UN Secretary General Ban Ki-moon. 'But they are even more terrifying because they are real.'[5]

★ ★ ★

Many Australian landscapes are already failing under the pressures we have placed on them and are nearing the limits of their tolerance. The effects of an average temperature rise of only 0.6 degrees Celsius over the past fifty years have already taken a toll, despite the fact that our unique flora and fauna has evolved to cope with seasonal high temperatures and limited or unpredictable rainfall, which have been the norm across 75 per cent of the continent. But, as shown with the mountain pygmy possum, not all our native species are so resilient. On the highest points along Australia's east coast, a range of plants and animals are strictly adapted to the cooler niches within the tropical north and to alpine landscapes in the south, and some among the latter even depend on a seasonal cover of snow to survive the winters. Plants and animals in ecosystems that occur at higher altitudes and therefore on the milder end of Australia's temperature range are among those whose survival are most threatened by the changing climate.

The changes in alpine climates will have consequences not only for the mountain pygmy possum but for most other alpine species, as well. More than two hundred and fifty plants are known to occur only in the small range between the treeline and the mountains' peaks.[6] As temperatures increase, the plants and animals dependent on the cooler conditions will try to move further up the mountains to escape the increasing warmth; the total distance between the current treeline and

Australia's highest peak, however, is only around four hundred metres. Once they have reached the top—provided they are able to move at all—these species will have nowhere left to go.

One tiny black alpine frog with distinctive greenish-yellow markings is particularly vulnerable to climate change. The southern corroboree frog is critically endangered and its few remaining populations are already under threat from chytrid fungus. Changing climactic conditions, however, have the potential to interfere with the frog's lifecycle in a number of ways. Corroboree frogs are unusual among frogs in that they lay their eggs (spawn) in encased clusters on thick layers of saturated sphagnum moss rather than in pools of water. Tadpoles initially mature within their soft egg cases before they hatch and move across rain-moistened ground to a nearby breeding pool. Warming temperatures have been responsible for an overgrowth of sphagnum moss at a number of breeding pools and may become a significant problem for the species' tadpoles if their access to water is impeded.[7] A bigger concern, however, is the effect of increased temperatures and drier weather on the pools. If it doesn't rain and the egg sites don't receive enough water, the tadpoles may not be able to move to the nearby pools. Another possibility is that the pools dry up before the tadpoles have metamorphosed into mobile froglets. Although the frogs breed in spring and early summer, a reduction in winter snow cover may also affect their breeding success. If egg clutches have been laid late in the season, some of the southern corroboree tadpoles remain in their egg cases over the winter and, like the mountain pygmy possum, rely on an insulating layer of snow to protect them from below zero conditions.[8] If the snow cover is reduced or non-existent when the temperatures drop, the tadpoles will freeze to death. The highly precarious future of the southern corroboree frog means that considerable investment is now being made in breeding this species in captivity to prevent its imminent extinction. The loss of its natural habitat because of climate change, however, makes the likelihood of its future release back into its current habitat a utopian fantasy.

★ ★ ★

From the alps to the tropics, plants and animals living at high altitudes face a gloomy future. Tropical Far North Queensland is home to some remarkable and rarely seen species found only in the cooler, moist remnants of the elevated tropical rainforest and the adjoining tablelands. Among these is the magnificent golden bowerbird, famous for its spectacular courtship displays performed outside a carefully constructed 'bower' of twigs and forest-floor debris that may reach up to three metres in height. Also there, but very elusive, are two mammalian tree dwellers, Bennett's and Lumholtz's tree kangaroo.[9]

Lumholtz's tree kangaroo, a frequent victim of cars and dogs on the ground, now occurs almost exclusively on isolated mountain tops on private properties of the Atherton Tableland. This makes movements between populations very difficult and means their conservation is almost entirely dependent on the goodwill of the landholders. As rising temperatures force the tree kangaroos further up these mountains, the fragmentation of this species will increase as populations have no means of interacting with each other. An increase of only one degree Celsius above what these animals are used to is sufficient to reduce their habitat to about one-third of its current extent; and a rise of two degrees Celsius would leave only 5 per cent of the animal's current range habitable.[10] Climate change also affects the quality of the animal's food source as increases in atmospheric carbon reduce the nutritionally important nitrogen content of the leaves while increasing the levels of tannins and other toxins that make the leaves less palatable.[11]

In the tropics, as in many other threatened habitats around Australia, highly specialised species of frogs are at the frontline of wildlife vulnerable to change. A total area of no more than two square kilometres in Queensland's Wet Tropics World Heritage Area is home to the mountain nursery frog and the Mount Elliott nursery frog. These diminutive frogs are the size of thumbnails and live in cloud-shrouded rainforest above 1200 metres. They are completely dependent on the moist, tropical conditions that are typical of this cloud forest. The reliable moisture of this environment means that the frogs breed by laying their eggs directly into damp leaf litter or underneath wet logs, from where they hatch directly into small froglets. Climate change, and in particular higher temperatures, may have a big impact on the mountain nursery frogs' environment. As the temperature increases, the cloud cover is likely to dissipate and leave the frogs' usually moist habitat much drier and less suitable for breeding. With the highest peaks at only 1350 metres, and with each degree of warming elevating the optimum habitat by 150 metres, an increase of less than even one degree Celsius will soon leave these mountain nursery frogs literally high and dry.[12]

The inability to tolerate more than a very small range in temperature is not an issue only affecting species in mountainous areas. The spectacular diversity of living coral structures and associated fish and sea-life communities that make up the Great Barrier Reef includes 35 million hectares of islands, seagrass beds and coastal mangrove communities, and close to 3000 coral reefs and cays that have been built by hundreds of different coral species.[13] This is one of the world's greatest natural wonders and the abundance of life supported by the Great Barrier Reef makes it one of Australia's biggest tourist drawcards.

Corals are small polyps that form large colonies. The hard coral structures are produced by lime-secreting polyps that create the surface on which other hard and soft corals can grow. Among the fantastically diverse structures of the hard and soft coral communities themselves, around fifteen hundred species of fish of all shapes and sizes—from trumpet fish to giant maori wrasse and clownfish to sharks—swim through underwater landscapes that also feature thousands of molluscs (clams, shellfish, snails and octopus) as well as sponges, anemones, crabs, prawns, worms, seastars, urchins, algae and seagrasses, marine turtles, dugongs and even whales.

The multitude of species of the Great Barrier Reef has evolved to suit very specific conditions and is vulnerable to *any* change. Until recently its greatest threat came from agricultural and urban run-off. Fertilisers, pesticides, soil nutrients, sewage, detergents, heavy metals, oil and a variety of toxic chemicals used by farmers and urban residents soak into groundwater or are washed into streams and end up in the ocean. Once there, they lead to algal blooms and increases in phytoplankton, which then boost the numbers of filter feeders that compete with the corals and upset the balance in the coral communities.[14] The impacts of threats such as run-off are being addressed, but the pressures on the Great Barrier Reef presented by climate change are much greater.

The many corals that grow near the ocean surface are highly sensitive to changes in temperature. This is because both hard and soft corals live in mutually beneficial partnerships with large numbers of tiny, light-dependent algae that cannot survive outside of a narrow temperature band. While the corals provide protection for these algae, the algae in turn generate food for the corals and give them their distinctive colours. A temperature increase of one or two degrees Celsius damages the algae and destroys the vital relationship between them and their coral partners. The result is coral bleaching, which becomes evident by the loss of the corals' vivid colours. After prolonged periods of elevated temperatures, this means the death of the coral communities within the warmer surface waters.[15] Once the corals have died, all that is left of their once colourful and vibrant structures are ghostly grey skeletons that can no longer provide suitable habitat for most of the fish and marine life. Two instances of coral bleaching have affected the Great Barrier Reef in the past ten years. In the second bleaching incident in 2002, well over 60 per cent of the reef was damaged, and in the inshore reefs almost 90 per cent of corals died.[16]

Around the world, coral communities are likely to lose much of their diversity and many of their habitat niches as temperatures rise. Adding to the corals' challenges, however, is the oceans' high concentration of carbon dioxide. Oceans are natural carbon sinks that absorb about a third of the carbon dioxide from the atmosphere. Excessively high levels of this greenhouse gas, however, make the seawater acidic. The acidity of the water dissolves the calcium carbonate skeleton of the corals and weakens the coral structures that support marine life. Unless atmospheric carbon dioxide is reduced, the oceans may become too acidic for corals to grow at all, a possibility that could take only fifty years or so to become real.[17] To date, no practical solution to this devastating threat to coral reefs and associated marine life has been found.

★ ★ ★

After more than seven years of El Niño-driven drought, severe water restrictions and escalating fruit, vegetables and meat prices, no one needs to be reminded of the effect that the prolonged absence of rain can have on every plant and animal—including ourselves. Climate change is set to affect rainfall patterns around the country, producing more rain in some areas and less in others.

In general terms, in south-western Australia and much of eastern Australia, annual average rainfall will continue to decline, while in the coastal areas and savannas of north-west Australia rain periods may become more intense and occur more often.[18] The implications of such changes are far-reaching. Where more rain falls the growth of some plants may improve, while those dependent on drier conditions may disappear and, over time, the suitability of habitat to local wildlife may change. This in turn may force animals to abandon their former ranges in search of more suitable habitats. More rain in large dumps will lead to increased floods and soil erosion, and more chemicals and nutrients will be washed into streams and affect freshwater and marine environments. On the other hand, reduced rainfall (coupled with continued overuse of water for industry and agriculture) will affect ecosystems such as wetlands and temperate rainforests that rely on regular downpours. In dry landscapes bushfires may occur more often and prevent natural landscapes and species from recovering from previous fires. This would change the species composition in those areas and lead to the loss of those plants and animals that are less tolerant of frequent fire.

The South West Botanical Province of Western Australia is particularly vulnerable to the impacts of reduced rainfall, which in the past three decades has already declined 15–20 per cent.[19] More than half of the plants in this region are found nowhere else and support equally endemic mammals (numbats, woylies, chuditches and red-tailed phascogales), the western bristlebird, reptiles such as the western swamp tortoise and almost two-thirds of the region's frogs.[20] More than 50 per cent of its spectacular flora, including hundreds of acacias and distinctive eucalypts like jarrah, karri, marri and tingle, is endemic. Despite its species diversity, eucalypts can only tolerate average yearly temperature fluctuations of 1–5°C.[21] As temperatures increase, the ecosystems they are a part of will shift southward where possible, and less heat-tolerant forest like jarrah will be replaced by hardier species in more open woodlands. One unwelcome beneficiary of the warmer conditions will be dieback-causing mould *Phytophthora cinnamomi,* which thrives in warm and moist conditions and will affect even more extensive areas of native forests and heaths and their hundreds of resident wildlife species.

★ ★ ★

In the decades and centuries to come, Australia's and the world's natural systems will be in a permanent state of flux. While many species already at their limits will follow the terminal path of the thylacine and the gastric brooding frogs, others will continue to shift and to seek more suitable niches elsewhere. Across Australia, each additional degree of average temperature rise will force landscapes to shift around 125 kilometres south or 100 metres upward in altitude.[22] The odds for plants and animals at high altitudes or in shallow seas are not good, but for myriad other species in continuous habitat ranges and with large gene pools they are significantly better.

In a healthy environment, these gradual and overlapping shifts by plants and wildlife might be hampered by obstacles (rivers, mountains, sea) or by competition with plants and animals that are less sensitive to the emerging climates. But because of the influences of human populations, migrating species of all ecosystems now face an obstacle course stacked with more challenges than the TV series *Survivor.* Streams and rivers near the coast and in agricultural regions such as the Murray–Darling Basin have been diverted, polluted, silted up and dammed, which has often blocked the movement of fish and other aquatic species into new areas. Coastal swamps and floodplains have been drained, cleared, fenced and 'reclaimed', and their wildlife residents isolated, evicted, or forced to live on the degraded fringes of their once accommodating habitats. Vast areas of formerly extensive and well-connected ecosystems like eastern Australia's expansive eucalypt forests have been cleared, cultivated, built out and separated into frayed fragments crowded out by cities, townships, roads, farms or mining operations. Weeds, feral animals and diseases have taken over most landscape remnants, leaving the remaining crowded strongholds of native habitats in a degraded and alien state. Far from being free to move to accommodate a changing climate, a large proportion of this country's native plant and wildlife populations and gene pools is stuck in restricted habitat patches and completely dependent on large-scale, innovative landscape restoration efforts for its survival.

One species of flying fox has become an unexpected early indicator of the impact of climate change on an already compromised group of animals. Until a few decades ago, the black flying fox (a native of Australia, Indonesia and New Guinea) had an Australian range that extended across coastal and near-coastal northern Australia from Western Australia to the Queensland–New South Wales border. In the south-eastern part of its range in Queensland, it overlapped with the northern reaches of the grey-headed flying fox, which occurs from about Rockhampton south to western Victoria. The black flying fox feeds on a variety of fruit, nectar and pollen, while the grey-headed flying fox prefers nectar; the former is therefore traditionally more sedentary than the latter. That said, where the two ranges cross, there is considerable overlap between their feeding and roosting habitats and both are often found roosting together at the same camp. Since observation of the species began in the early 1930s, the range of the more sedentary black flying fox has increasingly extended further south, with colonies appearing as far south as Sydney by 2007.[23] The exact driver for this southward extension is not known, but a likely hypothesis blames a combination of drought and the continuing clearing and development for housing and agriculture of the Queensland coast. During times of drought in particular, fruit and nectar in the Brisbane region can be extremely scarce and the individuals of both species are forced to travel long distances in the hope of finding a nightly feed.[24] Recently an intriguing observation was made on how the two flying foxes respond to increased temperatures. On very hot summer days when the mercury had topped 42°C, an increasing number of shared camps became the harrowing sites of mass die-offs as thousands of black flying foxes and their pups succumbed to the relentless heat.[25]

The signs of increasing heat stress in roosting bats are unmistakable. First there is a slow flapping of the wings to pass cool air over their rich blood supply, followed by wing licking, panting and increasing stress as the bats come down from the higher branches to seek shade among the foliage. With no relief offered, the parched and exhausted bats eventually lose their grip, slipping to the lower branches or dropping to the ground to die. As an observer of camps at these times, witnessing thousands of dying bats, from small pups to large adults, has been incredibly distressing as well as perplexing. Perplexing because the grey-headed flying foxes remained comparatively unaffected by the heat; they displayed a greater temperature tolerance than their black cousins of one or two degrees Celsius, despite the fact that the black flying fox originated in tropical regions. It appears that the southward shift of the black flying fox has driven it to the outer limits of its climatic tolerance into areas that experience more extreme heat spikes than the generally warmer tropics. Investigations have now begun to determine whether heat deaths are due to the temperatures per se or to a combination of factors that may include insufficient humidity or other micro-climatic variables. With a lack of food and natural habitat in its former range and an unsuitable climate in the newly settled reaches, eastern populations of the black flying fox are increasingly cornered. Flying foxes produce no more than one pup per year and continued mass deaths mean serious consequences for this forest keystone species unless concerted efforts are made to restore large sections of their habitat on public and private land.

★ ★ ★

In the Kimberley region of north-west Australia, climate change presents a different set of challenges. While drought will become an increasing issue in much of eastern Australia, the opposite is true in the north-west. Since 1950 rainfall in the Kimberley has increased 6–20 per cent per decade and this bigger volume of rain is causing much wetter monsoons.[26] More rain sounds desirable, but in the Kimberley the resulting, additional growth of woodlands, heath and grasses means more fuel for fierce, dry season wildfires. Fires have always been a formative part of the Kimberley landscapes and many plants and animals depend on irregular fires to germinate seeds and promote new seedlings and foliage. The problem is that fires are now occurring more often and more intensely than ever before, preventing plants and animals from recovering in the interim. A pattern of increasingly destructive fires that began in the mid 1990s resulted in one-third (140 000 km^2) of the entire Kimberley region being burned in 2000.[27] Fires that are too hot, too frequent and too extensive can destroy or permanently alter parts of the plant communities so that animals have to move much further afield to find suitable food and shelter.[28] And in addition to damage on the ground, the large-scale burning of vegetation also releases large quantities of carbon dioxide into the atmosphere, further contributing to the root cause of climate change. As climate change progresses, the careful management of the savanna landscapes with appropriate patch-burning regimes, controlled grazing and dedicated weed and feral management will be vital in protecting the natural diversity of the region, allowing it to adjust to the changing climatic conditions with fewer additional pressures.

★ ★ ★

The spectre of climate change has also impacted profoundly on the dedicated environment sector itself. Within a few short years, environmental protection agencies, scientists and non-government conservation organisations, many of which had focused on land clearing, the anti-nuclear debate and weed and feral animal control as threatened species conservation, have found their original agendas dwarfed by the grandaddy of environmental threats. What once were causes worthy of a lifetime's dedicated work in science and advocacy seem to have shrunk in importance. At a time when the future of all living creatures is under close review from the impacts of climate change, it could be argued that worrying about other, 'lesser' threats on individual suites of species or ecosystems at this time is like mending umbrellas to stave off Hurricane Katrina. That argument, however, is one deeply flawed. In the context of climate change, the resolution of the longer-standing environmental issues becomes even more important than before. In addition to its own direct temperature and rainfall-related impacts, climate change will accelerate existing threats and lead to faster habitat destruction and faster rates of extinction than any other threats in combination. Climate change and other environmental threats *must* be addressed simultaneously. To encourage the redirection of resources from other urgent threat abatement strategies solely to slowing the rate of climate change while ignoring the immediate needs of the environment would be grossly irresponsible.

The most sensible action that can and must be taken at this time to safeguard genetic and species diversity is holistic environmental conservation. Populations of plants and animals comprise the building blocks of evolution—the more diverse and healthy they are, the easier it will be for new ecological relationships to evolve and take shape. Never has commitment to a healthy environment been more important than right now.

Part II

WHERE WE ARE HEADING

8

IS IT ALL AN ACT?

Environmental Law

Our stewardship of this country's natural assets over the past two hundred years has been appalling, and on the current trajectory of careless environmental pillaging, further massive decline would be a certainty. But as undeniably serious as the current situation is, all is not yet lost.

Work *is* now being done to try to slow the decline of our natural landscapes. In the past two years in particular, a significant shift in attitude and action has taken place. A soaring demand for renewable 'green' energy and more efficient water use, a more thoughtful processing and recycling of waste, and concerted efforts to reduce over-consumption are proof of a growing awareness of nature's limits. More and more ordinary individuals are turning their growing disenchantment about a grossly mistreated environment into action, be it by changing how they care for their own farm or garden, reducing their ecological footprint, joining landcare or bushcare groups or insisting that their local MPs make their deep concerns heard by those in power. Increasingly, too, it has become apparent that where positive change has occurred it has been driven largely by community or consumer demand and only rarely by industry. The power of the people is far greater and far more influential than most realise.

But change, let alone swift change on a monumental scale, is not easily embraced. Where awareness and understanding alone are not enough and current economic paradigms stand in the way, industries such as agriculture, pastoralism and the energy and mining sectors need to be drawn by motivating incentives (such as consumer demand or financial compensation) and at the same time fear the weight of legal retribution if necessary change is not forthcoming. In Australia, the development of legal frameworks to regulate environmental activities and monitor the changing health of plants and wildlife as indicators of how we're faring has been a much-needed but fairly recent development. Strong legislation is an essential driver of nature conservation and has the potential to achieve substantial long-term wins (or prevent losses) for the environment, but without a firm government commitment to enact the law, it is worth little more than the reams of paper it is printed on.

A Few Short Lessons in Law

In the past three decades a number of high-profile environmental campaigns have helped push the environment firmly into the public consciousness and onto the political agenda. The first of these was the lengthy campaign to prevent the damming and flooding of Tasmania's magnificent Lake Pedder to generate hydro-electricity.

After a 6-year battle between conservationists and the Tasmanian government, this cause was lost when Lake Pedder was flooded in 1972.[1] But despite this loss, the lessons learned galvanised a small but growing community of citizens worried about the government's ready sacrifice of environmental icons and in 1976 Tasmania's Wilderness Society was founded.[2] The Wilderness Society and other conservation groups soon found themselves fighting against the damming of the Gordon River upstream of its junction with the Franklin River. Once again drawing focus to Tasmania's pristine south-west, the success of this campaign made it a defining marker for Australian conservationism. After seven years of political wrangling and physical blockading, the Franklin campaign was ultimately won by calling on federal government intervention to protect the World Heritage value of the river system. The commitment to do so ultimately won the Australian Labor Party and its new leader, Bob Hawke, a number of important marginal seats and thereby election victory in 1983.[3]

Other high-profile campaigns followed and prevented the development of the ancient rainforests of the Daintree in the mid 1980s (to be World Heritage-listed in 1988) and spared Kakadu National Park from the cultural and environmental damage of uranium mining in the 1990s. More recently, three large campaigning efforts helped to save Victoria's old-growth rainforests from being turned into woodchips in 2000–01, stopped the building of an environmentally devastating marina resort at Ningaloo Reef in Western Australia in 2003 and placed one-third (11 million hectares) of the Great Barrier Reef in sanctuaries to guard against over-fishing and address pollution from agricultural run-off in 2004.[4]

Since the 1970s the state, territory and federal governments have been forced to acknowledge that the natural environment can sway votes and carries weight with their constituents. The protection of native species and iconic landscapes had to, however reluctantly, become part of their agenda.

Lesson 1: Laws are one thing, their implementation another

For a number of states and the federal government, the inaugural drafting of specific environment legislation signalled the intent to take this issue seriously. A raft of new environmental laws began to emerge. In 1988, Victoria introduced the *Flora and Fauna Guarantee Act* to focus on the conservation of threatened species and ecological communities and the management of potential threatening processes in that state.[5] Queensland followed suit with the *Environmental Protection Act 1994*, New South Wales and Tasmania with the *Threatened Species Conservation Act* and *Threatened Species Protection Act,* respectively, in 1995, and the ACT with the *Environment Protection Act 1997*. South Australia, long conscious of its severely degraded landscapes, had already incorporated threatened species as part of its *National Parks and Wildlife Act 1972*. Nationally, the first piece of dedicated environment law was the *Endangered Species Protection Act 1992*, which was replaced by the more comprehensive *Environment Protection and Biodiversity Conservation Act 1999* (*EPBC Act*) in July 2000. The *EPBC Act* consolidated a number of Acts relating to environmental management and was considered 'landmark legislative reform' by Senator Robert Hill, the minister responsible for its introduction.[6] As all of the environment and biodiversity-related Acts had similar objectives—identifying species and ecosystems under threat and taking action to improve their status—it seemed reasonable to expect improvements for the threatened plants, animals and landscapes under their jurisdiction. If unlikely to lead to the complete recovery of threatened species within a few short years, the rate of species decline should at least be demonstrably slowed or halted and lead to recovery with ongoing effort. The legislative road to species conservation and the programs it spawned, however, turned out to be paved with potholes. The first was in the leeway created by the weak wording of its objectives.

Lesson 2: What the law says it does

Environment legislation can focus specifically on threatened plants, animals and ecological communities, or it can cover a broader range of environment-related issues. The federal *EPBC Act*, for example, also includes the protection of World Heritage and National Heritage properties, wetlands of international importance (as recognised under the Ramsar Convention), migratory species, Commonwealth marine areas and the regulation of nuclear actions—including uranium mining—on its list of so-called 'protected matters'.[7] Regardless of whether these are found on public or private land, the Act recognises these matters wherever they have been identified. Once in place, and provided it is supported by a dedicated budget and administration, environment law provides the impetus for governments to meet their legal obligations. This is achieved by instigating and supporting conservation activities (such as those recommended in recovery or threat abatement plans, or the gazettal of national parks) and by regulating and monitoring activities that could have a negative impact on the matters protected under the law. The objectives of the *EPBC Act* are quite comprehensive: protecting the environment; promoting ecologically sustainable development, biodiversity conservation and a cooperative approach to environmental management; and recognising the role of indigenous people in conservation and sustainable use of biodiversity.

The *EPBC Act*'s stated intention was to involve and strengthen the role of the general community in grass-roots conservation, and to empower vigilant members of the public to serve as additional 'eyes and ears' for monitoring and reporting of potentially damaging activities. While enabling the public to share in the large task at hand, this would also give it greater ownership of the natural environment and its management at a local and regional level. However, the reality is that many of the strategies employed to fulfil these intentions have so far turned out to be little more than distractions to placate a voting public while allowing industry development to proceed unencumbered. To a battle-wise conservationist, promising objectives such as 'protect', 'promote' and 'recognise' have come to represent almost any activity short of directly sabotaging these aims. In their application, they have fallen far short of committing the government to the concerted and uncompromising effort needed to achieve real and lasting environmental outcomes.

Lesson 3: What it actually does

Chapter 1 established that legislation is the statutory framework around which conservation measures are built. If administered properly, legislation identifies conservation priorities and threatening processes, outlines strategies for addressing threats, justifies the allocation of funds and resources and measures how well (or otherwise) conservation efforts are progressing. Every program, policy or activity that relates to protecting the natural environment is captured under sections of the relevant state, territory or federal legislation, and there are many parallels between these laws.

Lists of threatened species and ecological communities provide the basic yardstick by which conservation can be prioritised and measured. As discussed earlier, the failure to keep lists up to date is one significant

shortcoming of the administration of the federal legislation. The drafting of recovery, threat abatement and other conservation plans is also
common in environmental legislation. In one form or another, recovery plans or the provision of succinct 'conservation advice' are a significant part of all of Australia's environment law. Each species or group
of species identified as threatened with extinction requires a plan that
explains its current status, its distribution range and habitat, the threats
that impact on it and what needs to be done to prevent its further
decline. Similarly, threats such as land clearing, predation by cats and foxes
or competition from rabbits that impact on entire suites of species and
ecosystems also require large-scale strategies to counteract them. These
strategies are the focus of dedicated threat abatement plans. Both recovery and threat abatement plans are fraught with challenges and very few
of the hundreds of existing plans have produced any lasting measurable
outcomes to date, yet this failure reflects flaws in how these plans are
implemented rather than in their underlying strategies.

Another policy that operates nationally is the designation and management of national parks and reserves. Each state and self-governing
territory has its own network of land-based reserves in addition to a
separate, national network, and collectively they comprise the National
Reserve System.[8] A comparable system also exists for national marine
protected areas. The aim of these reserve systems is to set aside a 'comprehensive, adequate and representative' amount of habitat for all
regional ecosystems and their plant and animal diversity across Australia.
A substantial system of government reserves, free from detrimental
development and land use, along with incentives for a complementary
network of private reserves and corridors that link up wherever possible is perhaps the single most important endeavour needed for all
species represented within these reserves. And the generous allocation
of reserves across the landscape has become more important than ever
with the looming impacts of changing climate and the likelihood of
large-scale migrations. But poor resourcing and a lack of political
commitment have undermined the potential of this sensible and scientifically sound policy. Instead of a solid national insurance policy of

protected land, it has so far produced a reserve network containing land that can easily be expended instead of areas strategically selected for their conservation value. Hearteningly, at the end of March 2008 the new federal Labor government provided a $180-million boost to the national reserve system, an early indication of the government's intention to realise what is perhaps the most important conservation strategy on offer.[9]

Despite its disappointments to date, the *EPBC Act* was a step in the right direction. One of the main gains of the legislation was the standing provision for third party enforcements, which allows non-government conservation organisations to take the government to court over poor environmental decisions that fail to meet the objects of the Act. This provision has, for example, enabled the Humane Society International, an international animal protection organisation, to challenge the environment minister's declaration of the southern blue-fin tuna fishery (with tuna stocks now at 5 per cent of their 1960s population) as an ecologically sustainable operation.[10]

A further positive outcome has been the substantial improvement of the management of Australian fisheries. The increased questioning of the environmental impacts of the fisheries led the Australian Fisheries Management Authority (AFMA) to develop plans and strategies that have resulted in a much greater accountability by this high-impact industry at a time when fish stocks have declined dramatically worldwide.

Lesson 4: What it should (also) do

The most important function of environment law is to ensure that environmentally damaging activities can be prosecuted. As legislation is usually drafted only once the environment is in trouble, this is paramount in preventing further damage. The Environmental Assessment and Approvals (EAA) process comes into play whenever anyone, including private landholders, governments or industries, refers an activity that could impact significantly on any of the seven protected matters (EPBC-listed threatened species and ecological communities among them). Such activities can include the clearing of habitat, the drainage of swamps and wetlands, the widening of a road alongside an already-threatened ecological community or the proposal to mine in ecologically sensitive areas.

Despite the potential of the assessment and approvals process, several factors have substantially weakened its powers. The first is that the EAA process relies on the person proposing the activity to estimate its likely impact (is it 'significant' or not?) before deciding whether or not to refer it to the government for assessment. Evidence has shown that the industries most likely to propose damaging activities—such as agriculture, fisheries and forestry—submit referrals less often than might be expected.[11] A large proportion of forestry activity has been conveniently exempted from assessment by the regional forest agreements, and in a recent review of the *EPBC Act* it was considered to have had very little effect on reducing the rate of land clearing over a 5-year period despite the fact that many of the regions where clearing occurred contained substantial numbers of *EPBC*-listed threatened species and ecological communities.[12]

The second factor hampering the EAA process is the lack of thoroughness with which proposals are assessed. In fact, the vast majority (two-thirds of all assessments completed in the first six years) were assessed without any on-ground investigation; only 25 per cent of activities had undergone a formal impact assessment to evaluate their immediate and/or longer term effects.[13] Activities that are approved, subject to conditions imposed by the government, have also provided little comfort amid concerns that they have often been 'vague and ambiguous', based on questionable science and not monitored to ensure they are adhered to by the proponents.[14] One example is that of allowing the clearing of mature trees that are many decades old on the condition that new seedlings of the same species are planted. The value of these trees to wildlife is almost entirely dependent on their great age and the formation of natural hollows; new seedlings will take around a century to replace the logged ones in their value to birds like the red-tailed black cockatoo.

Also of great concern is the minuscule number of activities refused after assessment. By June 2006, only four out of more than 150 referrals deemed to be 'controlled actions' and subsequently assessed had been refused.[15] While this might indicate that very few activities of significant impact had been submitted, a number of highly damaging proposals for dam constructions, residential development, tourism, agriculture and mining that were given the go-ahead suggest otherwise.[16]

The third factor hampering the environmental assessment and approval process is that the monitoring and enforcement of referred activities appears to have been disabled by an inadequate administrative infrastructure and a lack of field staff. A formal audit of the Act's ability to protect threatened species and ecological communities in 2006 made the alarming discovery that the department lacked the resources to monitor whether conditions imposed on proponents were being met or not.[17] The lack of compliance monitoring throughout the country is perhaps the most telling sign that there has been a fundamental inability (and unwillingness) to monitor, and if necessary, prosecute and upset individuals or industry sectors conducting potentially damaging activities. It has also ensured that the *EPBC Act* provides only a very limited disincentive to conduct environmentally damaging activities if it is unlikely that anyone will notice.

On occasion it has been left up to vigilant members of the general public to report damaging activities to the government in the hope that they will be investigated. One such case involved the prosecution of a Gwydir farmer in northern New South Wales who illegally cleared around 800 hectares that were protected under the Ramsar Convention for Wetlands of International Importance in 2003.[18] The decimation of the wetland was discovered and reported by neighbours and led to the first ever civil enforcement proceedings under the *EPBC Act* and a $450 000 fine for the landholder. Public reporting on illegal and environmentally damaging activities is, however, likely to be occasional at best and cannot be expected to operate in place of sound government monitoring and enforcement of its environment laws.

Lesson 5: If environment laws are not adequately enforced and the key threats not addressed on a meaningful scale, community conservation is a waste of time

Australia's burgeoning community of environmentally aware citizens may be the natural environment's greatest hope for a healthier future. There is a veritable army of enthusiastic people volunteering time and effort to protect native vegetation and wildlife across the country.

The enormous potential for harnessing this free and invaluable labour force was recognised by the federal government in its drafting of the *EPBC Act*, where community capacity-building was writ large and measures were designed to bring the community on board. One was the setting up of two community-focused funding schemes, the Envirofund and the smaller Threatened Species Network Community Grants. Through annual funding rounds, both schemes offer up to $50 000 to community groups wanting to undertake local restoration and conservation projects that concern one or more nationally listed species. Over the years diverse issues that have been tackled include cat and fox predation, disturbance of beach-nesting birds by dog walkers, the exclusion of stock from threatened grasslands, the protection of marine turtle beach-nesting sites, the trialling of environmental burning regimes and the closure of dams, as well as countless weed invasions of threatened species' habitats at a local scale. At face value, the government's efforts at promoting the Act and empowering the community to participate in conservation appear genuine. But after the initial enthusiasm from community members had settled it became clear that their efforts, however committed, would not add up to any lasting outcomes for the environment. The community groups ran out of funds after the initial 1- to 2-year set up and the prescribed project time frames were far too short to produce any measurable outcomes for species. And while the projects made some important contributions to building skills and raising awareness about threatened species in the environment, there were few signs of back-up by appropriate government-led strategies to tackle the real threats and drivers of decline. While a local community group might spend hundreds of hours weeding and restoring a degraded 2-hectare patch of rainforest habitat for endangered cassowaries in coastal north Queensland, developers only a few hundred metres away could legally clear hundreds of hectares of the same rainforest for new luxury housing. And, while in rural Victoria a group of committed landholders might band together to bait for foxes in order to protect malleefowl across a handful of adjoining properties, this activity could produce lasting benefits *only* if taken up by the entire catchment with ongoing funding. Hampered by such issues, dedicated groups hoping to make a contribution to a better future for Australia's threatened flora and fauna have found their efforts frustrated by government support that was anything but wholehearted.

Another way of engaging the community was through an extension program intended to inform and educate the public. The EPBC Unit (later the EPBC Project), funded by the Australian government and administered for some years collaboratively by the Tasmanian Conservation Trust, the Humane Society International and WWF-Australia, was set up specifically to answer public queries about the Act and explain its purpose to all sectors of the community. Over the years, it produced a range of guides for the public to further simplify this complex legislation. Although usually staffed by only one person (never more than three), the busy unit also held free community workshops that provided an overview of the Act, explained how to write submissions under the Act and outlined the National Heritage provisions and their application. But public submissions remained routinely unanswered, requests for information ignored, and the resounding impression of the community was that the department considered proponents of potentially harmful environmental activities as their 'clients' to be shielded from public scrutiny rather than critically assessed.[19] WWF-Australia, which had supported the *EPBC Act* and managed the unit in good faith, was forced to recognise that it had allowed its solid international reputation to be used to lend credibility to a community participation program that had been set up to fail. The unit was wound up in 2006, after running on a shoestring budget of less than $900 000 over six years, and the final report by disconsolate project officer Lyndall Kennedy likened the *EPBC Act* to 'a large and powerful dog that had been muzzled and kept on a short and tight leash'.[20]

★ ★ ★

One of the challenges of federalism is that each state and territory has its own laws and regulations in addition to the Commonwealth laws that apply to all matters under federal jurisdiction. While state and territory laws cease to apply at the boundaries with neighbouring states, federal legislation overlaps with that of the separately governed states in areas of Commonwealth jurisdiction such as defence land, World Heritage areas, Ramsar-listed wetlands, habitats of migratory species etc., and where it relates to nationally threatened species and ecological communities. This means that more than one jurisdiction may apply in instances such as where plants, animals or ecological communities are listed under more than one law.

In the context of broad-scale nature conservation, the separate administration of the states and territories is completely impractical. To a bird, mammal or reptile whose particular range is determined by climate, soils, water and suitable habitat, state and territory boundaries are no more than lines on maps. But where an individual plant or animal is found may determine whether it is considered threatened or not and what degree of protection it is entitled to under the law. A case in point is the black flying fox. Not considered to be threatened in the northern reaches of its range including in the Northern Territory, Western Australia and Queensland, its gradual southward expansion into New South Wales and subsequent occurrence in small (though now increasing) numbers in that state have seen it listed as 'vulnerable' there despite it being considered common across its range. Individuals that fly across the state border are therefore treated as common in Queensland and threatened in New South Wales.

The spectacled flying fox, on the other hand, is listed as 'vulnerable' in Queensland, and as its range is entirely confined to that state, it has also been recognised as 'vulnerable' under the *EPBC Act*. Even so, its protection under this legislation is spurious. To require a referral under the Act, an activity such as the clearing of habitat on private property must impact on an 'important population', an assessment that is beyond any ordinary person's qualifications to make. And should a population on qualified assessment not meet the criterion of 'important', the Act's protective powers don't apply. Never mind that flying fox populations are highly dynamic and could easily meet this criterion only a few short weeks or months later if larger numbers of bats arrive to occupy the site.

The relationship between state and territory laws and federal governments can be complex, and disputes over jurisdiction usually arise when one government accuses the other of negligence. The devastating consequence of the rabbit scourge on Macquarie Island following the eradication of feral cats is a recent example. While the Tasmanian government administers the island, its World Heritage listing also makes it the responsibility of the Australian government, yet the Australian government had formally passed its ongoing administrative duties to Tasmania. After neglecting to undertake a pest eradication program in time, neither government wanted to bear the financial burden of eradicating rabbits, rats and mice and restoring the island's unique value as a seabird breeding sanctuary of international importance.

The federal government, guided by the *EPBC Act*, still wields a vast amount of power over conservation matters across the country. And with a large federal budget at its disposal, funds dedicated to the environment could be expected to outweigh the contributions of the substantially smaller state, territory and local government budgets. This, however, is far from the case. In 2002–03 the proportion of the federal budget dedicated to the environment was 1 per cent (around $2bn); state governments, by comparison, spent around 6 per cent ($6bn) of their combined budgets on the environment; and local governments devoted an average of 25 per cent of their annual funds ($4.1bn)—raised primarily from council rates—to local environment protection and natural resource management.[21] While the former federal Liberal government's contribution had increased somewhat since then, it still comprised only a very small percentage of the overall budget.

★ ★ ★

In 1997, the sale of the first stage of the Australian government-owned communications company Telstra yielded a windfall for the environment. The sum of $3 billion was allocated to establishing the Natural Heritage Trust (NHT) to support the government's environment conservation policies over five years. A second major funding program, the National Action Plan for Salinity and Water Quality, was established in 2001 to invest $1.4 billion over seven years in regions most affected by salinity and declining freshwater quality.[22] Both schemes operated Australia-wide.

The Natural Heritage Trust was guided by the objectives of the *EPBC Act* and other legislation that reflected the Australian government's environmental policies. Its broad aims were to help conserve biodiversity, promote the sustainable use of natural resources, build the capacity of local communities to contribute to conservation efforts and promote institutional change towards restoring and conserving the natural environment and its resources.[23] Initially intended to run for five years, in 2001 the Trust's funding was extended another five years by another one billion dollars and topped up once more with $300 million in 2004, which was to last until 2007–08.

The funds of the Natural Heritage Trust were disbursed via three streams: strategically determined national priorities (such as 'biodiversity hotspots'); as competitive grants for community-driven projects (examples include the Envirofund and Threatened Species Network Community Grants); and to regional natural resource management plans. The vast majority of the Trust's funds were expended via the latter stream across the country. Natural Heritage Trust funding boosted considerably the investments made by state and territory governments.

To manage this country's natural resources, Australia's entire land surface was divided into fifty-six integrated natural resource management

(NRM) regions, each of which developed a plan to sustainably manage its soils, water, plants and natural landscapes and the agricultural industries dependent on them on a regional scale. While these regions are mostly natural catchments or bioregions, state and territory borders were also considered and each government has a role in overseeing the regions within its boundaries.

The funding provided by the former federal Liberal government was contingent on the signing of agreements between the Australian government and each separate state and territory government. In order to receive funding from the Natural Heritage Trust, state governments had to agree to a range of terms relating to their expenditure set out by the Australian government. Among the terms, much to the states' ire, was that funds provided by the federal government would have to be matched by the states; it comes as no surprise, therefore, that some of these bilateral agreements were signed with some reluctance, all the more so as the Labor state governments did not want to bow to the demands of a federal Liberal government. With the election of the Rudd government in November 2007, it is hoped that these government relationships improve and that the willing cooperation around environmental protection increases.

The size of the federal government's environment budget means that it has a lot of sway in deciding which threatened species and ecological communities are prioritised for recovery. Via the NRM plans, it gave the states most of the authority to decide themselves what conservation measures they should invest in. But in respect to the other two funding streams—for national priority projects and community-based conservation projects via Envirofund and the Threatened Species Network Community Grants—the Liberal federal government demanded that funds were spent on species and communities listed under the federal *EPBC Act*.

Federal funding is one of the primary avenues for local groups wanting to restore a piece of bushland habitat for local threatened fauna, propagate a rare orchid, undertake a survey of Gouldian finches or restore the riparian habitat of a freshwater tortoise by clearing it of weeds. As community groups are often more concerned with state-listed priority species, however, their projects were often not eligible for federal funding unless those species were also listed under the *EPBC Act*. Not receiving a listing under the EPBC Act, however, meant that many species and ecological communities were therefore ineligible for federal funding. Although the government would argue that it provided funds to the states via the NRM plans, these funds were only ever a fraction of what would be required to implement the plans in their entirety. To complicate things further, the regional bodies charged with allocating the funds were almost inevitably biased towards improving agricultural land-management outcomes and left little for conservation purposes. An audit of the *EPBC Act* by the Australian National Audit Office in 2006 concluded that 'biodiversity conservation had not been a high priority for all NHT funded regions' and that where it had been a priority, the low level of expenditure would achieve only 10–20 per cent of the high-priority conservation targets nationally.[24]

With the election of the new federal Labor government, the Natural Heritage Trust and its associated funding was officially wound up in July 2008, leaving existing projects to be completed over the following twelve months. It has been replaced with a new, consolidated funding plan called Caring for Our Country and $2.25 million has been allocated for the first five years.[25] This new initiative promises a more business-like approach to environment protection: it will demand greater accountability and assess the performance of environmental initiatives against set goals. The new initiative is focusing on six aspects with the help of its funds. Those directly related to species and ecosystem conservation include the consolidation of the national reserve system, the conservation of biodiversity and natural icons and the protection of coastal and critical aquatic habitats. Others that seek to improve broad-scale land management include the development of sustainable farm practices, better natural resource management in remote areas, and the engagement of the wider community through the building of knowledge and skills.

The intentions embedded in these priorities are sound, though their value will depend on how well they are delivered.

★ ★ ★

At this critical time, when a changing climate is set to exacerbate all other long-standing threats to an already exhausted environment, legislation must amount to more than just literature in a law library. Legal loopholes must be closed, and ambiguous wording that weakens the intent of the law must be replaced to ensure that the environment is the foremost beneficiary of its implementation. All aspects of the law and its related policies must be well resourced, uncompromisingly administered, environmental activities closely monitored and transgressions appropriately punished. Recent history has shown that until the law is taken seriously and adhered to by all sectors whose activities contribute to environmental decline, Australia has no hope of conserving what's left of its natural capital. None.

9
———

SOUNDS LIKE A PLAN

Deciding What to Save and How

A range of industries continues to place pressure on the natural environment and, despite a legal framework created to support and protect
the environment, vast numbers of species and their communities and
habitats are in serious trouble. So how is it possible to take up this challenge without being swamped?

Our own healthcare system provides a fitting analogy for the manner
in which plant and wildlife 'patients' in need of aid are treated. A species
in danger is rushed to the 'emergency department'—usually a scientific
committee that considers the evidence and assigns it to a threat category.
Each 'patient' requires careful assessment of the nature and causes of its
illness so that it can be added to a patient list and an appropriate course
of treatment can be determined. For most species this will entail the drafting of a recovery plan that, provided it is implemented properly, should
lead to recovery or at least a notable improvement in the species' condition. In recent decades, however, wards have become over-crowded,
with some patients waiting years to be assessed. Even once a diagnosis
has been made, insufficient funding prevents the most sensible but often
more costly treatments from being applied and many in the ward will
miss out on treatment altogether.

The decision-making processes that determine which species receive 'treatment' and which don't are emotionally charged. Even among scientists and conservation managers, the sobering premises that underlie these decisions—that conservation efforts are mostly inadequate, that some species are beyond salvation—are avoided like the famous elephant in the room. Discussing the extinction dilemma openly is further complicated by the pervasive view that 'people don't want to hear bad news'. While an unwillingness to confront bad news may be true for a large sector of the community, it is profoundly unhelpful in dealing with our ailing environment.

In planning an important conference held in Sydney in July 2007, organisers for the 'Biodiversity Extinction Crisis Conference: A Pacific Response' found funding hard to come by as the topic was considered too grim for sponsorship. And to add to this frustration, a journalist approached to cover the conference felt that issues such as land clearing and weed and feral invasions, which of course are central to many of the presentations, were yesterday's news and had all been 'done'. Such prevailing attitudes ensure that species' extinction is not only hastened by ignorance and inaction but that it occurs quietly offstage while the factors that threaten their survival continue. And yet these very factors affect our own future in equal measure.

★ ★ ★

To date, the main prerequisite for a species to be listed (and the possible initiation of a recovery plan) is that its habitat or entire community is declining in extent or quality according to a set of criteria drawn up by the World Conservation Union (IUCN). The faster its decline and/or the smaller its remaining populations, the higher its conservation rating or threat status. Under the *EPBC Act*, a species can be listed as 'conservation dependent', 'vulnerable', 'endangered' or 'critically endangered', and beyond that as 'extinct' or 'extinct in the wild' where a handful of individuals are being kept alive in captivity.[1] Yet the species or communities assessed for evidence of decline are largely subjective.

Inevitably, plants or animals found to be declining in number are those studied by scientists or closely observed by conservation managers. Not surprisingly, large and attractive plants and animals appear on lists of threatened species more often than small and cryptic species, and mammals, birds and reptiles more often than invertebrates or small marine species. It is almost a given, however, that the declining status of many of the larger species under observation is representative of the decline of other parts of their ecosystems and not of their suffering in isolation. While the inherent bias in threatened species lists is commonly acknowledged[2], the lists represent the only reliable means of identifying at least some of the species that urgently require protection. Provided that strategic conservation activities are put in place to help them, other undiagnosed but similarly threatened creatures of the ecosystem may also benefit. The restoration of a native patch of eucalypt woodland for a population of koalas, for example, would also benefit a large number of birds, mammals and other nectar feeders, as well as (unstudied) invertebrates and small reptiles that live among the trees or in the grassy understorey or soils of this habitat.

To be considered for active conservation a plant or animal must be:

- noticed and monitored
- found to be declining or in very small numbers
- nominated for listing
- assessed and supported by a scientific advisory committee
- listed as threatened.

The next phase adds a further layer of complexity. With more than 1600 living plants, animals and ecosystems on the *EPBC Act*'s lists alone and hundreds of additional ones on state lists, what should be saved given the wholly inadequate conservation budgets? Traditionally this decision has been based predominantly on threat status—species that are 'endangered' or 'critically endangered' take priority over those that are vulnerable or conservation-dependent and may have a slightly longer stay of grace. As newly extinct species don't make for good public relations, focusing the small conservation budget on those most likely to prove embarrassing by dropping off their perch makes good sense to an incumbent government. Given the large number of species that occupy the highly threatened categories, however, this reactive approach to conservation has achieved little in the bigger picture. Species that are under the greatest threat (this applies to animals and ecological communities more than plants) are often more difficult to recover (or no longer recoverable at all) and divert resources from those with a better chance of recovery at less effort and expense.

★ ★ ★

One threatened Australian species with a very high profile is the critically endangered orange-bellied parrot. This beautiful grass-green parrot with the distinctive orange chest is endemic to southeastern Australia and has been the focus of one of the longest running recovery programs in this country. Although it is uncertain how large the populations of the orange-bellied parrot were prior to European settlement, it was once considered to be locally common and its range extended from Yorke Peninsula in South Australia along the mainland coast to Sydney and along the west coast of Tasmania.[3] Orange-bellied parrots are known to breed in the hollows of only two eucalypt species in coastal southwestern Tasmania in the summer months before migrating to the Victorian and South Australian coasts for the winter. On the mainland, the parrots traditionally feed in coastal saltmarsh, beach dune vegetation and other plant communities typically associated with coastal wetlands and dunes. It is the fragmentation of these habitats through the drainage of wetlands for grazing, industrial and urban development of the saltmarsh, land clearing and poor fire management that has likely caused the parrot's decline. Introduced weeds, among them a plant toxic to wildlife, have also played a part, as has the invasion of precious nesting hollows by feral populations of the honey bee and competition for food from introduced birds like the sparrow and European finches. Most recently, the construction of wind farms along the bird's migration route and in their coastal winter range have become an obstacle that could cause multiple deaths if flocks of the parrots were to collide with the turbines. By the early 1980s, a comprehensive survey of the bird's range revealed the total number of parrots to be fewer than two hundred individuals. This figure prompted the production of the first recovery plan for the species that began to be implemented in 1984; subsequent plans commenced in 1991 and in 1998.[4]

Given the narrow distribution range occupied by the bird and the pervasiveness of the threats within it, the ability to help the orange-bellied parrot is limited by the capacity to address these impacts, a situation that has been acknowledged by the recovery team.[5] Nevertheless, a recovery team across three states has been operating for more than twenty years to halt the bird's decline through monitoring and research, the cultivation of native food plants in the winter habitat, the exclusion of stock from feeding sites, controlling cats, foxes and rabbits, installing nest boxes, managing a captive breeding program and raising public awareness.[6] Funds expended during that time add up—direct federal government contributions from 1989 to 2003 totalled $1.09 million, and since then, further monies were spent via the regional natural resources management plans. The money provided by the federal government was only a proportion of funds sought; over the period 1998–2002 alone, the proposed budget for recovery actions comprised more than $2.73 million.[7] In 2006 a further $3.2 million was pledged over two years, despite the fact that a current recovery plan no longer exists. None of these funds takes into account the additional contributions of the many volunteers who conduct annual winter censuses as well as searches for the bird's nest sites in Tasmania's south-west.

Yet for all the focused attention this bird has received since the early 1980s, its status has not changed. Although more than three hundred captive-bred birds have been released over a 15-year period[8], estimates of the current population continue to hover around two hundred individuals, including around fifty breeding pairs—the same as it was almost twenty-five years ago. While it's true that unflagging commitment and resources have helped keep this highly threatened species alive, they have produced no signs of *improving* its chances of survival. The orange-bellied parrot's future continues to depend entirely on ongoing recovery efforts and substantial investment.

The orange-bellied parrot is by no means the only species in the category of those practically beyond salvation, or 'living dead'. The western swamp tortoise, Gilbert's potoroo, the Christmas Island pipistrelle and dozens of other species are also barely hanging on. Most highly threatened species are the subject of active recovery plans. Some have been reduced to small, semi-captive and highly managed populations in fenced-off and isolated remnants of their natural habitat. The western swamp tortoise, probably not abundant even in its original range of the Swan Coastal Plain, now exists only in two fenced nature reserves and a third intensively managed area where a trial introduction is under way. Its natural habitat has been almost entirely converted to farmland, urbanised or mined for the clay soils preferred by the tortoise.[9] While the populations in two of the three nature reserves are boosted by tortoises bred in captivity at Perth Zoo, the four hundred-odd remaining individuals of this species are no more than much-loved, carefully managed relics, kept alive in the ever-optimistic hope that future technologies may yet see it recover.[10]

The Christmas Island pipistrelle, a small insect-eating bat endemic to the island's rainforest, is also under real threat of extinction and without the safety net of captive-bred back up. Still widespread and common in the mid 1980s, surveys in the 1990s revealed that their populations had substantially declined and contracted. The precise causes of the bat's decline are as yet uncertain and its future survival depends on the successful implementation of its recovery plan to determine what the specific threats are and to try to contain them. Among the likely suspects are colonies of the exotic yellow crazy ant, and introduced predators like the wolf snake, the cat, the black rat and the naturalised Nankeen kestrel.[11]

★ ★ ★

A recovery plan is only one component of a conservation strategy that must take into account the bigger environmental picture to produce sensible and sustainable outcomes. No one species can be propped up by recovery actions forever. By definition, recovery aims to improve significantly the status of a species so that it can resume its intended role in the environment; keeping it alive with no real prospect of recovery amounts to little more than palliative care.

An investment in individual species must be measured against investing in suites of species or in whole-of-landscapes conservation wherever this is feasible. Disappointingly, highly threatened species become easy pawns in the game of politics. An extraordinary example of this occurred in 2006 when the environment minister Senator Ian Campbell found himself in political hot water for refusing to approve a wind farm in the orange bellied-parrot's range. Under considerable media pressure he then changed his mind and approved the farm, pledging an additional $3.2 million over two years towards the bird's conservation.[12] This pledge was considered to be a distraction from the minister's backflip on first disallowing the construction of the project— a campaign promise to a vital marginal seat—using the convenient excuse of the parrot's conservation.[13] While the extra funding for the parrot may have seemed generous from a public perspective, many other threatened species and ecosystems would have provided a much higher return on the investment.

The eminent ecologist Hugh Possingham has mourned the lack of vision and pragmatism in conservation decision-making worldwide.[14] In a 2001 paper entitled 'The Business of Biodiversity', he likens investing large sums of money in the most threatened species to 'Hadrian's last stand, [by] buying time before the inevitable avalanche of extinctions'.[15] A more sensible approach, he proposes, would be to acknowledge that many species will become extinct and to focus recovery efforts on those whose status *can* be improved and without exorbitant expense.[16]

A more business-like approach to conservation is ultimately inevitable but some conservationists are concerned that this approach would be too shortsighted, and that abandoning threatened species to save others simply makes the fate of the former a self-fulfilling prophecy. They are concerned too that this approach discounts the possibility of future technology and knowledge that may help those species that have been dismissed.[17] While this may be a valid point of view, only a limitless conservation budget would be able to resolve this situation to everyone's satisfaction.

The story of the orange-bellied parrot illustrates how difficult the attempted recovery of a highly endangered species can be. What needs to be estimated early in the decision-making process is whether the threats to any given species can be sufficiently contained to enable its recovery. Considerations must include the physical possibility of removing or reducing the threat/s, obtaining sufficient funding for the duration of the recovery process and the degree of political support for the species. Often, lobbying efforts for money and support are likely to be required.

The decision *not* to invest focused conservation efforts in a species or ecological community is, sadly, often made by default (as limited funds are spent on other species) but occasionally by design. Other considerations in addition to how threatened the species is include whether the species is of significant cultural value (especially Aboriginal culture), whether it is a keystone species and whether it would cause a negative public reaction if it became extinct.

Bias against the recovery of a threatened species happens where the species is the source of conflict with the public or particular industries. The lamentable treatment of two species of flying foxes left on the conservation backburner so as not to antagonise the fruit growing industry or urban residents in areas where the bats are seen as a problem are a case in point. The spectacled and grey-headed flying foxes are officially recognised as vulnerable to extinction, yet in an almost unfathomable paradox, fruit growers in New South Wales and Queensland are able to obtain permits to 'harm' them if they feed in their orchards. Protected by their permits and confident that compliance monitoring is all but non-existent, many fruit growers are known to shoot many times their seasonal quota and to be contributing to the species' decline. Ironically, the practice of killing flying foxes provides no relief for the fruit crops;

the killing of the bats merely vacates their spot for other hungry bats by night and flocks of equally hungry birds by day until the food source has been exhausted.

Indisputably, one objective of drafting recovery plans for these two flying foxes would be to cease the issuing of permits to kill the bats that forage in orchards. Following the national listing of north Queensland's endemic and vulnerable spectacled flying fox in May 2002, a recovery team was formed and the drafting of a recovery plan commenced in 2003. While awaiting the circulation of a draft for comment by the Queensland government, however, the recovery team discovered that the state government had put the plan on hold. No explanation was given. The stunned team was left in limbo and the licensed killing of this vulnerable species continued unabated for another two seasons. Then, as suddenly as it had been abandoned, the draft plan—minus the recovery team—was resurrected in 2005 amid a flurry of bad publicity about the use of electric grids to kill bats in orchards. Keen to be seen to be taking action, the Queensland government hired a consultant and gave him just four weeks to contact relevant experts and complete a report. But as the negative publicity abated, the completed plan was promptly buried. As of October 2008, the recovery plan for the spectacled flying fox had not been published and its recommendations had not been officially acknowledged. An issue that has contributed nothing to overcoming this delay is that the state of Queensland refuses to recognise the spectacled flying fox as threatened; therefore, it does not regard it as a priority for recovery. But without the aid of a recovery plan, the future of this species is in doubt.

The grey-headed flying fox is similarly in limbo. Listed nationally (as well as in New South Wales and Victoria) since 2001, its recovery plan was completed through extensive consultation in mid 2005 but it has yet to see the light of day. Deeply frustrated by this delay, the plan's author, prominent flying fox ecologist Dr Peggy Eby, writes that 'the listing of the grey-headed flying fox had thus far had no practical impact on the management of affected crops, [and] tentative deadlines for the phasing out of the killing of the bats had not been met'.[18]

Dedicated community groups are working to help the slow-breeding species but funding is limited and the task is practically impossible without government buy-in.

★ ★ ★

There are close to 1700 living species and ecological communities currently listed under the *EPBC Act*[19], yet fewer than four hundred plans (covering around 420 species and thirteen communities) have been completed to date, and only a proportion of those are being implemented. The time-lags and costs of writing recovery plans as well as the time it takes before seeing a species listed have often been criticised for absorbing funds that could be better spent on on-ground action.

A graphic example of lag in process is the tragic case of the southern corroboree frog. Until 1970 it was considered abundant within its small range in the Kosciuszko National Park.[20] A severe and prolonged drought in the 1980s led to increased monitoring of its decline, however, it took until 1989 for the first major survey of the distribution and abundance of the frogs to be published, which in turn delayed publication of the first species management report until 1991. By 1997 the frogs had gone from 70 per cent of their known range. The immediate funding of conservation activities focused on identifying the cause of the decline, which continued unabated. But despite the urgency a formal recovery plan for the southern corroboree frog was not published until five years later (2001), and by 2003 only a single viable population remained in the wild. This species is now expected to become extinct in the wild within less than a decade.

There have been numerous instances of serious delays in the formal recovery process; however, the information gathered for recovery plans is vital for decision-making and to track changes in the status of the species as a result of conservation activities. To reduce the time and cost of producing recovery plans, the federal government recently amended the *EPBC Act* so a plan is not necessary for each listed species. Instead, conservation activities for listed threatened species are to be guided in the first instance by 'conservation advice' that lists the key threats, the actions necessary to ameliorate them, and the degree of urgency with which a recovery plan should (or not) be drafted. The concern is that, in instances where recovery plans are not written, the information contained in the conservation advice is insufficient to guide or measure the success or otherwise of the recovery effort. And while detailed information about the biology, lifecycle, former and current distribution ranges and so on, usually contained in a comprehensive recovery plan, can now be provided as background documentation, collating this information will still require time and resources. A better compromise for minimising time-lags would be to publish conservation advice and focus immediately on the abatement of known threats while ensuring that all possible species information is gathered within a minimum time frame such as six months. The real challenges to recovery success remain adequate resourcing, strategic expenditure of funds and the targeting of the key threats.

★ ★ ★

Recovery plans remain a sensible conservation strategy for the majority of species and ecosystems. A thorough conservation plan provides a baseline of the species' status, that is, population estimates and/or estimates of the extent and condition of its habitat, against which progress can be measured. If recovery strategies are working, future declines should cease and improvements in population estimates or habitat expected within a certain period of time. This period may be a number of years or even decades.

Tracking recovery success is complicated by the difficulties of accurately estimating species or population numbers. Unless a species has declined to such a drastic extent and in such readily observable circumstances that the exact numbers of remaining individuals are known—as with the northern hairy-nosed wombat and Gilbert's potoroo—scientists rely on population estimates or proxy indicators (such as the rapid decline or destruction of the species' habitat or a notable increase in weeds or feral animals) to decide on their conservation status. Consequently, changes in species are measurable when they are substantial but much less so when they are subtle. There is also a risk that, where a species has been listed due to the rapid loss of its habitat and individuals are difficult to monitor, the regeneration of that habitat may be considered evidence of the recovery of the species, though this is not automatically the case. Sometimes individuals find it difficult to recolonise habitat, or their numbers are kept low, by physical obstacles such as roads constructed after the initial loss of habitat. These complications make it all the more important that good assessment and monitoring methods are established to identify changes as quickly as possible during the recovery process.

★ ★ ★

Different types of plans are needed in different circumstances. There are currently three general types of recovery plans: plans that address the conservation of a single species, others that focus on a suite of similar species, and those that address conservation at a landscape level within a particular geographical region or catchment.

The most common plan is the traditional single-species plan that provides all relevant available knowledge about a species and outlines what needs to be done to reverse its decline. The benefits of single-species plans are in the detail they provide, while their biggest downside is that it's simply not feasible to draft individual plans for each threatened species. Single-species plans are best suited to plants and wildlife with specific recovery requirements (such as isolated populations of plants), or those that are flagships for a particular ecosystem whereby the measures taken for their recovery benefit the entire ecosystem. In the latter case, a landscape plan may also be an option.

A multi-species plan is most appropriate for species biologically similar or related, or that occupy the same or overlapping ranges and are affected by the same threats. Where this is the case, one plan avoids repetition in conservation strategies, aligns and coordinates conservation activities and maximises efficiency. This recovery approach is being used for a suite of large threatened seabirds that feed and breed in the Australian Fishing Zone (AFZ). Eighteen species of albatross and giant petrels that forage in the AFZ are threatened by the commercial practices of long-line fishing that occur in the southern parts of this zone. Between 50 and 100 million hooks are set in long-lines each year in the Southern Ocean alone, and large numbers of birds are drowned or ingest hooks while trying to retrieve the bait attached to the lines.[21] In addition to those species that forage in the AFZ, four species of albatross and giant petrel also breed on Macquarie Island. With significant overlap in the biology of the species and their ranges and threats, recovery strategies that lead to changes to fishing gear and effective catch mitigation in the AFZ (as well as the eradication of rats, mice and rabbits from Macquarie Island) will benefit all of the listed species and are best captured in one plan. Another multi-species plan guides the recovery effort for seven species of stream-dwelling frogs in Queensland's Wet Tropics.[22] The plan's focus in the first instance is on determining the cause of numerous population crashes and how (and whether) further crashes can be avoided in the future.

Multi-species plans are also well suited to the local recovery of many plants. In Tasmania, for example, eight endemic species of flowering shrubs of the genus *Epacris* have been incorporated into one recovery plan. Although the species each have small distributions and occur at different sites and habitats across the state, all are susceptible to poor fire regimes and the root-fungus *Phytophthora cinnamomi*, and some are also threatened by habitat alteration, clearing, weeds and trampling and grazing by stock.[23] Although many of these threats have to be tackled on a site-by-site basis, the plan outlines recovery actions for each, enables a coordinated approach to protection and management and simplifies the plants' funding allocation.

In south-west Western Australia, the conservation of hundreds of threatened and near threatened plants is being tackled on a district-by-district basis. The large geographic areas covered by some of these plans allow for the better broad-scale management of threatening processes but as before, an identified downside was that less detailed information was provided about the individual plant species encompassed in each plan. To get around this issue, the Department of Conservation and Land Management has allowed for additional single-species plans to be written where individual plants require more specific recovery actions.[24] In this way, the advantages of both types of plans were combined in a flexible arrangement with the aim of producing the best-possible conservation results for the species they address.

Landscape plans are useful where the same threat impacts on different species and the ecology of a given region. By definition, landscape-focused recovery plans place a greater emphasis on addressing the various threats to particular ecological communities and seek to maintain their collective function, that is, the interactions and connectedness of plants and wildlife across an extensive—though often fragmented—area. The 'Recovery Plan for the Endangered Natural Temperate Grasslands of the Southern Tablelands of New South Wales and the ACT' seeks to protect a highly diverse flora dominated by tussock grasses of varying heights and densities, as well as forbs (sedges, orchids, lilies and herbs) and occasional eucalypts.[25] Left undisturbed, these grasslands produce a glorious flowing carpet of violet, purple, yellow and white flowers in the summer months and are natural grazing grounds for kangaroos, wallabies, wombats and other native herbivores as well as habitat for invertebrates. Reptiles such as the striped legless lizard and the grassland earless dragon share this ecosystem with skinks and frogs, and birds such as quail and the internationally protected Latham's snipe. Since European settlement, the grasslands in this agricultural area have been so degraded that today only around 3 per cent of the initial extent of the grasslands maintain a degree of ecological integrity.[26] Recovery actions to date have included the mapping of remnants on public and private land, the establishment of reserves, and the design of 'best practice' management guidelines for landholders, whose involvement is vital to help conserve what's left of this grassland community.

The multi-species and landscape plans are not yet ten years old, so it's too soon to make a call on their effectiveness. Australia's approaches to species conservation, however, mirror those in other countries. In the United States, the performance of recovery plans was extensively reviewed in 2002, and the results of this study served as a benchmark for a preliminary assessment of the three types of plans in Australia. This pilot study, undertaken by scientists from Murdoch University[27], confirmed that the newer types of plans had tried to cut corners on the amount and quality of information they provided to the detriment of their performance. The status of species addressed via multi-species plans evaluated in the United States, for example, was almost four times less likely to improve than those for whom single-species plans had been put in place.[28] And landscape plans lacked detail in terms of biological information, recovery actions for identified threats and performance assessment.[29] Like the findings from the USA[30], Australian single-species plans were more thorough and contained more of the ecological and biological information vital to assessing recovery success than the multi-species plans, while landscape plans fared worst in this aspect.

In contrast to the American plans reviewed, Australia was found to have embraced the involvement of the general community in its recovery actions. Recovery team members interviewed for this pilot study were enthusiastic about community engagement and recognised the immense value in enlisting landholders' help to conserve local biodiversity.

To date, the record of recovery success for species has been gravely disappointing. Species and communities are continuously added to the threatened lists while none has been permanently removed as a result of an improvement in status.[31] One almost-success was the downgrading of the Western Australia's woylie (brush-tailed bettong) from a national listing of 'endangered' to one of 'lower risk' in 1996. This small marsupial bounced back as a result of effective fox control and the subsequent reintroduction of individuals to fox-free habitats. Ten years after being removed from the list, however, the woylie's populations are once again declining.[32]

★ ★ ★

The success of recovery planning as a core conservation strategy depends on the high quality of the plans, regardless of whether these focus on one species, suites of species or a geographical area and its living components. Well-constructed recovery plans, such as Western Australia's Western Shield Project *can* and *will* produce conservation outcomes provided they are able to meet a number of essential conditions that take account of the political realities in the conservation challenge. First and foremost, the conservation of the species or community must have the support of the relevant governments and, where threatened species occur on public land or land contested by developers, that of the local councils. The publication and implementation of recovery plans and their financial and administrative support is impossible without the support of the relevant government departments and the support of local authorities. And the power of community groups and individuals in influencing governments cannot be underestimated—*no* organisation speaks as loudly as the voting public. Public support for recovery efforts (or against harmful environmental activities) could and should be voiced through phone calls, letters and even personal visits to local members of the state and federal governments, relevant ministers and local authorities. Better conservation outcomes rely on active public lobbying for government support and can only be achieved through the collective power of the people who elect them.

The second condition for the success of recovery programs is that ongoing causes of a species or community's decline are emphasised and addressed. But this should not mean a redirection of funds towards threat management alone; for many plants and wildlife species, other important recovery activities might include the captive breeding of individuals for release, raising public awareness and the active rehabilitation of habitat once threats have been removed. Effective threat management should provide the backbone that justifies the community's on-ground efforts in aid of species recovery.

The final conditions to help ensure recovery success include a realistic analysis of the likelihood of recovery (including a projected time line for improvement in status), sound estimates of the funds required

to reach that goal (and the likelihood of obtaining them), a clear definition of what constitutes 'recovery' and, most of all, an assurance that
the plan will be implemented. The definition of recovery once again calls
for a large dose of pragmatism. For the majority of critically endangered
or endangered species or communities this goal can at best be expected
to be a measure of improvement, such as the downgrading of a species'
threat status from 'endangered' to 'vulnerable', and the maintenance of
this improved status with continued investment and management. More
often than not, even this goal may be unrealistic, as the example of the
orange-bellied parrot has shown. Without doubt, the best odds for a full
recovery are held by those vulnerable or conservation-dependent species
whose decline could be halted by removing obvious threats such as cats
and foxes, or the destruction of habitat.

10

A BAND-AID WON'T DO

Tackling the Threats

In January 2002 a number of experts were assembled under the auspices of the Prime Minister's Science, Engineering and Innovation Council (PMSEIC) to ponder how the nation's biodiversity might best be conserved for current and future generations. Set with this ambitious task, the group identified a unique opportunity to reset conservation priorities to incorporate not just the components of nature but also the value of the services provided by healthy ecosystems to all living beings.[1] Vitally important products of a healthy environment—fresh air, clean water and soil nutrients among them—thus far had no recognised value in the current economy. Consequently, their inherent worth could not be weighed against that of marketable resources and the industries –forestry, agriculture, pastoralism and tourism among them—that depend on the health of the environment. The group recognised that as long as there was no price placed on ecosystem services and their life-giving commodities they would continue to be taken for granted, and this would interfere with environmental conservation efforts.

A second concern of the experts was the inefficient way in which limited conservation funds were being spent.[2] In making this point, the group emphasised the enormous cost that natural ecosystems, once extensively damaged, incur both to the environment and to the economy. In 2002, the cost of agricultural production lost to the symptoms of degradation—salinity, water pollution, ferals, weeds and disease—amounted to around $1.2 billion. At the same time, funds spent on programs attempting to repair often highly damaged natural systems and to protect their biodiversity were around $1.5 billion, around 25 per cent of what would be required for a wholehearted restoration effort.

The working group argued that it would be much more cost-effective to invest in protecting ecosystems that were still relatively healthy rather than to try to restore those that were profoundly damaged. (Without doubt, the Murray–Darling Basin as an example of the latter was uppermost in their minds.) The best way to do this, the group concluded, was to combat the underlying causes of environmental decline.[3] On considering the range of threats and the breadth of their impacts, PMSEIC recommended the further reduction of land clearing, limiting the over-extraction of fresh water from rivers, and controlling the spread of feral pests, weeds and diseases into new areas as sensible investment options. Adding to this, the group emphasised the importance of developing means for incorporating the value of ecosystem health into the products that nature yields for consumers, so that it would no longer be economically cheaper to degrade the environment than to preserve it.

The contribution of PMSEIC and its working group resonated strongly with conservation organisations and government agencies and many of its recommendations were adopted. Large-scale clearing now mainly occurs in Tasmania and the Northern Territory. The over-extraction of water, as yet a monumental challenge in the south-west and south-east of the country, is being pre-empted in Australia's north via efforts to conserve the still largely 'wild' rivers of the Northern Territory and Far North Queensland. The goal of reducing the spread of invasive species became the driver for a review of quarantine practices nationally and across the states—the nursery trade can now no longer sell several thousand invasive plants, and another 3300 have been banned from importation as of 2005.[4] Preventive measures, however, cannot be the only response to Australia's environmental crisis. And while PMSEIC justifiably argues for spending available funds more wisely, others might argue for *more* funds rather than resign themselves to the politically convenient assumption that funding could never resource the necessary efforts required.

★ ★ ★

Dealing with the big-ticket items—the ubiquitous threats and large-scale drivers of decline—requires a broader and often much more visionary perspective than that necessary for recovery planning. But neither strategy will work in isolation. Some plant or animal populations on a rapid downward spiral need additional help to overcome the long-term impacts of those causes, even when they have been removed. Small desert mammal populations preyed on by cats and foxes, for instance, may become too small and isolated by the time the predators have been contained and continue to decline without additional aid. In some cases, captive breeding and reintroductions to the wild may boost the numbers and genes of such populations to overcome this hurdle to their recovery. This was the case for the bilby, whose populations plummeted since the 1970s, and which is variously listed as vulnerable or endangered under state/territory and federal legislations.[5] Fortunately for the bilby, it has bred well in captivity and has since been released on predator-free islands off Western Australia and reintroduced to other wild and semi-wild sites within its natural range.[6]

Often, more than one threat is affecting a species or community and each needs to be addressed for recovery to become possible. The southern cassowary, north Queensland's large, flightless forest forager is threatened primarily by the loss and fragmentation of its rainforest habitat from coastal development and agriculture. Largely as a result of this fragmented habitat, it is now also threatened by vehicular traffic, dogs, feral pigs, as well as by cyclones and disease.[7] The preservation of the remaining lowland rainforest would be an essential step towards the cassowary's long-term survival, but other recovery actions—the removal of dogs and pigs and the control of traffic—would also be necessary to prevent its further decline. Although secondary threats may need to be addressed for the conservation of many species, *without* the concerted, long-term containment of the large, overarching threats and drivers of decline, most recovery efforts will fail.

Recovery and threat abatement planning are complementary processes; both require biological knowledge and technical skills, an ability to engage relevant stakeholders, a number of clear sequential objectives, performance and review measures and an adequate budget. But the sheer scale of a state-based or national threat abatement effort demands the wholehearted support of federal and state governments as well as that of those landholders and industry bodies whose practices are exacerbating the scale or severity of the threat. The adjustment of fire regimes to aid landscape and biodiversity conservation, for example, may entail working closely with individual landholders over extended periods of time to convince them of the benefits of irregular patch-burns. Where the aim is to stop large-scale land clearing, by comparison, active government regulation is a necessary strategy to ensure that landholders take this seriously. These challenges are not for the faint-hearted.

The distinction between species recovery and threat abatement becomes blurred when the former is entirely dependent on the latter. The recovery of large seabirds such as albatross and petrels threatened by long-line fishing[8], for example, is almost completely dependent on the amelioration of the threat of long-line fishing that is the aim of the seabird bycatch threat abatement plan.[9] But such complementary plans do not often exist.

The federal government reserves the right to create a threat abatement plan only if it considers it 'practicable', though the lack of a plan for a recognised key threatening process has a number of implications. Of the seventeen Key Threatening Processes currently recognised under the *EPBC Act*, eleven have approved abatement plans.[10] Of these eleven, most are threats related to introduced predators (cats, foxes), landscape degraders (pigs, goats, rabbits), lethal invertebrates (yellow crazy ant, red fire ant) or diseases and pathogens (chytrid fungus in frogs, beak and feather disease in parrots, Phytophthora dieback in native vegetation) whose containment would benefit both the environment and agriculture or at least not interfere with agricultural practices.

Those threats that don't have plans are related to harmful but lucrative commercial practices and include land clearing, loss of habitat from greenhouse gas emissions and two marine-based threats of incidental bycatch of marine turtles during otter-trawling (or large net-dragging) operations in northern Australian waters and the impact of harmful marine debris on marine life.[11] There is, however, a plan currently in the pipeline to combat the impact of marine debris, which will have to involve the tricky issue of dealing with the origins of that debris. Thorough surveys and cataloguing of debris have revealed that much of it—including fishing nets, floats, buoys, plastic bottles and thongs— originates from fishing operations in the Arafura and Timor seas, which are flanked by Indonesia to the north and Australia to south.[12] The containment of this threat to turtles and other marine life that can choke or drown from these items will involve dealing with both legal and illegal fishing operations in that area.

Two other threats without formal plans to date are the control of predation by exotic rats on offshore island fauna and of cane toads on the mainland. Rats, of which there are three exotic species in Australia, are opportunists in their dietary habits and prey on birds, small mammals and lizards and their eggs, as well as large insects, snails and plant seeds and seedlings. They are known to have played a large part in the extinction of birds in New Zealand and the Hawaiian Islands and, in Australian waters, on Lord Howe Island and Norfolk Island. The drafting of a rodent abatement plan was initiated via an expert workshop held in mid 2007 and is now under way.[13] Embarrassed by the highly publicised degradation of Macquarie Island from rats and rabbits once cats had been removed, the Tasmanian and Australian governments agreed to share the $24.6 million cost of eradicating rodents and rabbits.[14] A formal plan will help to tackle this issue across the many other islands under Australian jurisdiction on which native wildlife is similarly threatened.

The cane toad, which is now encroaching on ecologically priceless new frontiers such as Kakadu National Park proves to be a massive threat to native wildlife. As it continues to expand its range, the toad falls prey to wildlife unaware of its toxicity and leaves a trail of death in its wake. In the absence of a formal abatement plan, several projects coordinated by the Invasive Animal Cooperative Research Centre are working on developing abatement techniques to control toad numbers—something that hasn't been achieved since its introduction seventy years ago. Researchers are focusing variously on the toad's biology, breeding, diet and habitat needs to identify possible points at which to pierce its biological armour. Baiting and trapping options and genetic means of reducing the number of breeding females are also being investigated.[15]

A national Cane Toad Taskforce was established in 2004, followed more recently by an additional committee of stakeholders to oversee the strategies for toad control. The taskforce's aim in the first instance is to prevent it entering Western Australia and to protect vulnerable landscapes like the Kimberley from the advancing throng, but also to combat its march southward along the east coast. Interestingly, the non-existence of a national abatement plan in this case has not prevented the cane toad from being tackled with determination. In fact, the lack of a federal plan may be somewhat beneficial—all relevant governments (including federal) have contributed funds, and by not having a national plan the ownership of on-ground activities remains with each state, which can choose how best to act within its jurisdiction. This situation highlights that national threat abatement plans become important when little funding or impetus for action exists. Where sufficient funds are available, strategies are readily agreed to and relevant state and territory governments are motivated, the formal framework of a plan becomes less important provided that sensible on-ground actions are initiated.

★ ★ ★

The most glaring omission on the official lists of biodiversity threats and abatement strategies is the profound land degradation caused by domestic stock and poor agricultural practices. Both are root causes of the parlous state of Australia's environment and have been confirmed as such by reams of government reports. Regrettably, the findings of those reports are not always adequately or accurately publicised, allowing these practices to continue unhindered.

In 1992, a ground-breaking report commissioned by the newly established Endangered Species Unit of the then Australian National Parks and Wildlife Service (now Australian government Department of the Environment, Water, Heritage and the Arts) reviewed the impact of all introduced animal species, both feral and domestic, and ranked them in accordance with their impact on native species.[16] The results were illuminating. Among aquatic species, the predatory brown trout native to Europe had the most significant impact on its environment[17], affecting the status of six native species of fish and numerous invertebrates. Of the many introduced birds, the highly adaptable common starling topped the list of baddies with a detrimental impact on five native bird species, including eastern rosellas and blue-winged and orange-bellied parrots whose tree-nesting hollows they appropriate.[18]

The most serious impact of all known introduced animals by an order of magnitude, however, was that of domestic sheep. With a detrimental impact on thirty-five native birds and mammals—an extremely conservative figure in some opinions[19]—with half that number now listed as threatened, the mark of sheep on the Australian landscape was more than twice that of its nearest competitors, the black rat and the feral cat. As the report's author, Martin Denny, pointed out, this assessment did not include the sheep's impact on reptiles and plants, which in his opinion would have further strengthened its status as 'the undisputed leader in recorded impacts on native species'.[20] Foxes, widely acknowledged to be one of the gravest threats to native species, ranked fourth overall and affected an estimated ten to twenty native species. Sheep had been found to have actively affected the habitats of the rurally iconic malleefowl, the boodie, the ground parrot, turquoise parrot, regent parrot and, among mammals, the long-footed potoroo, bridled nail-tailed wallaby and bilby.

Denny, who spent almost two years consulting close to sixty scientists with extensive expertise in the management of native and introduced species, was dismayed to find that the department was not prepared to accept the politically nightmarish findings of the report. Denny was asked to change the list, a request that he duly refused. The department was then forced to accept the report as it stood, but promptly buried it deep in the vaults of its library, away from public scrutiny and public calls for action. Some years after its completion, however, the Australian Bureau of Statistics unearthed the report as it was preparing to compile an overview of Australia's environment at that time.[21] Disconcertingly, the report's most critical findings were not made public from this rediscovery. The Australian Bureau of Statistics quoted extensively from Denny's report and listed the range of introduced species and their impacts bar two—neither sheep nor cattle received a mention.

At the time of the original report, large investments were being made to control introduced predators; there was pressure to place cats and foxes at the head of the list to justify this expenditure rather than acknowledge the damage caused by the economically important sheep. Needless to say, a listing of domestic sheep (or the now perhaps even greater impact of cattle) continues to elude the political agenda to this day. Any government that refuses to acknowledge its responsibilities to current and future generations with respect to resolving this fundamental issue can never expect to earn genuine environment conservation credentials.

★ ★ ★

Under the federal legislation, the first batch of abatement plans completed in 1999 set its sights on the control of feral goats, rabbits, cats and foxes. Like all threat abatement plans, these were written for an implementation period of five years, after which the outcomes of each were reviewed and decisions made about whether a further plan was needed. The politically and technically complex nature of reducing the threats that are formally recognised as Key Threatening Processes makes it inevitable that this is the case; quite simply, none are even remotely resolvable in a 5-year term.

The authors of the first abatement plan for predation by the European red fox made it explicit that its main goal would be 'consolidating and coordinating the long-term process of managing fox impacts on native fauna' during its 5-year course.[22] The plan also recognised that the national challenge to control fox populations would have to continue *indefinitely* and consume considerable resources in order to yield results for native species. While this may sound daunting, the enormous conservation gains to be made by the number of species whose populations would be better off should warrant *any* investment necessary to protect species and living systems from this stealthy introduced predator. Interestingly, the incentive is equally large for the pastoral sector, where up to 30 per cent of lamb stocks can be lost to foxes.[23]

In keeping with strategic abatement planning guidelines, the first plan to address fox predation outlined the problems caused by foxes, and listed actions for addressing them that would apply at local, regional and national levels. The plan also identified a number of obstacles and strategies for dealing with these. In the case of fox control by baiting (the easiest option), there are animal welfare issues related to the killing of the foxes, the likelihood of also killing native animals attracted to the meat bait, and the risk of an increase in rabbits, cats and dingoes once fox numbers decline. With these in mind, the various actions recommended to help fulfil the plan's objectives were divided into four main streams: fox management actions (fencing, baiting), as well as actions to conduct further research into humane control methods; ongoing information-gathering about fox interactions with other pest species; education and information about the project to those whose financial and technical support is required, such as landholders, community groups, local government and pest management agencies; and the independent evaluation and review of the project to inform the next 5-year iteration of the plan.

The fox threat abatement plan was reviewed in 2005 and the resulting recommendations, mostly of a technical nature, were incorporated
into the new draft plan.[24] One expert reviewer commented that the
reporting of outcomes had been inadequate and it had been difficult to
assess the full return on investment from the first plan.[25] This issue has
pervaded conservation projects for a long time. Apart from addressing
the technical detail of the reviewers' recommendations, the continued
challenge for threat abatement programs is to raise sufficient funds and
support to maintain momentum until long-term objectives can be
achieved. That said, two factors work strongly in the fox plan's favour:
foxes have no industry stakeholders who would lobby against their control (unlike the threats of land clearing or greenhouse gas emissions) and,
while the native wildlife that foxes threaten cannot be accurately valued
in monetary terms, industry stakeholders are known to incur substantial environmental and agricultural losses each year.

In 2004, the estimated cost of the damage by foxes to the environment and agriculture was more than $227 million.[26] Of that sum, the gov-
ernment primarily bore the cost of environmental protection while the
private sector, affected by the economic losses of sheep, covered the bill
for protecting its stock. From 2002 to 2006, the Australian government
invested a total of $1.5 million in projects related to fox management
undertaken by the CSIRO Sustainable Ecosystems, Western Australia's
Department of Conservation and Land Management, the Arthur Rylah
Institute for Environmental Research, the Bureau of Rural Sciences and
others. This funding was only a fraction of the annual cost to the environment and agriculture borne by state governments or landholders. While
the states are generally more willing to fund hands-on actions within their
jurisdictions and through their own state-focused abatement plans, the
federal government's funds should provide strategic support by ensuring
that fundamental research is appropriately resourced and the outcomes
passed on to all. Both are essential elements of threat abatement that can
only be measured against clearly specified and costed goals.

★ ★ ★

South-west Western Australia's unique flora and fauna includes num-bats (Australia's only exclusive ant-eaters), exquisite honey possums, chuditches, woylies, a suite of honey-eating birds, nearly thirty species of frogs and remarkable forests, woodlands, shrub and heath. If these species are lost from this area, they're gone for good.[27] But this geo-graphically isolated location has also presented a wonderful opportu-nity to trial large-scale conservation efforts. Two of the key threats to south-west Australia's wildlife are predation by foxes and cats, which have driven a number of its species to the edge of extinction.

In 1996 the Western Australian Department of Conservation and Land Management launched the Western Shield Project, the largest wildlife conservation program undertaken in Australia, situated in the South West Botanical Province. Its aim has been to recover at least thir-teen species of wildlife across 3.5 million hectares of land and the action implemented to do so has included the comprehensive baiting of foxes, increased research into cat control and its application, and, once pred-ators were contained, the reintroduction of native fauna into suitable, predator-free habitats.[28] Effective means of controlling cats is taking longer than anticipated but, as has been mentioned earlier, heartening results were seen after only seven years of concerted fox baiting. The status of three medium-sized mammal species listed as seriously threat-ened had improved sufficiently to enable their down-listing. A number of other mammals like the bilby, chuditch and western barred bandi-coot, and birds such as the western bristlebird and malleefowl also had brighter futures, with new populations established via translocation of wild or captive-bred individuals once the fox numbers had been contained.[29]

Several factors have assisted in the project's success. For one thing, it operates with the support of its state government, a non-negotiable condition for a recovery/threat-abatement plan. The department respon-sible for the work also owns the parks and reserves on which the bait-ing takes place, so landholder permission for baiting is not an obstacle. And the support of neighbouring landholders is required only in so far as domestic dogs have to be kept away from the baited areas to avoid unintended fatalities. Another favourable factor is that native wildlife in Western Australia is immune to the 1080-poison used for the baiting and killing of foxes. And a final, rare factor of the project is that the department was always prepared to commit to the project over a long period of time.

And yet during the 12-year duration of this ongoing project there have been hiccups. The woylie (or hopping bettong), peculiar for building domed nests to live in and using its curled tail-tips to carry grass and other building material, was once listed as endangered under Western Australian legislation. In 1996, as a result of fox control, it had been down-listed to the category of 'lower risk'. But despite ongoing fox control and active translocations as part the Western Shield project, woylie populations have once again declined, in some areas to alarmingly low levels. The possible causes of this decline are being investigated; the suitability of the translocation sites is being questioned, as are the possibility of increases in other predators' numbers, the efficiency of baiting, and diseases in the populations.[30] The control of cats has also been problematic, largely because cats respond to bait that is also attractive to other native carnivores. With some refinement, however, the Western Shield Project may provide a feasible model for conserving fox-threatened marsupials across other large sections of the country.

★ ★ ★

The principle of solving a problem by addressing its causes is hardly revolutionary and the absence of passionate political commitment to this goal has not been due to an absence of logic. The tasks of containing invasive animal and plant populations and diseases, *and* changing traditional industry practices to better protect the natural environment are truly herculean. Investment in research and technology must be undertaken before invasive species and diseases can be tackled on the ground; and lengthy negotiations and the delicate promotion of a longer term view on issues such as land clearing, habitat fragmentation, burning regimes of native vegetation and commercial fishing methods that cause the deaths of seabirds and turtles needs to be undertaken for behaviour to change. Even so, the responses are likely to be vehement resistance along with demands for financial compensation. And even with the promise of compensation, changes in practices inevitably take time, as natural levels of inertia and a wariness of change have to be overcome. Education and awareness-raising are essential first steps that must be followed by negotiation with relevant stakeholders and the trials and subsequent promotion of alternative practices.

In the state of New South Wales 'high frequency fire resulting in the disruption of life cycle processes in plants and animals and loss of vegetation structure and composition' is one of thirty recognised Key Threatening Processes known to affect biodiversity in the state.[31] Instead of the threat abatement plans devised under federal legislation, New South Wales law requires the drafting of priority action statements to deal with state-listed threats.[32] The action statement outlines a number of strategies yet a key role in taking the issue of fire to the community has been taken up by an independently initiated project. The Hotspots Fire Project, managed by the New South Wales Nature Conservation Council, a non-government organisation representing one hundred and twenty community groups from around the state, was designed as a pilot project to meet the needs of landholders in promoting good fire management and to involve regional communities in protecting native plants and wildlife.[33] The project initially set up trial workshops in four regions of the state collaborating with fire fighters, science communicators, ecologists, government agencies and landholders in the hope that successful outcomes could be promoted elsewhere. The program covers fire ecology, fire legislation, the development of individual fire management plans as part of a broader landscape plan, and training in the physical aspects of burning, led by the Rural Fire Service. The latter also ensures that landholders work closely with the appropriate authorities and with the approval obtained under the *Rural Fires Act 1979*.

Three years down the track, more than 450 landholders and state agency staff had participated in the workshops, and more workshops were being requested on demand. The success of the project has produced sponsors willing to support the workshops, provided impetus for a range of follow-up activities and increased the landholders' awareness of the vulnerability of fire-threatened species such as brush-tailed rock wallabies. Most importantly, it has resulted in landholders of different tenures collaboratively planning for fire regimes across properties incorporating thousands of hectares of land. The projects manager, Waminda Parker, believes there are a number of reasons for the project's success: it is seen as an independent, non-partisan initiative; it is based on sound and understandable science; the workshops can be adapted to the relevant community, and they involve tangible, map-based planning. The engagement of diverse communities has dispelled myths and fears about fire management, enabled the formation of partnerships and engendered a sense of understanding and responsibility among landholders.[34]

Educating, teaching and motivating small groups of individuals to change the way they manage their land for the benefits of biodiversity is proving to be an excellent catalyst for bringing about similar change among a much wider group, demonstrating once again the power of the individual in the conservation game.

11

FUTURE BEQUESTS

Protected Areas and Reserves

On a chilly and overcast autumn day in the middle of writing this book, an urgent desire to reconnect with the Australian environment I was writing about drove me to abandon my laptop and head for the hills. In the company of two naturalist friends, and kitted out in well-worn hiking boots and luridly striped thermals, we set out to conquer Tasmania's wilderness track from Cradle Mountain to Lake St Clair.

Other than the often-waterlogged track and the huts and camping sites at intervals along the way, civilisation was a long way off. Mobile phones were out of range; televisions, radios, iPods or newspapers never crossed our minds; and even our emergency satellite phone remained silent.

Over five glorious days, the track led us through buttongrass plains, whose tall buttoned-stems swayed in the breeze, and myrtle beech forests full of brilliant golden-yellow and amber-rust leaves about to drop from the trees' branches. Below us were crater lakes, so still that reflections of the sheer walls that framed them were unbroken and clouds appeared to glide across their surface. Small birds flitted urgently through the trees along the track, chasing small insects and each other, utterly oblivious to us.

This was my first experience of a native environment in Australia almost entirely as nature had created it—without weeds, without feral animals, without roads, without development, domestic stock or agriculture and, almost, without people. Meandering through ancient wet rainforest and laughing at the crazy assortment of garish-coloured fungi that had sprung up from the rain to compete for attention, I found myself wishing for a crack in time and the chance to see the many other parts of this country as they once were.

★ ★ ★

Anyone inclined to spend time in a national park, reserve or wilderness area will appreciate the enormous cultural and aesthetic values these areas have. Whether they are areas of dense rainforest, sprawling savanna woodlands, lively eucalypt communities or arid expanses of desert, it is here that Australia's ancient pulse still maintains its slow and steady beat. For many people like myself, bushwalking or camping is the perfect antidote to a hectic city lifestyle, a chance to exhale, unwind and feel the comforting embrace of Mother Nature. Knowing that intricate webs of life unaltered by human influence exist among craggy rock plateaus, contour-hugging grasslands and in parched fields of sand and gibber is both grounding and reassuring—it provides perspective. In fact, appreciative human visitors to national parks and nature reserves contribute billions of dollars to the economy. In Queensland, it has been estimated that each dollar invested by the government in the management of a protected area brings more than forty dollars of economic activity to the state.[1] As protected landscapes have considerable economic value in their own right, they can in fact be compared with the financial value of other land uses. The most important purpose of natural reserves, however, is the conservation of their many forms of life along with the services they provide to sustain themselves and us humans.

Large natural areas that are allowed to remain undeveloped are one of the greatest legacies that any modern civilisation can leave its descendants. Much more than simply a physical and cultural inheritance, the bequest of healthy living communities of plants and wildlife contains within it a future of possibilities. A plethora of plants, animals, fungi, water, soils, moulds and microbes and their many complex relationships constitute a genetic investment that maximises the ability to evolve on a planet in constant flux, never more so than through periods of rapid climate change. While the science tells us that there will be casualties from climate change and some can be predicted, it is not clear which species will do well and which will disappear. Consider the possibility that some species best able to adapt to the new conditions are lost to poor stewardship before they are able to take on important new roles among evolving ecosystems. How long might it take for those gaps once again to be filled? One of the major long-term benefits of setting aside natural reserves and protected areas now is that it helps to ensure that the loss of the foundations of the future is not on our conscience.

★ ★ ★

In 1992 the Earth Summit in Rio de Janeiro ushered in the international Convention on Biological Diversity (or CBD) to which Australia is one of 168 signatories.[2] Among the many objectives captured under the articles of the convention, Article 8 ('In-situ conservation') identifies protected areas as 'central elements' of any nation's strategy to conserve biodiversity.[3] The convention urges all its signatory countries to set aside protected areas, carefully deciding on which ecosystems to include so that these networks of reserves protect 'comprehensive, adequate and representative' samples of all possible regional ecosystems and their living components.[4] The designated time frame to have completed this is 2010–15; nevertheless, while this is extremely ambitious, if signatory countries continue to pursue this target, the convention maintains that the current rate of species loss should be substantially reduced to the benefit of nature itself and of its human population.[5]

Australia still has some way to go. Among thirty OECD countries recently assessed, Australia ranks sixteenth in terms of the percentage of land in reserves (10.1 per cent). The top three countries on this scale, Austria (36.4 per cent), Germany (32.7 per cent) and Switzerland (28.7 per cent) have each reserved around a third of their landmass, while the United States, with a more comparable size and settlement history to Australia, has set aside 16 per cent of its land.[6]

The expansion and management of Australia's network of reserves—of national parks, indigenous protected areas, private nature reserves, nature conservation areas and World Heritage areas—is a critically important conservation strategy. And given the many different tenures of valuable land across the country, it is an undertaking in which governments, conservation organisations and private landholders all have large stakes. For a land responsible for protecting an internationally important megadiversity of species and living systems, and with many of its precious coastal regions already extensively cleared, the construction of a reserve system that is representative and with reasonably sized and well-functioning components is no modest ambition.

Guided by Australian environment policy, priority areas earmarked for protection in reserves include those containing high numbers of endemic species or a rich diversity of species, as well as habitat for threatened species and ecological communities or other groups such as migratory species.[7] At the present time, the largest areas of protected land in Australia are located in the central and southern arid regions, most of them in South Australia.[8] A large protected area also covers about a fifth of Tasmania, while on a national map the patchwork of small reserves of coastal south-western and eastern Australia is most dense in Victoria and the Australian Capital Territory.[9]

The concept of a protected area may seem pretty simple, but there are dozens of different kinds of protected areas that make up the reserve system in Australia. Although all are designated under a common theme of protection, what they protect, to what extent and for what purpose varies greatly. Reserves include botanic gardens, conservation parks, forest reserves, game and hunting reserves; reserves to conserve particular

natural features such as a cave or river; and various types of nature conservation reserves, wilderness protection areas, indigenous protected areas
and private nature reserves. Each type of reserve is defined by its primary purpose and by the types of activities that are permitted within
it. While some are managed mainly for nature conservation, such as
national parks and wilderness protection areas, others allow for the
reserve to have a number of uses but maintain nature conservation as a
primary objective and include private nature refuges, game reserves and
indigenous protected areas.

Indigenous protected areas (IPA) are areas that are voluntarily put
forward as reserves by their Aboriginal owners who may continue to
live and hunt on these lands and to carry out traditional practices. Before
being designated as a protected area, a formal management plan has to
be developed to identify the valuable floral and faunal components and
to list the threats that need to be managed to protect its biodiversity
values. While recognition as an IPA makes a reserve eligible for some
management funds, ongoing funding security to enable indigenous
owners to combine their traditional practices with modern land management skills and control the many detrimental influences on their lands
remains a challenge.[10] On the upside, however, the sheer size of some
indigenous protected areas means that if funds *can* be found to manage
them properly, they may protect several bioregions at once. In Western
Australia, a single indigenous protected area belonging to the
Ngaanyatjarra people covers an astounding 9.8 million hectares of land
and is by far the largest protected area in the country.[11]

Building a network of reserves across the nation relies on the
cooperation of all governments and the very important contributions
of private organisations and landholders. Australia has nine separate protected area networks, one in each state and territory and one of a small
number of federally managed reserves. Collectively these make up the
National Reserve System (NRS), which was formalised in 1992 and is
complemented by a similar network of marine protected areas in
Australian waters. 'Building the National Reserve System' is a strategy

document that sets out national guidelines for NRS reserves and a national plan of action with reserve acquisition targets and time frames.[12]

A review of how well Australia is meeting targets set in the early 1990s evaluated progress in terms of the comprehensiveness, adequacy and the standard of management of the reserves set aside by 2004.[13] Evaluating how well reserves are managed is critically important, as reserves, like all other Australian landscapes, are prone to degradation from weed infestations, the impacts of feral animals, poor fire management and other factors. Overall, the Australian Capital Territory and Tasmania scored best across all three measures by having comprehensive, large and well-managed reserves, while Western Australia, Queensland and the Northern Territory performed poorly on all measures. Although Western Australia, the best of these three, had a reasonably large protected area system, it was anything but comprehensive and it mostly consisted of two large multiple-use indigenous protected areas whose long-term protection and management was of ongoing concern.[14] Queensland's reserves, despite a state government commitment to building a reserve system dating back to the mid 1980s, were far too small, not comprehensive and poorly managed. Substantial areas of the Wet Tropics, south-east Queensland and Cape York Peninsula have been gazetted as reserves since the report was published, but although they have added more than 574 000 hectares to the reserves[15], concerns remain that a truly representative reserve system must be built across all regions of the state.[16] With the exception of the reserves managed by the federal government in the Northern Territory, a jurisdiction still comparatively less degraded than other states, the Territory also had a long way to go on all reserve performance measures.

The remaining states yielded mixed scores. Victoria, which has a large reserve network, rated poorly on comprehensiveness due to the amount of land that had been cleared soon after settlement.[17] Poor vegetation mapping in South Australia's north made it difficult to assess the comprehensiveness of the reserves in that state, although they were large in extent and covered a substantial area. Similar issues complicated the assessment of New South Wales, which appeared to have a reason-ably comprehensive network but consisted of mainly small reserves.

The federal government is responsible for five land-based reserves: Kakadu and Uluru–Kata Tjuta national parks in the Northern Territory (both co-managed with traditional owners), Booderee National Park in New South Wales, the National Botanic Garden in the ACT and the Calperum and Taylorville stations in South Australia. These five reserves were not rated in terms of their comprehensiveness or adequacy in adding to the national estate, but the standard of management was high—largely as a result of the resources invested by the federal government.

★ ★ ★

The National Reserve System might be the formal framework for pro-tected areas in Australia, but it is not the only system under which land can be recognised for its unique natural values. World Heritage Areas such as the Tasmanian Wilderness are internationally recognised areas that have also been deemed to warrant special protection.

The degree of that protection, however, depends more on whether the area is also managed as part of the National Reserve System than on its World Heritage tag. Although management plans are intended for each of the seventeen Australian World Heritage properties, World Heritage listing does not impact on the rights of the owners of the land, which can be of a wide variety of private and public tenures. As a consequence, grazing, recreational and commercial fishing (in marine World Heritage areas) and other commercial practices are generally per-mitted. In Kakadu National Park there is uranium mining. The future of these operations in the park is now in doubt, however, not as a con-sequence of its legal protection as a reserve but due to the veto-rights of the lands' traditional owners, the Mirrar people, who are opposed to the continuation of mining beyond the current lease period.[18] The Great Barrier Reef, the world's largest World Heritage area, was open for damaging commercial uses across more than 95 per cent of its range until late 2003, when a public campaign led by WWF–Australia saw a third of it declared as marine sanctuaries and protected from fishing while the remainder remains open to multiple commercial uses.[19]

World Heritage status offers a lot in terms of promoting the natural values of the sites they occur on but very little in the way of active protection against their decline, despite the international scrutiny these sites invite. Rightly or wrongly, protection relies on the effective management of the areas where they are a part of the National Reserve System.

★ ★ ★

Governments manage around 23 per cent of Australia's land. A further 63 per cent is managed by members of the non-indigenous community through freehold (private ownership) or crown leasehold land (owned by government but under long-term leases to individuals or industry), and the remainder is freehold, leasehold or reserves held by Aborigines or Torres Strait Islanders.[20] While many landholders whose properties contain wetlands, important patches of bush or specific ecological communities may choose to manage all or some of that land for the benefit of native flora and fauna, their concern is often that the land may not be so thoughtfully protected once it is sold or passed on to a new owner.

An increasing awareness of the need to protect their properties into the future has led a growing number of landowners to seek out private protection agreements over the last twenty years or so. As with the different types of publicly protected areas, private landholders have a number of options at their disposal.

Land protection schemes such as voluntary conservation covenants can be administered by government agencies or government authorised bodies such as Victoria's Trust for Nature and the Nature Conservation Trust in New South Wales and are usually permanent and legally binding. Apart from a selfless desire to protect a small piece of Australia in perpetuity, there are a number of other incentives designed to motivate a landholder to take this proactive step. Depending on the scheme, covenants may entail the mapping of the vegetation to be protected, professional advice and assistance with its protection and management, as well as some financial assistance towards legally securing the site. In some cases, tax concessions are also offered to help compensate for any potential loss in land value that may result from a binding covenant restricting the land's potential uses.[21] On the whole, however, a covenant acts as a kind of insurance policy that the good stewardship of a property, often fostered over several generations of one family, is not laid to waste by the lesser environmental ethos of a future owner.

Although properties put up for covenanting are not necessarily part of a strategic reserve plan, covenanted land can and does contribute to the totality of the reserve estate. Covenanting bodies have to be discerning about land that merits active protection and not all properties will meet their criteria. Land for which a covenant is meaningful has to be of high conservation value. It may form part of a larger regional wildlife corridor, serve as a natural buffer zone between a national park and unprotected commercial land or contain populations of declining species or communities. Assessment criteria will also include the size and shape of the land, the diversity of plants and animals that inhabit it, the status of these species, and the level of management needed to maintain the land.[22]

Since the mid 1980s, Victoria's Trust for Nature has approved covenants for over 840 properties across 35 000 hectares of Victoria[23], protecting such different ecosystems as box-ironbark in Victoria's Goldfields, grassland and grassy woodlands in the Riverina and Basalt Plains Grassland, and wetlands in the Glenelg–Hopkins region. Although the landowners initiate many of these covenants, the program is not entirely guided by the altruism of landholders. Occasionally Trust for Nature staff may initiate contact with owners of a property they consider to be of high conservation value.

Individuals who place protective covenants on all or parts of their property make a significant contribution to Australia's future, and provide heartening proof that financial compensation is not necessarily the only driver that will secure privately managed parts of natural landscapes.

To a growing number of people the bequest of a living, breathing, functioning patch of nature with its diverse collection of living plants and creatures to future generations is all the incentive they need.

★ ★ ★

Despite the commitments of the governments and the voluntary contributions of a growing number of forward-thinking individuals, goals set for the acquisition of reserves in the early 1990s have not been met. Ecologists and conservationists remain deeply concerned at the ongoing rapid commercial development of natural landscapes, and this frustration has led to a number of not-for-profit organisations being founded to speed up the reserve process.

These organisations may focus on purchasing significant properties to maintain and manage in perpetuity, or on establishing 'revolving funds' through which properties can be purchased, placed under conservation covenants and sold on to owners who are sympathetic to the binding conditions of the covenant and willing to abide by them. Apart from the Northern Territory, every state and the Australian Capital Territory has a revolving fund that enables the purchase and on-selling of properties with important ecological features. The money needed to buy the properties is raised via donations and bequests as well as from governments and charitable grants, and these funds are boosted by any profits made from the sale of newly covenanted land.

Victoria's Trust for Nature is an organisation that, in addition to placing covenants on privately owned land and purchasing properties to keep and manage, also operates a revolving funding stream for the purchase and on-sale of land. The success of the Trust's model has provided the incentive for similar revolving funds to be established in other states. The Tasmanian Land Conservancy (TLC), for example, has purchased a number of properties on King Island and on Tasmania's mainland, and now also administers the federal government's Forest Conservation Fund, which seeks to protect 45 000 hectares of old-growth forest on private land via purchase, covenanting and resale to suitable owners.[24] Among other acquisitions, this has enabled the aptly acronymed TLC to protect a swathe of delicate orchids and an endangered woodland community through the purchase of a reserve near Port Sorrell on Tasmania's north coast. Once the property had been safely protected by a covenant, it was sold to orchid lovers, who are now the proud stewards of thirty-three species of their favourite flowering plants, including one species that occurs exclusively on their property.[25]

One of the benefits of covenants and revolving funds is that they enable members of the community, with the support of expert organisations, to play a hands-on role in the conservation of their environment and its future that helps strengthen the connection between people and the land in a non-utilitarian context. The downside of covenanting, and in particular of the incentives often required to achieve covenants on private land, however, is that the cost is often comparable to that of buying the land outright.[26] This makes the social considerations of ownership and who bears the ongoing management costs a deciding factor between the two options for the covenanting organisation.

Two of the biggest non-government organisations that acquire land to maintain and manage in perpetuity are Bush Heritage Australia (formerly the Australian Bush Heritage Fund) and the Australian Wildlife Conservancy. The former was founded in 1990, when now Greens senator Bob Brown used a $50 000 environment prize to purchase the Fund's first property. Bush Heritage's vision is to protect 1 per cent of Australia by 2025; as of August 2008, it had acquired thirty-one properties totalling more than 946 000 hectares of land.[27] Strategic acquisitions include the Charles Darwin Reserve in south-west Western Australia that features stands of ancient salmon gum, York gum and gimlet woodlands; a licuala fan palm forest in North Queensland's Daintree rainforest; and Ethabuka Station, a 200 000 hectare arid-zone property in Queensland that provides vital habitats for desert mammals, reptiles and birds.[28] In the 2005–06 financial year, as a result of a large influx in donations and grants, the organisation doubled both its budget (to $13 million) and the area of land it owns and manages across the country.[29]

The Australian Wildlife Conservancy also purchases important parcels of land that contain precious natural ecosystems. In only six years, it has acquired more than one million hectares of land that is managed across fifteen sanctuaries and covers ecosystems of tropical savanna, wet eucalypt forest, rainforest, estuarine lagoons and semi-arid grasslands.[30] One of its flagship properties is Brooklyn Sanctuary in North Queensland, which covers around 60 000 hectares of the Wet Tropics and Einasleigh Uplands and is home to around fifty species of threatened wildlife, more than forty-five species of threatened plants and forty threatened ecosystems.[31] Northern quolls, southern cassowaries and shy Lumholtz's tree kangaroos all call Brooklyn home, and the property claims to give shelter to around 40 per cent of all Australian bird species and close to 30 per cent of all mammals, which in conservation terms makes it one of the most valuable pieces of land in the country.

Bush Heritage Australia and the Australian Wildlife Conservancy both recognise the immense challenge to achieve the necessary scale of conservation effort across the country. While purchasing and managing (or on-selling) ecologically valuable properties is a good strategy, there are limits to how much land can and perhaps ought to be managed in this way. With this in mind, both organisations promote their vision and practices to the wider community. The AWC prides itself on the range of conservation and land-management research conducted on its properties in the belief that it will yield lessons of value to adjoining property owners, motivate them to adopt sounder practices and thereby result in landscape conservation on a larger scale. Bush Heritage, on the other hand, also seeks firmer engagement with strategic stakeholders such as indigenous communities and large pastoral companies to develop better environmental outcomes. Given how much land these two groups own alone, this objective has enormous potential. Large companies like the Australian Agricultural Company (AACo) run cattle across an astonishing 8 million hectares of land across Queensland and the Northern Territory (more than 1 per cent of Australia's total land mass).[32] Working with pastoral companies such as AACo, NAPCo (the

North Australian Pastoral Company) and Kidman would be a sound way for Bush Heritage to leverage its experience in caring for Australian country and could yield outcomes at a vastly greater scale.

Bush Heritage is also a collaborator in the groundbreaking Gondwana Link project in south-west Western Australia. Over a distance of 1000 kilometres from the coastal karri forest to the edge of the Nullarbor Plain, this project aims to reconnect the fragments of natural ecosystems that over the decades have been isolated by agriculture. Initiated by the Wilderness Society in 2002, Gondwana Link relies on the cooperation of a number of conservation organisations, among them Greening Australia (WA), The Nature Conservancy and the Fitzgerald Biosphere Group, as well as the efforts of local volunteer groups and the input of scientists. In addition to purchasing and managing bushland where possible, Gondwana Link provides incentives to landholders for the better management of private properties, lobbies for stronger legal protection of public lands, undertakes revegetation of cleared land and even works to develop local industries that operate in harmony with the local environment.[33]

Bush Heritage Australia, in partnership with others, has purchased a number of properties within the range of the Gondwana Link project. One property, situated between two national parks on the southern edge of Western Australia's wheatbelt, is a sanctuary for an amazing assortment of plants that include many unique species of dryandras, acacias, banksias, grevilleas and eucalypts that grow across the 900 hectares of this property. Another land parcel of similar size on the eastern boundary of the Stirling Range National Park was co-purchased by Bush Heritage and Greening Australia and is now subject to an extensive restoration project to revegetate around two-thirds of it.

★ ★ ★

The effectiveness and importance of land acquisition has been acknowledged internationally by organisations with an interest in preserving Australia's natural values as part of the global heritage. While foreign involvement in Australian affairs is not always readily welcomed, the advantage of this interest has led to a healthy injection of funds into large-scale conservation efforts. Two United States-based charities, the Pew Foundation and The Nature Conservancy, have joined forces in Australia to initiate the Wild Australia Program with a focus on protecting important parts of the Australian bush, deserts and marine areas.[34] Although both have equal financial stakes in the program, the Pew Foundation is responsible for its management over a 3-year period. While this is the first time the Pew Foundation has invested in Australia, The Nature Conservancy has been here since the later 1990s and also offers land acquisition and management funds to partner organisations like Bush Heritage.

While these two US organisations bring with them a substantial funding base, some of their Australian counterparts have found their finances increasingly mired in uncertainty. Until 2002, the federal government's policy regarding funds raised by state-based revolving funds was to match them 2:1; for every dollar raised the government provided another two dollars to the fund. In September 2002[35], the government's contributions were scaled back to close to a 1:1 ratio, reducing the state and territory purchasing budgets by one-third and making it necessary for more of the donated funds to be spent on further fund-raising efforts. Smaller governments now have less incentive to continue to build their contributions to the reserve system or to manage them properly.[36] This is particularly frustrating as the buying of strategic land for conservation purposes has been shown to be extremely cost effective at around $10–$12 per hectare; the costs of repairing degraded land, by comparison, have been around twenty-five times higher.

While the unerring focus of non-government reserve purchasing and covenanting organisations helps ensure sound long-term management of the properties either briefly or permanently in their care, the governments primarily responsibility for protecting the natural landscape are lagging behind on what may well be the most valuable means of safeguarding biodiversity. The recent allocation of $180 million over five years to expanding the National Reserve System by the Rudd government is a promising indication of intent but still amounts to only a fraction of what's needed. The failure to adequately protect and maintain the resilience of a sufficiently large proportion of Australia's native landscapes and their living diversity across all bioregions may very soon become one of this country's biggest regrets.

12

GUARDS ON OUR WATCH

Environmental Players

For people working in the conservation industry, who understand the true state of our landscapes and are committed to doing something about it, environment conservation is—in its truest sense—a game of survival. There are many teams, and players on all teams can influence the game (environment) in positive or negative ways. And, taking this analogy a step further, there can be no pretence of a level playing field: a small number of influential players are doing deals with the referee; others are simply trying to understand the rules, and yet another lot appear to be changing the rules in the middle of play. But what's most worrying is that the major environment player, the general public, is not playing its part—indeed, it hasn't even turned up to play. In a game that depends on the numbers of pro-environment players on each team and where the profits-at-any-cost players remain extremely strong, those who place economic gain above the future of the planet are exploiting the public's absence. And no Australian is exempt from this game. It is not a game one can choose not to participate in: participation begins at birth.

The role of the individual as part of the broader public can have far more influence than he or she may have thought. And it is through each of us voicing our concerns that the future of Australia's environment will be decided.

As a consumer, each choice we make—from the food, clothes or household items we buy to the housing we choose and our mode of transport—sends a signal that we support the company, practices and policies that produced these goods and services. So it makes sense to stop and consider our choices. As members of the community, we can also speak to our local councillors and MPs of our concerns about poor environmental decisions. It is the job of politicians in particular to ensure that the views of their constituents feature in parliament and are heeded when making decisions. The greater the number of people concerned about a particular issue that politicians are made aware of, the more weight their concerns collectively acquire. Every voice counts.

★ ★ ★

We know that governments wield a lot of power in the conservation of Australia's landscapes and species. But the environment is only one of many government portfolios, and other issues (education, employment, public health, housing and transport) may be considered to be more important to the voters, and therefore more likely to influence election outcomes. In recent years, however, environmental issues have regained prominence with growing public concern about climate change and the country's environmental future.

Governments pass laws that have the power to prevent all manner of environmental damage and they regulate industries and approve or block potentially damaging developments and industry ventures. Alongside local councils, governments and their environment agencies are responsible for the management of public lands and protected areas. Governments have the financial resources to invest in many aspects of conservation such as the purchase of reserves, incentives for good stewardship, the recovery of threatened plants and wildlife, and tackling environmental threats.

The federal government, in addition to the matched funds provided to the states and territories as part of the regional natural resource management budget, offers a number of competitive funding options to the general community. These programs match money or in-kind contributions put up by community groups that collaborate with companies, conservation organisations or local councils to undertake practical on-ground conservation projects. Thanks to their control of the national and state/territory budgets and the law, governments are therefore in many respects pivotal to the future of the natural environment. So how can that future be assured?

★ ★ ★

The nature of government is that it is fraught with difficult decisions that juggle competing interests. At every turn, politicians are lobbied by the advocates of every imaginable business and interest group. Pharmaceutical lobbies and industries such as coal, gas, minerals, forestry, fisheries, wheat, dairy, livestock, war veterans' support groups, refugee and human rights charities, the renewable energy sector and thousands of others are all fighting to have their interests represented and backed by the political agenda.

Many industry groups station professional lobbyists in Canberra to build relationships with ministers and their advisers so that they can be assured of a place at the negotiation table when important issues arise. Lobbyists may explain, persuade, negotiate, coerce, or perhaps even threaten with the political voting power of the groups they represent. The most effective lobby groups tend to be those that have the most to offer the government—the most votes, the most jobs, the most revenue, the most kudos for decisive leadership. Jobs and revenue (regional development and export income) certainly played a part in the approval of the Anvil Hill coal mine in the Hunter Valley in June 2007. Despite great concerns about the mine's impact on the local environment and the burning of its coal on exacerbating climate change, the offer of several hundred new jobs along with $380 million in royalties to the New South Wales government ensured that planning minister Frank Sartor gave it the go-ahead.[1]

While political advocacy is also a large aspect of the work of non-government conservation organisations, they have often been unable to compete with the large industry sectors in what they could offer the government and the economy in return for stronger environmental protection. New jobs are rarely on the table, and the promise of votes can be a double-edged sword. Marginal seats featured successfully in the environmental campaign of the Franklin in Tasmania in the early 1980s, but pro-environment policies can also produce negative political outcomes. This was the case in the 2004 federal election when the Australian Labor Party pledged to review forestry practices and protect large areas of old growth forest in Tasmania.[2] The pledge was seen as a threat to timber industry jobs in the state and lost the party important seats and any hope of governing. More recently, however, direct revenue, which had given industries the upper hand, is beginning to feature in the options offered by conservation organisations. In addition to the fact that conserving unique regions of the natural environment is invaluable to tourism, and healthy ecosystems to the living resource-dependent industries, carbon taxes and/or licensing could potentially provide a growing stream of income for the economy while containing harmful practices. The political currency provided by the natural environment is rapidly changing and will continue to gain value with increasing demand for better environmental management.

★ ★ ★

Some of the most powerful industry lobbies, besides coal, are those of the agricultural sector. Farmers represent around 3.5 per cent of the Australian working public and generate a small and steadily decreasing proportion (currently about 2.7 per cent) of the country's GDP[3], but the long history of farming and the debt ostensibly owed to this industry since European settlement have meant that the farming lobby has remained highly influential. Through the National Party, farmers have direct representation in the realms of the federal government and in the agricultural states of Queensland, New South Wales, Victoria, South Australia and Western Australia, and the National Farmers Federation is the sector's strongest lobby group. The ongoing pressure exerted on governments by the farming lobby has, however, come at a large financial cost.

More than any other industry, farmers have benefited from rescue packages, disaster funding, drought relief and interest rate subsidies to keep afloat what many would argue are economically—let alone environmentally—unsustainable sectors of the industry.[4] Over the first six years of the drought alone, more than $2.8 billion was allocated to drought relief.[5] So far, however, there has been scant evidence of any attempt to streamline the industry and shut down unprofitable areas. Astonishingly, about 80 per cent of the profits derived from agriculture come from less than 1 per cent of Australia's agricultural land! This makes the remaining 99 per cent of land used not only largely unprofitable but its cost to the environment all but indefensible.[6] The closest the Australian government has come to encouraging a large-scale change in land-use practices has been the offer of exit packages to enable farmers to voluntarily leave the land in the face of increasing drought-related debt.[7] But even with the aid of this scheme, the farmers and the land they abandon face uncertain futures.

Clearly, there are different reasons why industries play a big part in influencing government decisions on the environment. So how can industries and governments be motivated to make environment conservation an absolute priority on their respective agendas? The answer to this lies with industries' dependence on the humble consumer and shareholder and the subsequent power of both to influence their practices.

★ ★ ★

Industries, for the most part, were never set up to consider their environmental impacts. In fact, as business analysts and economists have pointed out, benefiting the greater good of society seems to run entirely contrary to the principles of modern corporations, which are set up solely to benefit themselves and their shareholders.[8] Implicit to this perception as discussed by Milton Friedman, however, is that it is the shareholders or business owners (or boards) who determine the way in which the company operates.[9] If their interests go beyond financial gain and incorporate social or environmental benefits at some potential reduction in their profits, then the principles of the corporation still hold firm. Accordingly, what is now driving industries and corporates to give some serious thought to better environmental practices is not a demand for greater financial profits but an increasing demand by their shareholders for environmental and social accountability of the ventures they are prepared to invest in. How much of their profits they may be willing to sacrifice to this end, and indeed whether or not a large financial sacrifice will be required if the markets are forced to adjust to better practices across the board, will be fascinating to observe in the coming decades.

Industries and companies that aim for better environmental performance usually do so under the banner of 'corporate social responsibility'. Their progress on this front is reflected in triple bottom line reporting, which considers the performance of a business in terms of its economic prosperity as well as its environmental sustainability and means of ensuring social justice.[10] The tenets of corporate social responsibility (CSR) call on companies to conduct their business in ways that benefit not just themselves and their shareholders but also do not come at a cost to the environment or the general community. Practising CSR may involve simple adjustments to how a company's offices are run—changing to renewable energy, purchasing consumables such as paper from sustainable sources, reducing electricity and water consumption, offsetting staff air-travel—or more substantial changes to the transactions chain of the business—supporting fair trade practices and not using underpaid labour in developing countries, minimising physical damage to the environment, reducing packaging and waste, reducing energy consumption and carbon emissions by adjusting the transport chain and sourcing raw materials from socially and environmentally responsible suppliers. This last option can be particularly powerful when considering international fast-food chains, supermarkets and department stores that, because of the vast quantity and volume of their products, can influence how responsibly their suppliers source or produce them. The philosophical underpinnings of CSR were taken up and promoted by the member countries of the United Nations when they adopted the Millennium Development Goals in 2000. The eight goals, one of which specifically targets the need for environmental sustainability, put the onus on large international corporations to contribute to the alleviation of poverty and hunger in developing countries.[11]

★ ★ ★

An increasing number of progressive companies are embracing CSR and helping to define this new paradigm. Oxfam and the UK's Body Shop have for decades led the way in promoting fair-trade practices in the developing countries that produce the ingredients that go to make its product ranges. Tesco, a large UK-based supermarket chain, has committed to reducing its carbon emissions, reducing water and energy consumption, testing renewable energy options and minimising waste. In addition, it is also reviewing its supply chains, compelling suppliers to operate to high environmental standards and has developed a range of transparent policies to enable public monitoring of its progress over time.[12]

Similarly, Australia's Coles and Woolworths chains are in a position to improve the environmental sustainability of food production in this country. According to the Australian Bureau of Agriculture and Resource Economics (ABARE), supermarkets and grocery stores account for approximately 62 per cent of all food and liquor sales and Woolworths and Coles account for around 75 per cent of that market.[13]

Just over two-thirds of all beef consumed in Australia is sold through retail outlets while the remainder goes to restaurants, food services and processing.[14] Thirty per cent of beef sold through retail goes to Woolworths and 18 per cent to its rival Coles, while butchers take up around 28 per cent. Woolworths similarly dominates the domestic sheep meat market with just under 31 per cent compared with 29 per cent going to butchers and 19 per cent to Coles. The potential for the large supermarkets to positively influence the production of meat to reduce its large environmental and carbon footprints is immense.

At present, however, the large supermarkets' singular goal is to supply produce and groceries as cheaply as possible. Supermarkets are not only able to squeeze the profit margins of their suppliers (making sustainable production less viable) but also to demand year-round availability of seasonal foods (costly to produce locally and often supplied from overseas markets via carbon-emitting transport) standardised in quality and appearance (requiring high-level use of fertilisers and pesticides). And if the food is not already wrapped in plastic, many shoppers insist on placing fresh foods in plastic bags, adding another detrimental aspect to supermarket purchases. In 2002 Australians were still using around 6.9 million new plastic bags a year; more than half came from supermarkets.[15]

In the United Kingdom, the government's Advisory Committee on Consumer Products and the Environment undertook a 2-year review of all aspects of farming and its resulting food products, including carbon emissions during production, packaging and transport, use of resources and production of waste.[16]

On the report's completion in 2002, the committee found the negative impact of food production to be considerable and it recommended better consumer awareness, including comprehensive environmental product information and more tools for simplifying choices higher in the supply chain, including minimum industry standards and policies for retailers. Its main recommendation was a new approach (called an Integrated Product Policy approach) to the environmental impacts of 'products' (including foods) that would consider their entire lifecycles from production and processing through to use and disposal.[17] It also identified the market clout of large supermarkets as 'one of the most powerful drivers in influencing the market for greener goods' and recommended two critical means of achieving this—via transparent and sustainable supermarket procurement (stock purchasing) policies, and via environmental product information.[18] Both recommendations are equally applicable in Australia, where comprehensive information about the sources of groceries and other consumer goods are still too difficult to come by.

★ ★ ★

In 2002, twenty-three of Australia's largest one hundred companies did not have any publicly available information on their environmental policies or issues of concern and were unwilling to participate in a preliminary survey of their reputations based on these measures.[19] In that number were Foster's Group, ConAgra Holdings, Mayne Nickless, Toll Holdings, the Australian Wheat Board, James Hardie Industries and Qantas. This did not necessarily imply that these companies' practices were poor, but it did raise doubts and uncertainty among shareholders and environmental watchdogs, a fact that was likely to force these companies into greater transparency.

A company may choose to adopt improved environmental practices to satisfy its socially conscious shareholders, to improve its reputation and public image (and thereby its sales), to improve the morale of its employees or to demonstrate leadership among its industry peers. Acting on any of these drivers is ultimately intended to keep the business healthy. What improved environmental practices must not do, however, is impinge on the company's profitability or competitiveness. Consequently, a company is likely to act responsibly in the long term only if the costs of doing so are offset by the protection of profits. Inevitably, industry accountability will have to be regulated by law, which brings the onus for determining the impact of industry back to the government. In the meantime, however, there is the pressure of shareholder demand. The community-led emergence of CSR indicates the willingness of a frustrated general public to take matters into its own hands. Shareholders, consumers, taxpayers and other groups of community stakeholders are driving greater transparency and accountability in business practices and the demand for triple bottom line reporting.[20] Some shareholders have even formed activist groups to raise the profile of their concerns such as the large mining and forestry companies such as BHP, Boral, North, PaperlinX, Wesfarmers and Gunns. All of these groups have the option of withdrawing support (and funds) from the companies whose practices they are not satisfied with to spend them elsewhere. The more this option is exercised, the more likely it is that environmentally sustainable business practices and social justice considerations will become part of business culture.

★ ★ ★

Although the greatest positive changes for the environment will depend on the commitments of governments and industry, the weight of public expectation to help make this happen is felt most acutely by the independent, non-government conservation organisations (NGOs) that are dedicated to the environment. While governments juggle a vast range of competing agendas and industries struggle to reconcile their broader accountabilities with their profit margins, the agenda of conservation organisations has a singular focus: to ensure that the interests of nature feature heavily in the minds of all those whose actions can either damage or protect it.

Conservation organisations are seen as the staunchest watchdogs of the national conservation game and are often dismissed as 'tree-huggers' by those they criticise. To lump them all together though would be doing them a disservice. Some organisations like Greenpeace and The Wilderness Society have favoured hardline, vigilante-style campaigns that play out alongside whaling ships on the high seas or in death-defying tripods among the canopy of old-growth forests, while at the other end of the spectrum the Australian Conservation Foundation and WWF-Australia more often engage in low-profile negotiations with industry bodies, government agencies or ministers to work out practical solutions to specific issues. In the recent past, one issue that has been negotiated in this manner and without fanfare is that of a clean-energy future as science-based organisations such as WWF have lobbied for the adoption of their own blueprints for reducing carbon emissions.[21]

Each of these styles has its merits. The first ensures ample media coverage and raises the profile of specific causes such as logging, whaling or uranium mining with the aim of causing public outrage and political engagement. In the process, it also drums up financial support for the organisation fighting for these causes and for the causes themselves. The second approach by comparison invests in the careful negotiation of compromises or solutions. And while the softly, softly approach often yields results, the nature of such negotiations means less exposure, lack of publicity and therefore lack of public funds needed to keep the organisation afloat. Different yet again are Bush Heritage Australia and Trust for Nature, organisations that have carved out a niche in the legal and physical protection of natural ecosystems and that work closely with other landholders.

Another role of NGOs draws on legal and political processes to lobby for the rigorous application of environmental legislation. At the forefront of this role is the Australian office of the Humane Society International (HSI). As one of several organisations that lobbied hard for the introduction of the federal *Environment Protection and Biodiversity Conservation Act 1999 (EPBC Act)*, it takes an active interest in its application and takes the government to task if the interests of the environment are being neglected in political decisions. If necessary, HSI takes or supports legal action to ensure that poor environmental decisions are reconsidered. Among the issues it has fought for in the past eight years is the greater legal protection for southern blue-fin tuna, the cessation of the culling of grey-headed flying foxes, and for incidentally caught (but commercially sold) threatened fish species, sea lions, sharks and albatross caught by an Australian scale-fish fishery.

The Humane Society also nominates species and ecological communities for listing under the *EPBC Act* so that their declining status can be formally recognised. While any qualified member of the public can legally make nominations, it is an arduous process more easily undertaken by an organisation with the necessary resources. Since the commencement of the first federal environment legislation in 1992, HSI has nominated more than forty-eight species (forty were listed, five remain pending) and thirty-four ecological communities (seven were listed, twenty-four are pending) for listing, and further triggered the promised federal assessment of five hundred communities for inclusion in the *EPBC Act*.[22] HSI was responsible for the listing of five Key Threatening Processes out of a total of seventeen currently on the federal list[23], and also provided the Australian government with data to support the listing of critical habitat for over sixty listed species that, to its dismay, were ignored.[24] Although the nomination and pursual of listings can be exhausting, these listings secured the first step in the legal protection for a whole raft of native species under threat.

★ ★ ★

On the vast playing field occupied by environment groups, there is much ground to cover. If properly positioned in the game, conservation organisations can make substantial contributions. Their political independence means that scientists, corporates, community groups, industry bodies and even government agencies will often look to them for support to help further their environmental objectives. NGOs like WWF-Australia, which aims for practical, science-based solutions, can often serve as invaluable partners in bringing about the appropriate changes.

Unfortunately, the ethical, green image of high-profile conservation organisations is delicate and can easily be tainted. Considerable risks include poorly managed associations with governments or companies looking to green-up their own image without any genuine long-term commitment to the environment. As the public interest in the protection of the environment continues to grow, so does the value of the expertise and kudos that a small number of conservation organisations can offer. And with this position of increasing power comes both opportunity and responsibility. International conglomerates with large budgets and poor environmental images like oil, mining or pharmaceutical companies are particularly interested in the improved public image that comes with the support of a well-known conservation organisation.

In exchange for a financial, often project-based and highly promoted contribution that is absurdly small in relation to the company's profits, the joined logos of sponsor and recipient can provide an invaluable boost to the sponsor's image. Of concern is that this may extend well beyond the scale of the sponsored project and appear to endorse the company's wider environmental practices. Care must be taken by NGOs in considering such a partnership with careful scrutiny of the terms and conditions so their own ethical and credible image is maintained.

Community groups and members of the public often look to independent conservation organisations to exert pressure on governments and business and promote solutions. Some people, however, may place unreasonable expectations on what these organisations can do: if they are financial supporters of an NGO, their expected return on their modest financial 'investments' may indicate a complete lack of understanding of the realities and complexities of nature conservation. It is not uncommon for donors of relatively small amounts of money to, within say the space of a year, expect a report demonstrating that one or more favoured wildlife species have been rescued from the brink of extinction. Such expectations are bound to lead to disappointment and, unreasonably, the possible redirection of their funds to other causes. To produce the desired outcomes of healthier environments and less threatened species, large environmental NGOs' efforts focus on tackling the big threats rather than the comparatively smaller symptoms. This sets them apart from some human charities like Médicins Sans Frontières or World Vision that focus primarily on helping the victims of poverty and war and can produce visible results of improved livelihoods more quickly. Nevertheless, loaded up with the public's hopes and expectations, some NGOs feel compelled to set themselves goals that surpass the realm of the feasible and to stretch their limited resources so thinly across a large range of issues that no one issue is adequately backed. Pursuing even one issue such as more sustainable fishery practices or stronger quarantine laws to a meaningful point of resolution depends on a long-term strategy (often of five to ten years), ongoing financial resources and qualified, experienced and committed advocates.

Miracles are beyond the scope even of NGOs and clear goals and strategies and the nurturing and retention of valuable staff are the only way to avoid drowning in a sea of overwhelming expectations.

★ ★ ★

Two other key groups in the conservation game are governmental environment and land management agencies (such as the Environment Protection Authority or the Parks and Wildlife Services) and the army of scientists who conduct the research and supply the information on which conservation practices depend.

The environment agencies of each state and territory are responsible for the management of public land, the administration of conservation plans and the public's engagement in this process—these are critical activities for conservation success, but they are largely bound by the policies of their current government and caught up within internal cumbersome bureaucracies.

Surprisingly, the place of science and scientists in conservation has become an ambiguous one, despite the fact that research is the foundation of any conservation strategy. Every aspect of the protection of living systems relies on science—understanding their needs, their threats, their past and current status and any changes that occur over time. But as the human population-driven pressures on the planet increase and the necessary environmental solutions offered by science are becoming increasingly costly and cumbersome, it seems that scientists are being pushed into the background by politics. Too often, scientific reports recommending changes in environmental practices (sometimes years in the making) are published and promptly ignored, their findings praised but their recommendations not, or not adequately, implemented. For a large number of natural scientists who have dedicated their lifetime to understanding ecological relationships in order to argue for their preservation, finding their work shelved and its subject matter sliding towards extinction has been deeply demoralising. Eminent scientists working for prominent research organisations such as the CSIRO or for universities dependent on government research grants are unable to speak out during their working careers because their organisation's purse-strings are held by the very government they wish to criticise. So it is often through independent conservation organisations that critical scientific findings and/or solutions are promoted to relevant stakeholders and the broader community and persistently advocated to governments. For organisations like WWF, close relationships with climate scientists, ecologists, marine scientists, botanists and zoologists have become rewarding for both, giving added meaning to each other's respective roles as solution finders and solution advocates.

Understanding the conservation game and its players is vital for any participant hoping to be effective. And the most important thing to understand is that the game is not about the environment at all, nor is it about scientific certainties. It is, and always will be, about people.

13

HEADING IN THE RIGHT DIRECTION

As this era of abundance takes its toll, protecting nature will become the primary consideration in everything we do. Our lives are sure to become increasingly affected by climate change and the physical limitations of the environment. We now have some idea of what this will mean, so it's essential that we turn our attention towards our stewardship of nature as the only means of ensuring a future for humans on this planet.

The ways we produce food will continue to dominate much of our thinking. With ever more mouths to feed, food and clean water will be among the primary currencies of the world's economies. In Australia, declining water and unsuitable conditions for farming across most of the continent, and the harm many agricultural and pastoral practices cause to biodiversity and the processes of nature will force a drastic rethink of these sectors. Neither agricultural nor pastoral practices can continue in the way they have, by using, abusing and mismanaging nature's resources beyond its capacity to regenerate. In protecting the future of these necessary industries, the most scientifically sensible—if politically challenging—approach would be to master plan and regulate both across all states and territories, selecting areas naturally suitable for specific agricultural land-use (cropping, horticulture, pasture) country-wide and banning them elsewhere. With the aid of new technology that enables the careful assessment of soils and water availability at a continental scale, the value of natural assets and biodiversity can be factored into any land-use equation. Keeping in mind the altered weather patterns predicted by climate change, the regions where agriculture, horticulture and pastoralism might be maintained could therefore be logically determined. Inevitably, this would mean that in some regions certain costly land uses would have to be minimised or phased out entirely, and overall yields of, for example, meat and irrigated produce would be reduced. In some coastal regions agriculture could be intensified, while in others as yet less degraded, the soils could be allowed to regenerate and to support generous corridors of native ecosystems to improve their connectivity and natural functions. Wherever agriculture does remain environmentally feasible, a combination of technology and a better understanding of natural soil building and nutrient cycling processes could go a long way to reducing its impact on nature.

A relatively new concept in agriculture that can contribute to better land-use practices is that of 'precision agriculture'. The term originated in the United States in the early 1990s and began to be incorporated into some sectors of Australian agricultural thinking shortly thereafter. In essence, precision agriculture recognises that our landscapes and soils are not uniform (even on a small spatial scale such as a paddock) and that agricultural practices can benefit if they take these differences into account. While the aim in the first instance is an improvement in agricultural crop and pasture yields, the initial definition articulated its desired outcomes as 'increased long term, site-specific and whole-farm production efficiency' with the minimisation of impacts on wildlife and the environment.[1]

Precision agriculture came into being with the availability of Global Positioning System (GPS) and Global Information Systems (GIS) technology that could be used to monitor crop yields via satellite. In conjunction with soil sensors and yield monitors, fertiliser regimes could then be adjusted to the needs of the soil within individual crop fields. Its broader potential application, however, includes its ability to help to match land uses to the capability of the land, which can optimise crop yields in areas where the land is productive.[2] Although this type of farming was initially developed for grain crops, it has also proved useful for the wine-growing and horticultural industries and has been applied across a range of landscapes. The positive implications of this technology are considerable: the use of fertilisers can be minimised and carefully targeted, crop yield can be maximised and soil chemistry factored in when planning crop distributions. As such, in addition to identifying more sustainable means of agricultural production systems, precision agriculture can be used in environmental auditing, from individual paddocks on farms to entire landscapes.

Many farmers across the country are using another tool that has long been available to those who know how to use it: commonsense. The fact that much of Australia's farming land has been exhausted in a few decades has prompted many to look back to understand how the Australian landscape worked and regenerated before Europeans arrived. A better understanding of natural processes such as hydrology and nutrient cycling, and a willingness to experiment and take time to read the land have produced some remarkable results. One example is an innovative approach to do away with chemicals entirely. Developed over two decades of experimentation, 'natural sequence farming' has been put into practice on a horse stud in Denman in the Hunter Valley. The stud's manager and farmer Peter Andrews wanted to reduce the use of chemicals and fertilisers, to make better use of any available fresh water and to stop salinity on his land.[3] He developed and introduced this system based on two simple premises: that plants—any plants—were providers of essential nutrients to the soil and these nutrient levels needed to be fostered naturally, and that the leaching of soils over time could be prevented if fresh water were channelled to supply paddocks by means that resembled natural watercourses. On reading the land, Andrews decided to mimic the processes that had shaped Australia's natural landscapes in the first place and produced remarkable results. One radical departure was to incorporate the existing weeds on his properties into the rehabilitation process of the land. Instead of chemically poisoning the weeds and ploughing and burning the land, Andrews ceased all ploughing and disturbance of the topsoil and instead simply slashed the weeds and left them to mulch into the ground, gradually restoring the carbon that had been lost from the soil from constant grazing and stubble burning. The result was that the soil soon began to produce lush pasture without any chemical intervention or seeding. The value of naturally nurturing delicate topsoils is something long recognised by permaculturists, but was now proven to work on a large agricultural scale. Andrews also displayed ingenuity in managing natural water flows. After observing this precious resource rush through the property's deeply eroded watercourses and past most of his pastures, he began to block sections of the creek to create something of an obstacle course. Using organic matter and reeds to slow the water's flow enabled the formation of graduated ponds.[4] Once the water had pooled, he dug channels along contour lines of the property to allow the water to spread out and soak slowly into the natural in-ground water storages that would feed the landscape during drier times. In trialling these new approaches, Andrews noticed that the variety of plants (weeds included) in his paddocks played an important role in keeping salinity at bay. Not all plants were palatable and consumed by stock, and these prevented the over-grazing of the land and the rise of the in-ground water level. On adjoining paddocks planted with only one type of grass, the loss of vegetation from grazing had allowed the soil's salt content to rise so that water flowing through those paddocks would emerge much saltier.[5] In his book *Back from the Brink*, Andrews concludes that a variety of plant, animal and microbial life and its myriad interactions gave the environment a 'kind of collective strength' that made it better able to cope with stresses such as drought while allowing it to make the most of favourable times.[6]

Andrews is convinced that natural sequence farming could benefit other farmers and he outlines recommendations for farm planning to maintain soil fertility. On a basic principle of dividing a farm (or individual sections of it) into thirds, he advocates leaving one-third (preferably on higher ground) to natural scrub and bushland to produce nutrients and support wildlife, one-third to pasture interspersed with rows of decaying, soil-feeding mulch, and the last third as a recovery area (on lower ground) to catch any nutrients moved by leaching during rain. On a property used solely for grazing, the ratio could be amended to one-third bush and two-thirds grassland. Andrews predicts that on properties managed in this way, the productivity of the grazed/cropped areas will increase fivefold compared with that of properties where most or all of the land is utilised.

There are, of course, a number of concerns on the use of natural-sequence farming. One is that its suitability is largely confined to land with a natural slope to enable the dispersal of nutrients by water and gravity. A second is that water is a requisite in this equation, precluding the usefulness of this approach in regions of permanent drought or over-extraction upstream. A third argument might be that the benefits yielded for the natural-sequence farmer in slowing the flow of water through his property may disadvantage the farmers downstream, much as larger dams affect farms and wetlands downstream. However, those concerns acknowledged, where conditions are suitable and sequence farming implemented at perhaps the scale of an entire catchment, the potential benefits to both the natural environment—vastly reduced chemical usage, deliberate protection of substantial proportions of properties for biodiversity—and improved agricultural yields could be truly remarkable. Any land management regime that once again demonstrates the merits of working with instead of against the natural Australian conditions must surely warrant a closer look.

★ ★ ★

The development of cities with extensive housing options, transport systems, industrial and recreational areas and other infrastructure will continue into the foreseeable future. This means that the immense pressure on native biodiversity that exists in urban pockets of bushland or ecosystems adjacent to these cities will also continue to increase. But for a large number of the detrimental impacts that new and existing housing developments invariably have, there are ways and means of reducing them. The various strategies for reducing the carbon and ecological footprints of an existing household are by now common knowledge and include installing solar panels to supply hot water and other energy needs, reducing water by installing water-saving showerheads, front-loading washing machines and rainwater tanks, reducing energy consumption by choosing renewable electricity and fitting energy-saving light bulbs. But beyond adjusting our daily habits, the development process itself, including where and how development takes place, also offers many options that can reduce the negative impact on the surrounding and wider environment.

In most Australian capital cities, the Great Australian Dream of owning a house is rapidly moving out of the reach of a large proportion of the population as house prices rocket past even the remotest boundaries of their budgets. A detrimental result of this fading dream is that many people are moving away from the cities and are driving the development of the sensitive coastal ecosystems between these large hubs. The damage already done by excessive coastal development, preceded by land clearing and the drainage of critical wetlands, is enormous. Apart from the growing risk of inundation from tidal surges driven by climate change and rising sea levels along low-lying coastal areas, wetlands are vital filtering systems of pollutants; toxins and chemical run–off washed downstream from agricultural areas have a chance to be neutralised in these ecosystems only if they remain functional.

If house prices continue to rise, living arrangements will become more concentrated as people are forced to live in unit blocks or townhouses that take up less space than individual houses. Smaller, more densely built settlements and apartment buildings will become the norm for the larger cities in the coming decades. In the meantime, though, a range of measures can be taken to reduce the impacts of new construction. For the living environment, it is essential that urban spread is minimised and that development is primarily confined to already cleared areas and that remaining natural areas are protected and enhanced wherever possible.

Incorporating strong sustainability measures into housing in the planning stages is much easier than retrofitting existing homes. Wherever possible, new housing should be of a passive solar design and built to make the most of sunlight and breezes to heat and cool the interior. Cooling and heating contribute an average of 40 per cent to average household carbon emissions (not to mention energy bills) and this can be avoided through smart building design.[7] Building regulations in all states should insist that all housing is solidly constructed and well insulated, which reduces the need for energy-expensive and carbon-emitting cooling and heating.

Water tanks should also be installed to make the most of coastal rains and reduce the need to draw on water from the environment. And water recycling must be made easier for us as an immediate priority—the use of drinkable fresh water in toilet cisterns, washing machines and swimming pools is an offence that we will be embarrassed to admit to well before the end of the next decade. Domestic grey water recycling systems that enable the efficient reuse of water already exist and, along with tanks, should become an essential feature in all new housing.

In regions where wildlife habitat is being directly affected by commercial development, housing estate designs are being trialled and refined to benefit native species. One example is a coastal housing estate at Pottsville on the New South Wales north coast, an area whose fragile coastal ecosystems have been ravaged by the increasing demand for sea-change living. Conceived around an association between developers The Ray Group and the Australian Koala Foundation, this 365-hectare former cattle property was only partially developed to take into account the protection of the local koalas and of twenty-four species of threatened wildlife found on the property and in the surrounding region. To ensure ample habitat for these and other local species, no less than 75 per cent of the estate including largely intact bush and a creek was set aside for conservation. The development of the remaining cleared land was preceded by extensive surveys and assessments of the wildlife on the property to understand how the site was used by species like the koalas, glossy black cockatoos, bush thick-knees, blossom bats, insectivorous bats, planigales, wallum froglets and a number of rare plant species. Only once this had been determined and all areas of importance clearly marked out did the design and layout commence; construction followed in stages.

From the outset, the developers also imposed a number of conditions on the estate's future homeowners. As the entire estate is part of a larger koala habitat, koalas have right of way on local streets and strict speed limits apply at all times. Owners cannot own either cats or dogs; dogs are particularly known to impact on koalas, and as the building regulations on the site required that homes would use only koala-friendly fencing (fences with gaps at ground level), complete dog exclusion was necessary. In return for what some might consider unreasonable restrictions on homeowners, the developers contributed to the natural integrity of the site by enhancing (additional planting) existing native eucalypt and wetland vegetation. Owing to the local importance of the site to wildlife, the Tweed Shire undertakes regular fox-baiting on and around the property and reports on its results to the Koala Beach Wildlife and Habitat Management Committee, which comprises residents and is chaired by the Tweed Shire Council.

Today the final stage is almost complete and around five hundred homes have been built across the entire property.[8] The Tweed Shire Council together with local scientists and wildlife carers is still monitoring the native flora and fauna on Koala Beach and all species initially recorded on the site are still present. A recent survey of blossom bats on the site, for example, showed that the numbers that still regularly visit the site to feed among the banksia heath are equivalent to those observed before development commenced.[9] Incidental observations have also confirmed the continued presence of glossy black cockatoos, bush thick-knees and koalas and have even revealed the presence of a powerful owl, a species that had never before been seen at Koala Beach.[10] Despite the restrictions, only a few homes are still available and residents have developed a sense of stewardship for the property's precious living environment. Koala Beach is proof that developers and conservation agencies can move from a frequent climate of antagonism to innovative collaborations of much greater respect and value to native biodiversity.

★ ★ ★

There are many other fields of commercial endeavour where moves towards sustainability are being made or where environmentally friendly options are available for the consumer. Industry independent certification bodies such as the Forest Stewardship Council (FSC) and the Marine Stewardship Council (MSC) apply strict criteria before approving products to carry the FSC label for the use of sustainable timber products (including paper) or the MSC label on viable fish products, respectively. Wherever these labels appear, consumers are assured that the products that carry them are among the soundest available at the time. The Forest Stewardship Council is an international organisation that by its own account works with a wide range of stakeholders to promote good stewardship of the world's forests. In order to achieve this at a global scale, the FSC accredits third parties to certify forest managers and timber product producers to FSC standards in forty-five countries. In 2006, more than 90 million hectares of forest and several thousand timber-based products in more than seventy countries had been FSC-certified.[11] In Australia, the FSC has been active since 2001 and operates with the triple bottom line aims of environmental, social and economic sustainability of the certified products. The Australian website provides an up-to-date list of companies that have been FSC-certified either with Forest Management certificates or Chain of Custody certificates as well as a list of the products sold, including paper, printing and building materials.

Like the FSC, the Marine Stewardship Council operates independently and internationally. Its aim is to use consumer-purchasing power to promote the environmentally responsible stewardship of the world's seafood stocks and prevent the over-fishing of threatened fish stocks.[12] In a collaboration similar to that of the Koala Beach development venture, the MSC was developed via a partnership between the world's largest seafood buyer, Unilever, and the conservation organisation WWF. So far, close to nine hundred products have been MSC-labelled. In Australia, MSC-certified fisheries include Western Australia's rock lobster fishery and mackerel icefish fishery, and the Lakes and Coorong mixed fishery is currently being assessed.

The certification of products and businesses that are genuinely striving for better environmental outcomes has numerous benefits to recommend it. For the consumer or buyer of the product it provides transparency about how it has been produced and simplifies choosing a responsible product among the many options in the market. For the producer it provides a means of advertising his position as an environmentally responsible business and helps attract the growing market sector that seeks this assurance while providing no disincentives for the remainder of the market yet to be interested in reducing its environmental footprint. For those industries where certification schemes *are* available, the absence of a product label also identifies companies whose products may not, or not yet, be environmentally sound. This allows consumers to avoid them and brings pressure on those industry sectors to pull up their socks to retain a market share. But while certification is an excellent marketing tool, it is also open to abuse. The certification standards that underpin a label can vary dramatically and it is important to look out for the stamp of a reputable certifier. A current shortfall of many certified products is that their producers are far more concerned with a market advantage than with ensuring that their labelling translates into a healthier environment. It is vital then that consumers demand several things from certification: the clear identification of sound products; answers to how certification has contributed to the conservation of species and the living environment; ongoing transparency and regular updates on how this is being ensured.

At present, the voluntary nature of certification schemes means that producers are not pressured to join. The environment, however, cannot afford to wait for industry laggards to get on board. To create change at the necessary speed, mandatory certification and labelling schemes for all supermarket goods, for example, would be much more likely to motivate industries to improve their environmental performance within a meaningful time frame. Until certification by reputable certifying bodies becomes the norm across all industries, responsible consumers must do their own homework on the products they purchase while environmentally conscious companies must rely on consumer support of their products to remain viable in the short term.

★ ★ ★

Thanks to the age of the internet, finding out about sustainable practices, products and businesses is a matter of only a few keystrokes. Some of the most sensible advances in reducing the unsustainable taking of resources from the environment come from the burgeoning businesses that re-use previously used materials.

Re-using, whether by passing on an object to a new owner, finding alternative uses for it in a household or business or simply prolonging its current use, has a whole suite of environmental benefits; as does recycling, taking existing materials and reshaping them into new objects. Helping to extend the lifecycle of materials such as plastics, paper, cardboard, glass and aluminium cans has been widely embraced by urban communities where recycling services are offered. Forty-six per cent of our waste is currently being recycled.[13] Increasingly, these materials reappear on the market as recycled glassware and paper products, but there are some surprising transformations such as the ingenious biodegradable eco-coffins that are made from recycled paper pulp.[14] In some areas, whitegoods such as fridges, stoves and washing machines and other goods containing harmful chemicals, such as batteries, old paint, used oil, pool chemicals, pesticides, herbicides and wood preservatives and old medications can also be collected by local council services to be disposed of responsibly. Electrical goods such as televisions, computers, faxes, printers and stereos remain among the worst items to discard as they cannot be readily recycled and often end up in landfill even if collected by councils. While recycling helps it still entails some environmental costs in the form of the energy required and emissions produced in the recycling process. By far the best option for the environment is to re-use items without the need for reprocessing. Everything old must become new again.

New ways forward for the building industry have been briefly discussed, but it is worth noting that it, more than any other sector, is blessed with innumerable opportunities to re-use local reclaimed, materials. Doors, windows, tiles, flooring, plumbing materials and fixtures and fit-outs such as kitchens and bathrooms can often be salvaged prior to the destruction of an existing building to be sold and re-used elsewhere. Timber, bricks and pavers that remain intact are also re-usable and may be re-employed in the construction framework of a building or as rustic or elegantly aged features in the interior or exterior of a house. Using recycled materials reduces the impact on the environment that a new building has—not just from its construction but also from the manufacturing, sourcing and transport of its many materials. Businesses and agents specialising in building materials reclaimed from demolition sites can be found in all major cities and provide builders and renovators with options that produce few greenhouse gas emissions through transport (provided they are sourced locally), reduce the destruction of habitat for landfill sites, extend the lifecycle of environmentally costly raw materials such as timber and glass by decades.

A recent Australian–Japanese study found that there were convincing economic and environmental cases to be made for recycling and re-using building materials, but identified a number of obstacles that currently prevent it from becoming standard practice in the industry. They include a lack of government support and the need to promote the secondary building materials market, to standardise the building industry, to improve building demolition techniques and to increase community awareness of this sector of the industry.[15]

In the Californian city of San Jose, construction and demolition material made up a hefty 30 per cent of landfill. A waste diversion deposit program was established that, in a move to motivate developers and contractors to incorporate material reclamation into their demolition plans, charges a 'diversion deposit' fee that reflects the environmental cost of the amount of landfill produced if no materials are recycled. This fee, calculated per square foot of the size of the project (and which differs for residential and industrial demolitions), is fully refundable if all possible materials are reused or taken to a certified recovery facility.[16] To ensure no short cuts are taken, progress at certified demolition/building sites is regularly monitored by the city of San Jose.

One of the largest recycling successes involved the demolition of a shopping centre to make room for an enormous retail and shopping community. Reclaimed rebar, roofing materials, timber and metal stud framing and other materials included 310 tonnes of steel, 175 tonnes of tin and more than 30 000 tonnes of asphalt and concrete which were ground up and recycled on-site. This meant that more than 70 per cent of materials were recycled and reused or sold compared with the 15 per cent of standard recycling.[17] The application of a concept as simple as a diversion deposit resulted in a shift in the perspective of developers and contractors and many of them have now embraced the idea of recycling.

A more considered attitude to what we actually *need* in our lives— as opposed to the things we are told we *should have*—is making a timely comeback. Individuals and industries need to think of smarter, sustainable and far less environmentally costly ways to operate. The implementation of new ideas should be encouraged rather than stifled, and it is, as we have seen, often rewarded in many ways.

14

TEN WAYS TO MAKE A DIFFERENCE

The idea that the evolution of entirely new cultural trends can be initiated by the actions of only a few individuals was recently explored in *The Tipping Point*, Malcolm Gladwell's intriguing analysis of the origins and proliferation of modern consumer trends.[1] Gladwell found that changed trends and behaviours (such as the mass-purchase of a previously unfashionable brand of shoe) can result when a number of different social players who initiate, recognise and adopt and popularise a new fashion (termed mavens, connectors and salesmen, respectively) are able to trigger its large-scale adoption at phenomenal speed.

The heartening phenomenon that changed behaviours of only a few can trigger positive change in many continues to give hope to conservationists and others concerned with the ongoing degradation of the planet and of Australia in particular. An individual action can and does make a difference to the bigger picture, even if that difference seems minute and its ripple effect is not immediately apparent

And right now, it's up to us to start this change.

With governments and industries likely to remain locked into existing, environmentally destructive economic paradigms in the near future (despite promises of change), real change within these two sectors will not occur quickly enough to ensure a safe future. It may yet seem futuristic, but economic wealth and excessive consumption today *will* come at the price of food, water and clean air tomorrow. To bring about the political, industrial and individual changes needed for greater equity across cultures and generations, several changes in our attitude and behaviour must occur. Among them are an increased political engagement, more sustainable consumer choices, and the recognition that our lives in this wealthy western country are ones of extreme privilege.

As part of the global community, our entitlements encompass life, liberty, personal security against harm, the presumption of innocence until proven guilty, the right to move freely between states and countries, to seek asylum, to receive basic education and to work for equal pay.[2] These fundamental rights are, however, simply aspirations for the vast majority of the world's nations where hunger, extreme poverty and sometimes even genocide are the order of the day. Food and water are human rights; the year-round availability of every imaginable exotic fruit and vegetable at any environmental cost is not. Liberty and freedom of speech are human rights; four-wheel drives for the inner-city school run are not. Equality and protection against poverty are human rights; private home ownership, especially in regions under enormous environmental pressure, is not. Shelter from the elements is a basic human right; MP3 and DVD players, plasma televisions, personal computers and cars are not. An acceptance that the material abundance we have enjoyed in recent decades cannot continue is essential to fundamental environmental (and social) change. In pursuing the three basic principles of change listed above—political engagement, responsible consumer choices and an adjustment in our unrealistic and unsustainable Australian lifestyle expectations, there is much positive action that can be taken by anyone ready to embrace their part. The term 'consumption' has become synonymous with excessive living, but any activity that involves acquiring something constitutes consumption and most likely impacts on the environment. Choose more sustainable products whenever possible; the cumulative signal this sends will help make those businesses more viable and pull others into line.

1. Understand your personal footprint and commit to reduce it

Calculating our personal or household footprints can yield surprising insights into how large (or small) our patterns of consumption really are. A number of user-friendly footprint calculators can be found on various websites, including those of the Victorian government (www.epa.vic.gov.au/ecologicalfootprint/calculators/personal) and the Australian Conservation Foundation (www.acfonline.org.au/custom_greenhome/calculator). Identifying where the biggest reductions can be made from a few simple changes is a good way to get started. If a complete adjustment in lifestyle is too overwhelming, consider committing to just one major change per year—such as the installation of solar panels or a water tank, the switching to green energy sources or the purchase of a water and energy-saving washing machine. The sense of empowerment that comes with embracing one's personal social and environmental responsibility and adopting new sustainable practices is surprisingly habit-forming.

2. Buy local, seasonal produce and eat less red meat and dairy

The environmental impacts of diverting fresh water from rivers and wetlands to produce crops, fruit and vegetables is threatening the survival of countless birds, mammals, fish, invertebrates and entire plant and wildlife communities in many regions of the Murray–Darling Basin and elsewhere. Transporting produce from overseas (by plane) or beef or sheep from remote pastoral regions (by truck) contributes to greenhouse gas emissions. Buying locally grown, seasonal produce can go a long way to reducing the impact of essential foods on the landscape.

Cutting back on red meat and dairy products and making them a treat rather than a staple will ease the demands these industries place on the environment. According to the Australian Conservation Foundation, reducing our individual dairy intake by only two cups of milk a week could save 13 000 litres of water as well as 250 kilograms of greenhouses gases per person per year.[3]

3. Reduce, reclaim, re-use—maximise the lifecycle of everything you buy

Disposability, and products made cheaply to break down and be replaced after their twelve-month warranty expires are an environmental curse. The impact of the lifecycles of these products consist of the sum of the environmental costs of the resources they are made from—cotton, timber, oil-derived plastics—the processes that produced them, the energy many of them consume—coal-fired electricity or fossil fuel—and the space all nonrecyclable parts occupy in landfill or wherever they are dumped illegally into the environment. Repair and re-use or consider swapping instead. Another alternative is to buy quality used goods—clothes, furnishings, building materials, whitegoods or cars. This reduces the demand on new products along with your own consumer footprint.

4. Don't build or buy new property on a coastal floodplain

Australia cannot afford to lose another acre of its coastal ecosystems. Thousands of ecosystems and their flora and fauna are already under threat of extinction and require protection and rehabilitation. As sea levels rise, they will rely on room to move away from permanent inundation. We depend on the health of those ecosystems—don't contribute to their further demise. Do not support new development in coastal regions. Stick to areas already well-developed and serviced through infrastructure and avoid the clearing of unclaimed land.

5. Get to know your local politicians and councillors

Talking to your state and federal members and local councillors about your environmental concerns and requesting that action be taken are easy yet powerful actions. Politicians are well aware that their own positions and those of their parties depend on a satisfied electorate and look to the public mood as an indicator. Whether face-to-face, by phone, email or letter, voice your concerns about inadequate product-labelling, ensure that remaining green spaces and waterways are looked after, rehabilitated and maintained as wildlife habitats, and demand sustainable building practices and renewable energy over coal-fired power.

Read your local public notices to be aware of development proposals that may harm the environment and draft a letter before close of the public comment period. Whether you voted for them or not, make your local representatives defend the environment.

6. Write to the environment ministers

State and federal ministers (like local politicians) must take notice of the views of the community: the more people that speak out, the more likely it will result in action. Individual letters are more powerful than signing a petition, even if they are short and to the point. Write to voice your concerns about climate change and the securing of comprehensive nature reserves. Write to demand better industry regulation so that sustainable practices can be enforced. Write to demand that environment legislation serve the environment, not developers. Never assume that someone else is representing your concerns; 'someone else' is assuming the same thing.

7. Support a non-government conservation organisation

Different conservation organisations specialise in different environmental causes and are well informed and up-to-date on the issues they are working on. They also understand the political system and know how best to apply pressure on governments when pressure is needed. Choose a cause close to your heart—the protection of wetlands or rivers, the removal of feral animals or the recovery of certain plants, animals or a local bush remnant– and find an organisation that works on that cause to discuss what contribution you can make. Remember that much positive change to the environment begins in an office.

8. Invest in sustainable companies

Whether through your superannuation fund, a private share portfolio or both, choose your financial investments with the environment in mind. Investigate where exactly your money goes. Green funds such as Hunter Hall and Australian Ethical Investment and Superannuation are increasing in popularity and the returns of the sustainable options of larger investment companies such as BT, AMP and Perpetual are also starting to outperform the standard 'safe' options. If you can't resist the returns of one of the large extractive or agricultural companies, join an ethical shareholder group and put pressure on the company to improve its environmental performance. As a shareholder in the company, your voice counts. Make it heard.

★ ★ ★

To become involved at the conservation coalface and contribute to the restoration of a native ecosystem, there are further hands-on actions that can be taken.

9. Get your neighbours involved in local conservation activities

Pick almost any region in Australia and you will find species and landscapes under threat. Some may occur in your immediate neighbourhood or even on your property. Whether you live in a city or a country town, contact your local council or state environment department for information about the status of plants, wildlife and ecological communities in your area and any priority recovery actions that apply. Some may be as simple as installing some nest boxes or fencing, removing specific weeds or restraining your pets, but others such as fox control or the restoration of creek lines or bush are effective only on a larger scale. Find out what grants are available to support your community conservation efforts and whether any bushcare or landcare groups operate in your area. The building of continuous wildlife habitat corridors across all tenures of land will be a critical strategy for combating extinctions from further degradation and climate change. Contact your state environment department for advice on how you can play a part in this.

10. Don't contribute to environmental problems

Some of the easiest environmental contributions can be made in your own backyard:

- Do not let your pets roam where wildlife lives; it's in the nature of cats and dogs to hunt and kill. Never release unwanted pets of any kind or their young into the wild; contact your vet or the RSPCA for other options instead.
- Learn to identify noxious weeds in your garden (your local council can help) and remove them immediately. Control low-growing weeds by smothering them using newspaper covered in mulch. Plant local native or non-invasive plants instead.
- Do not use chemical pesticides or herbicides in your garden, use natural permaculture alternatives instead.
- Start a worm farm or compost and turn your fruit and vegetable scraps into rich, organic humus for your garden and pot plants in a matter of weeks.

The list of practical positive actions is long, but every contribution counts. The most important message, however, is that of political engagement.

★ ★ ★

On his first day in office Kevin Rudd, the new prime minister, signed Australia on to the Kyoto Protocol before heading to Bali to help negotiate the post-Kyoto future of 2012. Signing the protocol has released Australia from clutching the shirt-tails of the United States on the most far-reaching environmental issue of our time. This move has allowed Australia to be taken seriously in its contributions to developing strategies and regulations to cut carbon emissions globally.

And with climate change now firmly on the national agenda (indeed we have our own climate change minister), the government's commitment to other environmental challenges is also beginning to emerge. So far, the signs have been promising. There is a commitment to the continued funding of prioritised concerns such as biodiversity, the national system of conservation reserves and the protection of coastal and critical aquatic habitats, as well as pursuing improvements in sustainable farm practices.

The unprecedented firm stance taken by the government against Japanese 'scientific' whaling has demonstrated that it will not be cowed from opposing blatantly commercial slaughter in defiance of an international moratorium even by a major economic partner.

Relations between the federal government and the states have also improved, as seen in the March signing of the Living Murray Agreement, a water-conservation plan that had stalled amid tensions between Victoria and the previous federal Liberal government. While scientists remain concerned that the plan is inadequate for addressing the conservation of the Murray–Darling Basin's ecosystems with the necessary speed and decisiveness, it nevertheless represents a milestone in the difficult issue of water-sharing for consumption and environmental health.

The Rudd government is in a position to build an environmental legacy of unprecedented importance. This legacy should be built on commonsense and a vision that looks to the future of this country's landscapes to ensure that the economy can benefit from the health of the natural ecosystems that it currently destroys. Climate change is the most alarming of many signs that demonstrate that mismanaging nature results in catastrophic consequences. This Labor government will help determine how quickly and comprehensively Australia will respond to these signs. As the 2020 Forum has shown, the government has opened channels for the public to communicate its hopes, concerns and ideas for the future. The future of the environment is being decided on our watch, so make yourself heard.

NOTES

Introduction: A Day in the Year of the Dog

1   N Stern, *The Economics of Climate Change: The Stern Review*, Cambridge University Press, Cambridge, 2006.

2   A McIntosh & D Wilkinson, 'Environment Protection and Biodiversity Conservation Act: A Five Year Assessment', Discussion Paper no. 81, Australia Institute, Sydney, 2005.

3   Australian Government Department of the Environment, Water, Heritage & the Arts, 'Listing Advice, Southern Blue Fin Tuna (*Thunnus maccoyi*)', Canberra, 2005.

4   EA Hayes, 'A Review of the Southern Bluefin Tuna Fishery: Implications for Ecologically Sustainable Management', Traffic Oceania, www.traffic.org/species-reports/traffic_species_fish1.pdf.

5   P Sattler & C Creighton (eds), 'Australian Terrestrial Biodiversity Assessment 2002', National Land and Water Resources Audit, Commonwealth of Australia, Canberra, 2002, p. 44.

6   Australian Government Department of the Environment, Water, Heritage & the Arts, 'Threatened Species and Ecological Communities', Canberra, http://www.environment.gov.au/biodiversity/threatened/index.html.

7   ibid.

8   Australian Network of Environmental Defenders Offices, 'Submission on the Environment and Heritage Amendment Bill (No. 1) 2006', Canberra, 27 October 2007, p. 4.

9   ibid.

10 D Heinze, L Broome & I Mansergh, 'A Review of the Ecology and Conservation of the Mountain Pygmy-possum *Burramys parvus*' in RL Goldingay and SM Jackson (eds), *The Biology of Australian Possums and Gliders*, Surrey Beatty & Sons, Chipping Norton, 2006, pp. 254–67; L Broome personal communication: <7km^2 in article recently revised to <6 km^2.

11 Threatened Species Network, Factsheet: *Mountain pygmy-possum* Burramys parvus, WWF–Australia, Sydney, 2005.

12 P Menkhorst, Victorian Department of Sustainability & Environment, personal communication, February 2007.

13 L Broome, New South Wales National Parks & Wildlife Service, personal communication, February 2007.

14 'Flora and Fauna Guarantee Action Statement, Mountain Pygmy-possum *(Burramys parvus)*', Victorian Department of Sustainability & Environment, 2003.

15   Amendment C17, Alpine Resorts Planning Scheme, Victorian *Planning and Environment Act 1987*.
16   A Reid, 'Cold Comfort a Hot Investment', *Sunday Age*, 11 June 2006, p. 4.
17   R Brereton, S Bennett & I Mansergh, 'Enhanced Greenhouse Climate Change and Its Potential Effect on Selected Fauna of South-eastern Australia: A Trend Analysis', Biological Conservation, no. 72, 1995, pp. 339–54.

1 The Big Dry

1   Australian Government Bureau of Meteorology, Drought Statement, Canberra, 4 January 2007.
2   Australian Bureau of Statistics/Department of the Environment, Water, Heritage & the Arts, 'Water Use and Irrigation', *Yearbook Australia 2007*, Canberra, 2007.
3   SEQ Water Corporation, Dam Operations and Maintenance, www.seqwater.com.au/content/standard.asp?name=DamOperationsand Maintenance. There is no set maximum level of water restrictions. Restrictions are determined by each state government as necessary, and so implications for businesses and households may vary between states.
4   Brisbane City Council, Residential Water Restrictions, www.brisbane.qld.gov.au/BCC:BASE:1937616960:pc=PC_2162.
5   Queensland Department of Transport, SEQ Snapshot, viewed March 2007, www.transport.qld.gov.au/resources/file/ebb0b646593c161/ Transportgreenpaper_section01seq_snapshot.pdf.
6   Water Corporation, Western Australia, www.watercorporation.com.au.
7   Indian Ocean Climate Initiative, 'Climate Variability and Change in the South-West', www.ioci.org.au/publications/pdf/IOCI_CVCSW02.pdf.
8   Water Corporation, Western Australia, www.watercorporation.com.au.
9   Australian Government Department of the Environment, Water, Heritage & the Arts, Canberra, www.environment.gov.au/water/mdb/index.html.
10   Australian Government Department of Agriculture, Fisheries & Forestry, 'Murray–Darling Basin Policies and Programmes', Canberra, http://www.environment.gov.au/water/mdb/policies.html.
11   P Kerr, 'Water Buyback Nets $24m Rural Property', *Age*, 11 September 2008.
12   B Haisman, 'Macquarie Marshes, Murray Darling Basin, Australia', Contributing Paper for the World Commission on Dams Thematic Reviews, Murray–Darling Basin Commission, Australia, 2000.
13   Ramsar Convention on Wetlands, www.ramsar.org.
14   Australian Government Department of the Environment, Water, Heritage & the Arts, www.environment.gov.au/water/mdb/index.html.

2 A Snapshot of Australia

1   R Hough, *Captain James Cook: A Biography*, Hodder & Stoughton, London, 1994, p. 174.

2   'Overcoming Indigenous Disadvantage', Australian Bureau of Statistics, Canberra, Yearbook Chapter 8.

3   Australian Bureau of Statistics, 'Population Projections, Australia, 2004–2101 (cat. no. 3222.0)', Canberra, 14 June 2006.

4   CIA World Factbook, India, viewed February 2007, www.cia.gov/library/publications/the-world-factbook/index.html.

5   A global hectare as defined in the 'Living Planet Report 2006' is 'a hectare with world-average ability to produce resources and absorb waste'.

6   'WWF Living Planet Report 2006', WWF World Wide Fund for Nature, Gland, Switzerland, October 2006.

7   ibid., p. 30.

8   B Foran & F Poldy, 'Future Dilemmas: Options to 2050 for Australia's Population, Technology, Resources and Environment', Technical Report, CSIRO Sustainable Ecosystems, CSIRO, ACT, Australia, 2002.

9   CSIRO, 'Future Dilemmas for Australia's Population', Media Release, Australia, 4 November 2002.

10 'WWF Living Planet Report 2006', p. 14.

11 ibid.

12 Green Home—Eco Calculator, Australian Conservation Foundation, viewed 5 November 2007, www.acfonline.org.au/custom_greenhome/calculator.asp ?section_id=86.

13 ibid.

14 ibid.

15 Australian Government Department of the Environment, Water, Heritage & the Arts, 'Electrical and Electronic Stewardship Strategy', Canberra, www.environment.gov.au/settlements/waste/electricals/index.html.

16 Australian Bureau of Statistics, 'Human Activity Trends: Waste', *Australia's Environment: Issues and Trends 2007* (cat. no. 4613.0), Canberra, 11 January 2008.

17 Clean Up Australia, 'Climate Change Concern Increases Clean Up Day Action', Media Release, 4 March 2007.

18 HG Cogger, HA Ford, CN Johnson, J Holman & D Butler, 'Impacts of Land Clearing on Australian Wildlife in Queensland', Report to WWF-Australia, 2003, p. 15.

19 RJS Beeton, KI Buckley, GJ Jones, D Morgan, RE Reichelt & D Trewin, 'Australia State of the Environment 2006: Land', Independent report to the Federal Minister for Environment, Water, Heritage & the Arts, 2006, p.10.

20   ibid.

21   P Sattler, personal communication, March 2007.

22   ibid.

23   P Sattler & C Creighton (eds), 'Australian Terrestrial Biodiversity Assessment 2002', National Land and Water Resources Audit, Commonwealth of Australia, Canberra, 2002, p. 50.

24   RJS Beeton, KI Buckley, GJ Jones, D Morgan, RE Reichelt & D Trewin, p. 69.

25   ibid, p. 71.

26   Australian Government Bureau of Rural Sciences, 'Land Use in Australia: At a Glance', Canberra, October 2006, p. 3.

27   Australian Bureau of Statistics, 'International Merchandise: Trade', *Yearbook Australia 2007* (cat. no. 1301.0), Canberra, 2007.

28   Australian Bureau of Statistics, 'Landscape Trends: Land', *Australia's Environment: Issues and Trends 2007* (cat. no. 4613.0), Canberra, 2007.

29   E Farelly, 'Victories for the Environment Turn Up Heat', *Sydney Morning Herald*, 6 December 2006.

30   New South Wales Conservation Council, 'Proposed Anvil Hill Coal Mine', Media Release, 2006.

31   E Farelly, 'Victories for the Environment Turn Up Heat'.

32   'New South Wales Government Approves Anvil Hill Coal Mine', ABC News Online, viewed 7 June 2007, www.abc.net.au/news/newsitems/200706/s1945236.htm.

33   The burrowing bettong once occurred on the mainland but is now extinct; the golden bandicoot does occur on the mainland but is critically endangered. The four others are subspecies strictly endemic to the island.

34   'Environmental Advice on the Principle of Locating a Gas Processing Complex on Barrow Island Nature Reserve', Environmental Protection Authority, Western Australia, July 2003, p. 17.

35   P Gamblin, Senior Policy Officer Oceans and Coasts, WWF–Australia, personal communication, June 2007.

36   S Levy, 'A Top Dog Takes Over', *National Wildlife*, vol. 42 (5), 2004.

3 One Hundred Football Fields an Hour

1   C Johnson, *Australia's Mammal Extinctions: A 50,000-Year History*, Cambridge University Press, Cambridge, 2006.

2   BJ Traill, personal communication, October 2007.

3   C Johnson, H Cogger, C Dickman & H Ford, 'Impacts of Land-Clearing: The Impacts of Approved Clearing of Native Vegetation on Australian Wildlife in New South Wales', Report to WWF–Australia, 2007; Victorian

Department of Sustainability & Environment, 'Victoria's Forests', Factsheet, 2006. This figure refers to estimates from 1972; Australian State of the Environment Committee, 'Australia State of the Environment 2001—Land Theme Report', Australian Government Department of the Environment, Water, Heritage & the Arts, Canberra; Australian Greenhouse Office, 'Land Clearing: A Social History', National Carbon Accounting System, Technical Report no. 4, 2000.

4   State of the Environment Advisory Council, 'Australian State of the Environment 1996', Australian Government Department of the Environment, Water, Heritage & the Arts, Canberra, 1998; Australian State of the Environment Committee, 'Australian State of the Environment 2001', Australian Government Department of the Environment, Water, Heritage & the Arts, Canberra, 2001; P Sattler & C Creighton (eds), 'Australian Terrestrial Biodiversity Assessment', National Land and Water Resources Audit, Commonwealth of Australia, Canberra, 2002.

5   HG Cogger, HA Ford, CN Johnson, J Holman & D Butler, 'Impacts of Land Clearing on Australian Wildlife in Queensland', Report to WWF-Australia, 2003, p. 15.

6   Australian State of the Environment Committee, 'Australian State of the Environment 2001—Land Theme Report', Australian Government Department of the Environment, Water, Heritage & the Arts, Canberra, 2001.

7   Victorian Department of Sustainability & Environment, 'Victoria's Forests', Factsheet, 2006.

8   BJ Traill, 'Land Clearing in Queensland', The Wilderness Society, www.wilderness.org.au/articles/qld_landclearing.

9   Controls for rare vegetation types on leasehold land introduced in 1995 were followed by the same regulations on freehold land in 2000. The regulation for the cessation of large-scale clearing commenced in 2004 with a phase-out date of 2006; HG Cogger, HA Ford, CN Johnson, J Holman & D Butler, p. 4.

10   ibid., p. 4.

11   T Merito & S Ruane, 'Private Sector Conservation: Assisting Biodiversity', Department of Premier & Cabinet, Government of Western Australia, 2002.

12   ibid.

13   WE Wood, 'Increase in Salt in Soil and Streams Following the Destruction of Native Vegetation', *Journal and Proceedings of the Royal Society of Western Australia*, vol. 10, 1924, pp. 35–47, cited by the CRC for Plant-based Management of Dryland Salinity; HG Cogger, HA Ford, CN Johnson, J Holman & D Butler, p. 15.

14   B Walsh, 'Getting Credit for Saving Trees', *Time*, 23 July 2007.

15 'Red-tailed Black Cockatoo: About the species',Victorian Department of Sustainability & Environment, 2005.

16 D Quammen, *The Song of the Dodo: Island Biogeography in an Age of Extinction*, Simon & Schuster, New York, 1997, p. 1.

17 RJ Whelan, 'Landscape Management: Is It the Future?', Faculty of Science Papers, University of Wollongong, NSW, 2004.

18 D Driscoll, G Milkovits & D Freudenberger, 'Impact and Use of Firewood in Australia', CSIRO Sustainable Ecosystems Report, CSIRO, 2000.

19 'Removal of Dead Wood As a Key Threatening Process: An Overview', Threatened Species Information Sheet, New South Wales National Parks & Wildlife Service, 2003.

20 Australia and New Zealand Environment and Conservation Council, 'National Approach to Firewood Collection and Use in Australia', Australian Government Department of the Environment, Water, Heritage & the Arts, Canberra, 2001.

21 RJS Beeton, KI Buckley, GJ Jones, D Morgan, RE Reichelt & D Trewin, 'Australia State of the Environment 2006', Independent Report to the Federal Minister for the Environment and Heritage, 2006, p. 73.

22 ibid.

23 'Platypus and Pollution', *Ripples* 26, Australian Platypus Conservancy Newsletter, February 2004, www.platypus.asn.au.

24 ibid.

25 BJ Traill, 'Land Clearing in Queensland' The Wilderness Society, www.wilderness.org.au/articles/qld_landclearing.

4   Thirsty Work

1 Australian Bureau of Statistics, 'Agriculture, the Early Years', *Yearbook Australia 2001* (cat. no. 1310.0), Canberra, 2001.

2 Australian Natural Resources Atlas V 2.0: Rangelands Biophysical Resources: Australia, www.anra.gov.au/topics/rangelands/change/index.html.

3 T Grice & T Martin, 'The Management of Weeds and their Impact on Biodiversity in the Rangelands', Report of the CRC for Australian Weed Management, Townsville, 2005.

4 LR Brown, 'World's Rangelands Deteriorating under Mounting Pressure', Earth Policy Institute, www.earth-policy.org/Updates/Update6.htm.

5 R Paltridge & S McAlpin, *A Guide to Rare and Threatened Animals in Central Australia*, WWF-Australia, Sydney, 2002, p. 33.

6 Australian Government Department of the Environment, Water, Heritage & the Arts, 'The Feral Water Buffalo (*Bubalus bubalis*)', Factsheet, Canberra, 2004.

7 'Researcher Warns of Need to Reduce Feral Buffalo Numbers', ABC News, 26 February 2008.

8 B Myers, G Allan, R Bradstock, L Dias, G Duff, P Jacklyn, J Landsberg, J Morrison, J Russell-Smith & R Williams, 'Tropical Savannas', *Fire Management in the Rangelands*, CRC, Darwin, 2004.

9 P Sattler & C Creighton (eds), 'Australian Terrestrial Biodiversity Assessment 2002', National Land and Water Resources Audit, Commonwealth of Australia, Canberra, 2002, p. 50.

10 Williams et al, cited in Tait, 2001, p. 23 [WWF inhouse report by Tait; not published].

11 S Garnett & G Crowley, *The Action Plan for Australian Birds 2000*, co-publication Australian Government Department of the Environment, Water, Heritage & the Arts, Canberra, and Birds Australia, Melbourne, 2000.

12 R Paltridge & S McAlpin, *A Guide to Rare and Threatened Animals in Central Australia*, WWF-Australia, Sydney, 2002.

13 C James, J Landsberg & S Morton, 'Provision of Watering Points in Australian Rangelands: A Literature Review of Effects on Biota', CSIRO Division of Wildlife and Ecology, 1997.

14 ibid.

15 R Harrington, 'The Effects of Artificial Watering Points on the Distribution and Abundance of Avifauna in an Arid and Semi-Arid Environment', PhD Thesis, Department of Zoology, University of Melbourne, 2002.

16 D MacKenzie, personal communication via Michael Weston, May 2007.

17 P Olsen & M Weston, 'Water, Wetlands and Birds' in *The State of Australia's Birds 2004*, Birds Australia, Melbourne, 2004, p. 4.

18 B Bryan & S Marvenek, 'Quantifying and Valuing Land Use Change for Integrated Catchment Management Evaluation in the Murray–Darling Basin 1996/97–2000/01', Report to the Murray–Darling Basin Commission, CSIRO and Murray–Darling Basin Commission, 2004.

19 Other major land uses across the remainder of the country include nature conservation (6.9%), other protected areas including indigenous uses (12.8%) and minimal use land (15.2%).

20 ibid.

21 DJ Pannell, MA Ewing & AM Ridley, 'Dryland Salinity in Australia: Overview and Prospects', CRC for Plant-based Management of Dryland Salinity, 2004, p. 4.

22 ibid.

23 'Australian Dryland Salinity Assessment 2000: Extent, Impacts, Processes, Monitoring and Management Options', National Land and Water Resources

Audit, Australian Dryland Salinity, Land and Water Australia,
www.anra.gov.au/topics/salinity/pubs/national/salinity_aus.html

24 The three initiatives are the National Action Plan for Salinity and Water
Quality, the Cooperative Research Centre for Plant-based Management of
Dryland Salinity and Land and Water Australia's National Dryland Salinity
Program, which was completed in 2003.

25 G Walker, M Gilfedder & J Williams, 'Effectiveness of Current Farming
Systems in the Control of Dryland Salinity', CSIRO Land & Water,
Canberra, 1999.

26 ATP Ivey, 'The Current Cost of Dryland Salinity to Agricultural
Landholders', report to the Murray–Darling Basin Commission and the
National Dryland Salinity Program, 2002.

27 The Pesticide Impact Rating Index (PIRI), CSIRO, www.clw.csiro.au/
research/biogeochemistry/organics/projects/piri.html.

28 Australian State of the Environment Committee, 'Australian State of the
Environment 2001', Australian Government Department of the
Environment, Water, Heritage & the Arts, Canberra, 2001, p. 115.

29 Queensland Government Department of Natural Resources and Water, 'Soil
Acidification', Factsheet, 2006.

30 'Land Theme: Soil Acidification', State of the Environment Report 2007,
Western Australia, 2007.

31 T Davis, 'Agricultural Water Use and River Basin Conservation', WWF, 2003,
www.panda.org.

32 Murray–Darling Basin Commission, 'State of the Darling—Interim
Hydrology Report', www.mdbc.gov.au/news/darling_report_2007.

33 Cubbie Group Ltd, viewed June 2007, www.cubbie.com.au.

34 B Haisman, 'Macquarie Marshes, Murray–Darling Basin, Australia',
contributing paper for the World Commission on Dams Thematic Reviews,
Murray–Darling Basin Commission, 2000.

35 P Olsen & M Weston, 'South Eastern Australia', *The State of Australia's Birds
2004*, Birds Australia, Melbourne, 2004, p. 14.

36 'Save the Macquarie Marshes', National Parks Association of New South
Wales, www.npansw.org.au/web/conservation/marshes/marshes.htm.

37 'Macquarie Marshes Project Briefing Notes', National Parks Association of
New South Wales, www.npansw.org.au/web/conservation/marshes/
briefing.htm.

38 Soth, 'Agriculture and Environment: Cotton', 1999, cited on WWF website,
www.panda.org.

39   'Macquarie Marshes Project Briefing Notes', www.npansw.org.au/web/
      conservation/marshes/briefing.htm; J Oltjen & J Beckett, 'Beef:
      Environmental Impacts of Production, Water Use and Quality', cited on
      WWF website, www.panda.org. This figure is based on studies in the United
      States but is likely to be similar to Australian figures.

40   Australian Government Department of the Environment, Water, Heritage &
      the Arts, 'Water for Agriculture', Canberra, viewed August 2007,
      www.environment.gov.au/water/agriculture/index.html.

41   National Water Initiative, Australian Government National Water Commission,
      www.nwc.gov.au/nwi/index.cfm

5 The Bad and the Ugly

1   Australian Biosecurity Group, 'Invasive Weeds, Pests and Diseases: Solutions to
      Secure Australia', CRC for Pest Animal Control/Australian Weed
      Management and WWF-Australia, Canberra, 2005, p. 3.

2   ibid.

3   'Facts and Figures: Environmental and Agricultural Weeds', CRC for
      Australian Weed Management, www.weedscrc.org.au/index_flash.html.

4   'Weeds of National Significance, Weed Management Guide, Cabomba
      (*Cabomba caroliniana*)', CRC for Australian Weed Management, Canberra, 2003.

5   'Weeds of National Significance, Weed Management Guide, Salivinia (*Salvinia
      molesta*)', CRC for Australian Weed Management, Canberra, 2003.

6   'Native Plants as Weeds', Eurobodalla Shire Council, www.esc.nsw.gov.au/
      Weeds/NativePlantsAsWeeds.htm.

7   Weed Society of Victoria, 'Can Australian Native Plants Be Weeds?', viewed
      2 March 2001, www.wsvic.org.au/w_news.php#five.

8   Queensland Government Department of Primary Industries & Fisheries,
      'Umbrella tree (*Schefflera actinophylla*)', www.dpi.qld.gov.au/cps/rde/xchg/
      dpi/hs.xsl/4790_7369_ENA_HTML.htm.

9   A Glanznig, personal communication, June 2007.

10   Australian Government Department of the Environment, Water, Heritage &
      the Arts, 'Weeds of National Significance: Weed Management Guide: Rubber
      Vine (*Cryptostegia grandiflora*)', Canberra, 2003.

11   ibid.

12   ibid.

13   JF Chippendale, in AP Mackey (ed.), *Rubber Vine (*Cryptostegia grandiflora*) in
      Queensland*, Pest Status Review Series, Queensland Department of Natural
      Resources and Mines. 1996.

14 'Cumberland Plain Woodland', Endangered Ecological Community Information Factsheet, New South Wales National Parks & Wildlife Service, 2004.

15 'Weeds of National Significance: Weed Management Guide: Bridal Creeper (*Asparagus asparoides*)', CRC for Australian Weed Management, Canberra, 2003.

16 'Threatened Plants and Animals: Richmond Birdwing Butterfly (*Ornithoptera richmondia*)', Environment Protection Agency/Queensland Parks & Wildlife Service, www.epa.qld.gov.au/nature_conservation/wildlife/threatened_ plants_and_animals/vulnerable/richmond_birdwing_butterfly/.

17 A Petroeschevsky, 'Water Weeds', *Australian Farm Journal BUSH*, May 2004.

18 'Weeds of National Significance: Weed Management Guide: Cabomba (*Cabomba caroliniana*)', CRC for Australian Weed Management, Canberra, 2003.

19 'Facts and Figures: Environmental and Agricultural Weeds', CRC for Australian Weed Management, Canberra, www.weedscrc.org.au/index_ flash.html.

20 A Glanznig, personal communication, June 2007.

21 W Truss, 'Keeping Wild Camel and Deer on the Back Hoof', Australian Government Department of Agriculture, Fisheries & Forestry, Canberra, 2005.

22 Australian Government Department for the Environment, Water, Heritage & the Arts, 'The Feral Camel (*Camelus dromedariu*)', Factsheet, Canberra, 2004.

23 Australian Biosecurity Group, 'Invasive Weeds, Pests and Diseases: Solutions to Secure Australia', CRC for Pest Animal Control/Australian Weed Management and WWF–Australia, Canberra, 2005, p. 11.

24 CSIRO Australia, 'The Northern Pacific Sea Star', Information Sheet, CSIRO Marine Research, 2005.

25 Australian Biosecurity Group, 'Invasive Weeds, Pests and Diseases: Solutions to Secure Australia', p. 11.

26 ibid.

27 M Lintermans, 'Human-assisted Dispersal of Alien Freshwater Fish in Australia', *New Zealand Journal of Marine and Freshwater Research*, Wellington, 2004.

28 Australian Biosecurity Group, 'Invasive Weeds, Pests and Diseases: Solutions to Secure Australia'.

29 Australian Government Department of the Environment, Water, Heritage & the Arts, 'Feral Animals in Australia', Factsheet, Canberra, 2006.

30 Australian Government Department of the Environment, Water, Heritage & the Arts, 'European Wild Rabbit (*Oryctolagus cuniculus*)', Factsheet, Canberra, 2004.

31   R Paltridge & S McAlpin, *A Guide to Rare and Threatened Animals in Central Australia*, WWF-Australia, Sydney, 2002, p. 4.

32   ibid., p. 67.

33   State Library of Western Australia, 'Western Perspectives on a Nation: The Rabbit Proof Fence', www.liswa.wa.gov.au/wepon/land/html/rabbits.html.

34   'Rabbits Blamed for Penguin Deaths in Landslide', ABC News Online, viewed 21 October 2006; www.tnpa.asn.au/macquarie/Rabbitinduced landslides22006.pdf.

35   M-L Considine, 'Politics Adds to Macquarie Island's Pest Problem', *ECOS* no. 136, April–May 2007.

36   Australian Government Biodiversity Group Environment Australia, 'Threat Abatement Plan for Predation by Feral Cats', Canberra, 1999.

37   Australian Government Department of the Environment, Water, Heritage & the Arts, 'The European Red Fox (*Vulpes vulpes*)', Factsheet, Canberra, 2004.

38   Australian Government Department of the Environment, Water, Heritage & the Arts, 'The Feral Cat (*Felis catus*)', Factsheet, Canberra, 2004.

39   ibid.

40   'The European Red Fox (*Vulpes vulpes*)', Pest Animal Control CRC, www.feral.org.au/content/species/fox.cfm.

41   R Paltridge & S McAlpin, *A Guide to Rare and Threatened Animals in Central Australia*, WWF-Australia, Sydney, 2002.

6 Stealthy Threats

1   'Save the Tasmanian Devil: Tasmanian Devil Facial Tumour Disease', Department of Primary Industries & Water, Tasmania, viewed 4 December 2007, www.tassiedevil.com.au.

2   ibid.

3   ibid.

4   'Weeds, Pests and Diseases: Hard Evidence of Foxes Discovered in Tasmania', Department of Primary Industries & Water, Tasmania, 2007 (current at 21 December 2007).

5   'Weeds, Pests and Diseases: Threats Posed by Foxes in Tasmania', Department of Primary Industries & Water, Tasmania, 2007 (current at 21 December 2007).

6   Australian Government Department of the Environment, Water, Heritage & the Arts, 'Invasive Species: Phytophthora Root Rot', Factsheet, Canberra, 2004.

7   R Carter, *Arresting Phytophthora Dieback: The Biological Bulldozer*, WWF-Australia and the Dieback Consultative Council, 2004, p. 13.

8   ibid., p. 5.

9   'Biodiversity Hotspots—Southwest Australia—Unique Biodiversity—Diversity and Endemism', Conservation International, 2007; R Carter, p. 2.

10   R Carter, p. 2.

11   R Strahan (ed.), 'Yellow-footed Antechinus' in R Strachan (ed.), *The Mammals of Australia*, Smithsonian Institution Press, Washington, DC, 1995, pp. 86–8.

12   R Carter, p. 10.

13   C Weldon, LH du Preez, AD Hyatt, R Muller & R Speare, 'Origin of the Amphibian Chytrid Fungus', Emerging Infectious Diseases (online series), Centers for Disease Control and Prevention, Atlanta, www.cdc.gov/ncidod/EID/vol10no12/03-0804.htm.

14   Australian Government Department of the Environment, Water, Heritage & the Arts, 'Chytridiomycosis (Amphibian Chytrid Fungus Disease)', Factsheet, Canberra, 2004.

15   C Weldon, LH du Preez, AD Hyatt, R Muller & R Speare.

16   'Chytrid Fungus', Frogs Australia Network, frogsaustralia.net.au/conservation/disease.cfm.

17   R Speare & L Berger, 'Chytridiomycosis Status of Wild Amphibians in Australia', viewed 26 January 2005, www.jcu.edu.au/school/phtm/PHTM/frogs/chy-au-status.htm.

18   L Berger, R Speare, P Daszak, DE Green, AA Cunningham, CL Goggin, R Slocombe, MA Ragan, AD Hyatt, KR McDonald, HB Hines, KR Lips, G Marantelli & H Parkes, 'Chytridiomycosis Causes Amphibian Mortality Associated with Population Declines in the Rainforests of Australia and Central America', *Proceedings of the National Academy of Science USA*, 21 July 1998, 95(15), pp. 9031–36.

19   Australian Frog Database, Frogs Australia Network, www.frogsaustralia.net.au/frogs/millsap.cfm.

20   K McDonald, personal communication, December 2007.

21   '*Rheobatrachus silus*', Australian Frog Database, Frogs Australia Network, www.frogsaustralia.net.au/frogs/display.cfm?frog_id=84.

22   '*Rheobatrachus vitellinus*', Australian Frog Database, Frogs Australia Network, www.frogsaustralia.net.au/frogs/display.cfm?frog_id=85.

23   MJ Tyler, 'The Action Plan for Australian Frogs', National Parks & Wildlife Service, Canberra, 1997.

24   IR Lawler, WJ Foley, IE Woodrow & SJ Cork, 'The Effects of Elevated CO_2 Atmospheres on the Nutritional Quality of Eucalyptus Foliage and Its Interaction with Soil Nutrient and Light Availability', *Oecologia*, vol. 109(1), December 1996.

25   'Farm Pests and Diseases: Hendra Virus', CSIRO, www.csiro.au/science/
     HendraVirus.html.
26   'Hendra Virus (Equine morbillivirus): Emergence and Subsequent Equine
     Cases; Experimental Studies; Fruit Bats As Natural Hosts', Department of
     Primary Industries & Fisheries, Queensland Government, 2007.
27   H Field, P Young, Johara Mohd Yob, J Mills, L Hall & J Mackenzie, 'The
     Natural History of Hendra and Nipah Viruses', *Microbes and Infection* no. 3,
     2001, pp. 315–22.
28   HE Field, AC Breed, J Shield, RM Hedlefs, K Pittard, B Pott & PM Summers,
     'Epidemiological Perspectives on Hendra Virus Infection in Horses and
     Flying Foxes', *Australian Veterinary Journal*, no. 85, 2007, pp. 268–72.
29   BJ McCall, JH Epstein, AS Neill, K Heel, H Field, J Barrett, GA Smith,
     LA Selvey, B Rodwell, & R Lunt, 'Potential Human Exposure to Australian
     Bat Lyssavirus, Queensland, 1996–1999', Emerging Infectious Diseases
     (online series), Centers for Disease Control and Prevention, Atlanta, 2000,
     http://www.ncbi.nlm.nih.gov/pubmed/10827115.
30   ibid.
31   AW Philbey, PD Kirkland, AD Ross, RJ Davis, AB Gleeson, RJ Love,
     PW Daniels, AR Gould & AD Hyatt, 'An Apparently New Virus (Family
     Paramyxoviridae) Infectious for Pigs, Humans and Fruit Bats', Emerging
     Infectious Diseases, (online series), Centers for Disease Control and
     Prevention, Atlanta, 1998, www.cdc.gov/ncidod/eid/vol4no2/philbey.htm.
32   'Hendra Virus Has a Growing Family Tree', Media Release, CSIRO
     Livestock Industries and the Australian Animal Health Laboratory, 18 July
     2001.
33   Australian Biosecurity Group, 'Invasive Weeds, Pests and Diseases: Solutions to
     Secure Australia', CRC for Pest Animal Control/Australian Weed
     Management and WWF-Australia, Canberra, 2005, p. 12.
34   'Weed Management Guide: Siam Weed or Chromolaena (*Chromolaena odorata*)',
     CRC for Australian Weed Management, 2003.

7 More Frightening Than a Science Fiction Movie

1   KG McLeod, DL Whitney, BT Huber & C Koeberl, 'Impact and Extinction
    in Remarkably Complete Cretaceous-Tertiary Boundary Sections from
    Demerara Rise, Tropical Western North Atlantic', *Geological Society of America
    Bulletin*, vol. 119 (1), January 2007.
2   M Schulz, 'Cash Help Worth $8500 for Cranbourne Methane Gas Leak
    Victims', *Herald Sun*, viewed 12 September 2008, www.heraldsun.com.au.

3   'Climate Change 1995: The Science of Climate Change', IPCC Working
     Group 1, Intergovernmental Panel on Climate Change, Geneva, Switzerland,
     1995.

4   'Climate Change 2007: The Physical Science Basis', IPCC Working Group 1,
     Intergovernmental Panel on Climate Change, Geneva, Switzerland, 2007.

5   A Max, 'UN Panel Gives Dire Warning Forecast', ABC News Online,
     17 November 2007.

6   R Reynolds, 'Warnings from the Bush', Climate Action Network Australia,
     Sydney, 2001.

7   'National Recovery Plan for the Southern Corroboree Frog (*Pseudophryne
     corroboree*)', New South Wales National Parks & Wildlife Service, Department
     of the Environment, Water, Heritage & the Arts, Canberra, 2001.

8   G Gillespie, personal communication, December 2007.

9   JP Stanton, PD Bostock, KR McDonald, GL Werren & A Fleming,
     'Queensland Wet Tropics' in *Hotspots Revisited: Earth's Biologically Richest and
     Most Endangered Terrestrial Ecoregions*, Conservation International and
     University of Virginia, Washington, DC, 2004.

10   'Rainforests and Climate Change', interview with John Konowski, *Earthbeat*,
     ABC Radio National, viewed 4 September 1999, www.abc.net.au/rn/
     science/earth/stories/s51963.htm.

11   ibid.

12   'The Tipping Point', interview with Stephen Williams, *Catalyst*, ABC TV,
     viewed 25 May 2006, www.abc.net.au/catalyst/stories/s1647466.htm.

13   Australian Government Department of the Environment, Water, Heritage
     & the Arts, 'World Heritage: The Great Barrier Reef', Canberra,
     www.environment.gov.au/heritage/worldheritage/sites/gbr/index.html.

14   'Threats to the Reef: Water Quality and Catchment Run-off', CRC Reef
     Research Centre, viewed 9 January 2008, www.reef.crc.org.au/discover/
     threats/index.html.

15   'Biology of Coral Bleaching', CRC Reef Research Centre, www.reef
     .crc.org.au/discover/coralreefs/bleaching/coralbleachingbiology.html.

16   'Coral Bleaching on the Great Barrier Reef', Great Barrier Reef Marine
     Park Authority, www.gbrmpa.gov.au/corp_site/key_issues/climate_change/
     climate_change_and_the_great_barrier_reef.

17   J Loney, 'Acid Seas May Kill Coral Reefs in Fifty Years', ABC News in
     Science/Reuters, 14 December 2007.

18   'Climate Change Solutions for Australia', The Australian Climate Group,
     WWF-Australia and Insurance Australia Group, Sydney, 2004.

19   GJ Hughes, 'Meeting the Challenge of Climate Variability in a Major Water Supply System', *Water Supply*, vol. 3 (3), 2003, pp. 201–07.

20   'Biodiversity Hotspots: Southwest Australia', Conservation International, 2007, www.biodiversityhotspots.org/xp/Hotspots/australia/biodiversity.xml.

21   L Hughes, M Westoby & M Cawsey, 'Climatic Range Sizes of Eucalyptus Species in Relation to Future Climate Change', *Global Ecology and Biogeography Letters*, no. 5, 1996, pp. 23–9.

22   'Building Resilience to Climate Change for Australia's Species and Ecosystems', Threatened Species Network Factsheet, WWF-Australia, September 2006.

23   F Ratcliffe, 'Notes on the Fruit Bats (*Pteropus*) in Australia', *Journal of Animal Ecology*, no.1, 1932, pp. 32–57; N Markus, C Palmer & LS Hall, 'Black Flying-fox Pteropus alecto' in R Strahan (ed.), *Mammals of Australia*, Reed New Holland, Sydney, 2008, pp. 435–6.

24   N Markus & L Hall, 'Foraging Behaviour of the Black Flying-fox (*Pteropus alecto*) in the Urban Landscape of Brisbane, Queensland', *Wildlife Research*, (31), 2004, pp. 345–55.

25   J Welbergen, S Klose, N Markus & P Eby, 'Climate Change and the Effects of Temperature Extremes on Australian Flying Foxes', *Proceedings of the Royal Society*, doi. 10.1098/rspb.2007.1385, 2007.

26   Australian Bureau of Meteorology, as cited in A Reynolds, 'Warnings from the Bush', Climate Action Network Australia, Sydney, 2002.

27   Kimberley Regional Fire Management Project, as cited in A Reynolds, 'Warnings from the Bush', Climate Action Network Australia, Sydney, 2002.

28   C Palmer, as cited in A Reynolds, 'Warnings from the Bush', Climate Action Network Australia, Sydney, 2002.

8 Is It All an Act?

1   Lake Pedder Restoration Committee, www.lakepedder.org.

2   'History of the Franklin River Campaign 1976–1983', The Wilderness Society, viewed 2001, www.wilderness.org.au/campaigns/wildrivers/franklin/franklin/.

3   ibid.

4   'Logging Melbourne's Water Catchment', The Wilderness Society, viewed 2001, www.wilderness.org.au/campaigns/forests/victoria/central_highlands/water; The Save Ningaloo Campaign, Conservation Council of Western Australia, www.save-ningaloo.org/; Great Barrier Reef, WWF-Australia, wwf.org.au/ourwork/oceans/gbr.

5   *Flora and Fauna Guarantee Act 1988*, Department of Sustainability &
    Environment, Vic., www.dpi.vic.gov.au/DSE/nrenpa.nsf/FID/-
    0488335CD48EC1424A2567C10006BF6D?OpenDocument.

6   Senator Robert Hill, 'Environmental Cringe? Why Australia's Environmental
    Achievements Receive More Recognition Abroad Than They Do at Home',
    address to The Sydney Institute, 10 February 2000, viewed March 2007,
    www.deh.gov.au/minister/env/2000/spfeb00.html.

7   Australian Government Department of the Environment, Water, Heritage &
    the Arts, *Environment Protection and Biodiversity Conservation Act 1999*,
    Canberra, www.environment.gov.au/epbc/about/index.html.

8   Australian Government Department of the Environment, Water, Heritage &
    the Arts, 'Directions for the National Reserve System: A Partnership
    Approach', Natural Resource Ministerial Council, Canberra, 2004.

9   P Garrett, the Hon. Minister for the Environment, Heritage & the Arts,
    '$180 million to Build the National Reserve System', Media Release,
    viewed 31 March 2008, www.environment.gov.au/minister/garrett/2008/
    pubs/mr20080331.pdf.

10 N Beynon, M Kennedy & A Graham, 'Grumpy Old Greenies: Lament
    Waiting Lists, Wasted Opportunities and Wayward Pork-barrelling in
    Australia's Biodiversity Programs'. Paper presented at the Environmental
    Defenders Office (EDO) National Environmental Law Conference, Sydney,
    2005, p. 9.

11 *Environment Protection and Biodiversity Conservation Act 1999*, Activity Report,
    30 June 2006.

12 Regional Forest Agreements are documents that set out 20-year strategies for
    forestry use and management by all stakeholders including forestry and
    plantation industries, private landholders, conservation agencies and others.
    Ten agreements across four states—New South Wales, Tasmania, Victoria and
    Western Australia—were signed between 1997 and 2001 following ostensibly
    comprehensive assessments of the economic, social and environment values of
    each region and to provide surety of use for all concerned. The RFA process
    is an initiative that involved all Australian governments and the agreements
    are now administered by the states. For more, go to www.daff.gov.au/rfa;
    C McGrath, 'Review of the *EPBC Act*', paper prepared for 2006 Australian
    State of the Environment Committee, Australian Government Department of
    the Environment, Water, Heritage & the Arts, Canberra, 2006.

13 *EPBC Act 1999*, Activity Report, 30 June 2006.

14 A McIntosh & D Wilkinson, '*Environment Protection and Biodiversity
    Conservation Act*: A Five Year Assessment', The Australia Institute, Sydney, 2005.

15 *EPBC Act 1999*, Activity Report, 30 June 2006.

16 ibid.

17 'The Conservation and Protection of Nationally Threatened Species and Ecological Communities', Australian National Audit Office, Canberra, 29 March 2007.

18 Minister for the Environment & Heritage v. Greentree (no. 3), Federal Court of Australia [2004] FCA 1317, viewed 14 October 2004, www.austlii.edu.au/au/cases/cth/federal_ct/2004/1317.

19 L Kennedy, 'Wind up Report for the EPBC Project', unpublished report, WWF-Australia, 2006.

20 L Kennedy, personal communication, February 2007.

21 2002–03 is the most recent year for available figures on local government environmental expenditure; S Wild River, 'The Role of Local Government in Environmental and Heritage Management', article for 2006 State of the Environment Committee, Australian Government Department of the Environment, Water, Heritage & the Arts, Canberra, 2006, pp. 13–14.

22 'National Action Plan for Salinity and Water Quality', Australian Government, www.napswq.gov.au/.

23 Natural Heritage Trust, Australian Government, 2007, www.nht.gov.au/nht/index.html.

24 'The Conservation and Protection of Nationally Threatened Species and Ecological Communities', Australian National Audit Office, 29 March 2007.

25 'Natural Resource Management Funding: Caring for our Country', Australian Government, www.nrm.gov.au/funding/future.html.

9 Sounds Like a Plan

1 *Environment Protection and Biodiversity Conservation Act 1999*, Australian Government Department of the Environment, Water, Heritage & the Arts, Canberra, www.environment.gov.au/epbc/about/index.html.

2 MA Burgman, 'Are Listed Threatened Plant Species Actually at Risk?, *Australian Journal of Botany*, 50(1), 2002, pp. 1–13.

3 Orange-bellied Parrot Recovery Team, 'Orange-bellied Parrot Recovery Plan 1998–2002', Parks & Wildlife Service, Hobart, www.environment.gov.au/biodiversity/threatened/publications/recovery/orange-bel-parrot/index.html.

4 PB Brown & RI Wilson, 'Orange-bellied Parrot Recovery Plan', National Parks & Wildlife Service, Tasmania, 1984; L Stephenson, 'The Orange-bellied Parrot Recovery Plan—Management Phase', Department of Parks, Wildlife & Heritage, Hobart, 1991; 'Orange-bellied Parrot Recovery Plan 1998–2002'.

5   Orange-bellied Parrot Recovery Team, 'Background and Implementation Information for the Orange-bellied Parrot Recovery Plan', Parks & Wildlife Service, Hobart, p. 22, www.environment.gov.au/biodiversity/threatened/publications/pubs/orange-bellied-parrot-recovery-background.pdf.

6   'Orange-bellied Parrot Recovery Plan 1998–2002'.

7   ibid.

8   'Background and Implementation Information for the Orange-bellied Parrot Recovery Plan.'

9   A Burbidge & G Kuchling, 'Western Swamp Tortoise (*Pseudemydura umbrina*) Recovery Plan 2003–2007', Department of Conservation & Land Management, Western Australia, 2004.

10 T Friend, personal communication to Katherine Miller, March 2007.

11 M Schulz & LF Lumsden, 'National Recovery Plan for the Christmas Island Pipistrelle (*Pipistrellus murrayi*)', Commonwealth of Australia, Canberra, 2004.

12 I Campbell, The Hon. Minister for the Environment & Heritage, '$3.2 million to Save the Orange-bellied Parrot', media release, 29 August 2006.

13 'Campbell "playing politics" with Parrot', *Age*, 29 August 2006.

14 HP Possingham, The Business of Biodiversity: Applying Decision Theory Principles to Nature Conservation, Tela Series, Australian Conservation Foundation, 2001, p. 14.

15 ibid.

16 ibid.

17 A Burbidge, personal communication, August 2007.

18 P Eby, personal communication, August 2007.

19 *Environment Protection and Biodiversity Conservation Act 1999*—Threatened Species and Ecological Communities Listings, viewed May 2007, www.environment.gov.au/biodiversity/threatened/index.html.

20 'Southern Corroboree Frog', Threatened Species Information, New South Wales National Parks & Wildlife Service, 1999.

21 'National Recovery Plan for Albatrosses and Giant Petrels', Wildlife Scientific Advice, Australian Government Department of the Environment, Water, Heritage & the Arts, Canberra, 2001.

22 Northern Queensland Threatened Frogs Recovery Team, 'Recovery Plan for the Stream-dwelling Rainforest Frogs of the Wet Tropics Biogeographic Region of North East Queensland 2000–2004', report to Environment Australia, Canberra, Queensland Parks & Wildlife Service, Brisbane, 2001.

23 D Keith, 'National Recovery Plan for Tasmanian Forest Epacrids 1999–2004', Tasmanian Parks & Wildlife Service, 1997.

24 DJ Coates & KA Atkins, 'Priority Setting and the Conservation of Western Australia's Diverse and Highly Endemic Flora', *Biological Conservation*, no. 97, 2001, p. 257.

25 'National Recovery Plan for Natural Temperate Grasslands of the Southern Tablelands (NSW and ACT): An Endangered Ecological Community', Environment ACT, Commonwealth of Australia, 2005.

26 ibid.

27 S Moore & S Wooller, 'Review of Landscape, Multi-and Single Species Recovery Planning for Threatened Species', WWF-Australia, Canberra, 2003.

28 PD Boersma, P Kareiva, WF Fagan, JA Clark and JM Hoekstra, 'How Good Are Endangered Species Recovery Plans?, *BioScience*, no. 51 (8), 2001, pp. 643–9.

29 S Moore & S Wooller, 'Review of Landscape, Multi-and Single Species Recovery Planning for Threatened Species'.

30 JA Clark & E Harvey, 'Assessing Multi-species Recovery Plans under the *Endangered Species Act*', *Ecological Applications*, 12(3), 2002, pp. 655–62; LR Gerber & LT Hatch, 'Are We Recovering? An Evaluation of the Recovery Criteria under the US *Endangered Species Act*', *Ecological Applications*, 12(3), 2002, pp. 668–73.

31 Some species have in fact been removed from the lists, but not due to an improvement in conservation status. Removals have occurred where species have been reclassified and listed as a different population (such as the grey nurse shark with east- and west-coast populations; only east coast is critically endangered); found to be a hybrid, not a species (Albany woolybush); found to have restricted but stable populations (spiral-leaved daviesia); or where substantial new populations have been discovered (spiny bentleya).

32 A Burbidge, personal communication, September 2007.

10 A Band-aid Won't Do

1 S Morton et al., 2002, 'Sustaining Our Natural Systems and Biodiversity: An Independent Report to the Prime Minister's Science, Engineering and Innovation Council', CSIRO and Environment Australia, Canberra, 2002.

2 H Possingham, S Ryan, J Baxter and S Morton, 'Setting Biodiversity Priorities', paper prepared as part of activities of working group producing the report 'Sustaining Our Natural Systems and Biodiversity' for the Prime Minister's Science, Engineering and Innovation Council, 2002.

3 ibid.

4   *WWF-Australia Annual Report 2005*, WWF-Australia, p. 5, www.wwf.org.au/
     publications/annual_report_2005.

5   C Pavey, 'National Recovery Plan for the Greater Bilby (*Macrotis lagotis*)',
     Northern Territory Department of Natural Resources, Environment & the
     Arts, 2006.

6   'Bilbies Reclaim Homeland in WA's Goldfields', *Nature Base News*, 14 August
     2007.

7   'Recovery Plan for the Southern Cassowary (*Casuarius casuarius johnsonii*)
     2001–2005', Queensland Parks & Wildlife Service, Brisbane, 2002.

8   'National Recovery Plan for Albatrosses and Giant Petrels', Wildlife Scientific
     Advice, Australian Government Department of the Environment, Water,
     Heritage & the Arts, Canberra, 2001.

9   'Threat Abatement Plan 2006: Bycatch of Seabirds for the Incidental Catch
     (or By-catch) of Seabirds during Oceanic Longline Fishing Operations',
     Australian Government Department of the Environment, Water, Heritage &
     the Arts, Canberra, 2006.

10. The threat abatement plan for tramp ants incorporates the listed threats of
     the yellow crazy ant and the red fire ant.

11   *Environment Protection and Biodiversity Conservation Act 1999*, Approved Threat
     Abatement Plans, www.environment.gov.au/biodiversity/threatened/
     tap-approved.html.

12   'New Marine Debris Report and Net Kit Highlight Deadly Problem',
     WWF-Australia, media release, 21 June 2004.

13   J Miller, personal communication, August 2007.

14   M Turnbull, The Hon. Minister for the Environment & Water Resources,
     'Agreement to Eradicate Rabbits on Macquarie Island', media release,
     June 2007.

15   'Terrestrial Products and Strategies: Research Program—Cane Toad Research',
     Invasive Animals CRC, www.invasiveanimals.com/research/terrestrial_
     products_and_strategies/index.html.

16   'The Impact of Introduced Terrestrial and Aquatic Animals upon Native
     Fauna and Flora', Mount King Ecological Surveys Report to the Australian
     National Parks & Wildlife Service, April 1992.

17   The second introduced species of trout, the rainbow trout, was not
     investigated in this report but might have a similar impact to that of the
     brown trout.

18   'The Impact of Introduced Terrestrial and Aquatic Animals upon Native
     Fauna and Flora.'

19   BJ Traill, personal communication, October 2007.

20   'The Impact of Introduced Terrestrial and Aquatic Animals upon Native Fauna and Flora', p. 79.

21   *Australia and the Environment* (cat. no. 4601.0), Australian Bureau of Statistics, Canberra, 1996.

22   'Threat Abatement Plan for Predation by the European Red Fox', Biodiversity Group Environment Australia, Australian Government Department of the Environment, Water, Heritage & the Arts, Canberra, 1999.

23   The Fox in Tasmania: A Threat to Stock and Wildlife Alike', Factsheet, Parks & Wildlife Service, Department of Primary Industries, Water & the Environment, Hobart, 2002.

24   Australian Government Department of the Environment, Water, Heritage & the Arts, 'Draft Threat Abatement Plan for Predation by the European Red Fox', Canberra, 2007.

25   G Saunders, personal communication, September 2007.

26   R McLeod, 'Counting the Cost: Impact of Invasive Animals in Australia 2004', CRC for Pest Animal Control, 2004.

27   'Biodiversity Hotspots: Southwest Australia', Conservation International, Washington, DC, www.biodiversityhotspots.org/xp/Hotspots/australia/pages/biodiversity.aspx.

28   *Nature Base*, Western Shield Project, Department of Environment and Conservation, Western Australia, www.dec.wa.gov.au/programs/western-shield/index.html.

29   H Possingham, P Jarman & A Kearns, 'Independent Review of Western Shield: Report of the Review Panel', Department of Environment & Conservation, Western Australia, 2003.

30   A Burbidge, personal communication, September 2007.

31   'Ecological Consequences of High Frequency Fires: Key Threatening Process Listing', New South Wales Scientific Committee, NSW Department of Environment & Climate Change, 24 March 2000.

32   Department of Environment and Climate Change, 2007, 'Introducing the New South Wales Priority Action Statement (PAS)', DECC, Sydney, http://www.environment.nsw.gov.au/resources/threatenedspecies/threatspecpas07168.pdf.

33   Hotspots Fire Project, Nature Conservation Council of New South Wales, www.nccnsw.org.au/index.php?option=com_content&task=view&id=1115&Itemid=642.

34   W Parker, personal communication, September 2007.

11 Future Bequests

1   S Driml, cited in 'Directions for the National Reserve System: A Partnership Approach', Natural Resource Management Ministerial Council, Australian Government Department of the Environment, Water, Heritage & the Arts, Canberra, 2004.

2   'Sustaining Life on Earth: How the Convention on Biological Diversity Promotes Nature and Human Well-being', Convention on Biological Diversity and United Nations Environment Program, viewed 8 August 2007, www.cbd.int/convention/guide.shtml.

3   'Protected Areas', Programmes, Secretariat of the Convention on Biological Diversity, viewed 18 September 2007, www.cbd.int/protected/intro.shtml.

4   'Directions for the National Reserve System: A Partnership Approach', Natural Resource Management Ministerial Council, Australian Government Department of the Environment, Water, Heritage & the Arts, Canberra, 2004, p. 13.

5   ibid.

6   PS Sattler & A Glanznig, 'Building Nature's Safety Net: A Review of Australia's Terrestrial Protected Area System 1991–2004', WWF-Australia, Sydney, 2006, p. 21.

7   ibid, p. 24.

8   'Directions for the National Reserve System: A Partnership Approach', Natural Resource Management Ministerial Council, Australian Government Department of the Environment, Water, Heritage & the Arts, Canberra, 2004, p. 15.

9   ibid.

10 PS Sattler & A Glanznig, p. 53.

11 ibid, p. 51.

12 'Directions for the National Reserve System: A Partnership Approach.'

13 PS Sattler & A Glanznig.

14 ibid.

15 Gazetted SEQFA and Wet Tropics forest reserves, Environmental Protection Agency, Queensland Government, viewed 6 November 2007, www.epa.qld.gov.au/publications?id=2016.

16 P Sattler, personal communication, October 2007.

17 PS Sattler & A Glanznig.

18 'Aborigines Win Veto on Kakadu Uranium Mining', Sydney Morning Herald, viewed 25 February 2005, www.smh.com.au/news/Business/Aborigines-win-veto-on-Kakadu-uranium-mining/2005/02/25/1109180079111.html.

19   'Fish Boats Barred from One-third of Great Barrier Reef', Environment News Service, viewed 1 July 2004, www.ens-newswire.com/ens/jul2004/2004-07-01-06.asp.

20   'Land Tenure', *Geoscience Australia*, viewed 25 September 2007, www.ga.gov.au/education/facts/tenure.htm.

21   'Covenants for Conservation', Information Leaflet, Australian Government Department of the Environment, Water, Heritage & the Arts, Canberra, 2004.

22   FAQs: What Land Can Be Covenanted?, Trust for Nature, www.trustfornature.org.au/faqResult.asp?id=17.

23   M Gooey, personal communication, October 2007.

24   Tasmanian Land Conservancy Newsletter, issue 14, Spring 2007, p. 4.

25   ibid.

26   PS Sattler & A Glanznig.

27   700,000 hectares is equivalent to about 0.0009 per cent of the country.

28   'Our Reserves', Bush Heritage Australia, www.bushheritage.org.au/our_reserves.

29   ibid.

30   'What Does AWC Do?', viewed October 2007, Australian Wildlife Conservancy, www.australianwildlife.org/whatwedo.asp.

31   Brooklyn Sanctuary, Australian Wildlife Conservancy, www.awc.org.au/AWC-Sanctuaries/Brooklyn-Sanctuary.aspx.

32   'Land—Environment', Australian Agricultural Company, 2005, viewed 16 November 2007, www.aaco.com.au/Environment.aspx.

33   Gondwana Link, www.gondwanalink.org.

34   'Global Conservation Groups Announce Major Effort to Protect Australia's Bush, Deserts and Oceans', media release, The Pew Charitable Trusts, viewed 23 July 2007, www.pewtrusts.org/news_room_ektid26436.aspx.

35   PS Sattler & A Glanznig.

36   ibid, p. 9.

12 Guards on Our Watch

1   Centennial Coal, 'Anvil Hill Mine Approved', media release, 7 June 2007.

2   2. 'Latham Pledges to Save Trees and Jobs', ABC News, viewed 4 October 2004, www.abc.net.au/news/stories/2004/10/04/1212801.htm.

3   'Agricultural Economies of Australia and New Zealand', Australia Bureau of Resource Economics, viewed 23 October 2007, www.abareconomics.com/interactive/ausNZ_ag/htm/au_overview.htm.

4   P Hartcher & M Wade, 'Time to Walk Away', *Sydney Morning Herald*, 29–30 September 2007, p. 23.

5   S Marris, 'Farmers to Be Paid to Leave the Land', *Australian*, 25 September 2007.

6   P Hartcher & M Wade.

7   S Marris.

8   B Banerjee, *The Problem with Corporate Social Responsibility*, International Graduate School of Management, University of South Australia, 2004.

9   M Friedman, 'The Social Responsibility of Business Is to Increase Its Profits', *New York Times magazine*, 13 September 1970.

10   J Elkington, 'The Triple Bottom Line: Sustainability's Accountants', in *Cannibals with Forks: The Triple Bottom Line in Twenty-First Century Businesses*, New Society Publishers, British Columbia, 1998.

11   'Millennium Development Goals', United Nations Development Programme, viewed 16 October 2007, www.undp.org/mdg/basics.shtml.

12   'Green Choices', Tesco Corporate Responsibility Review 2007, www.tescocorporate.com/crreport07/11_charitiescom/charity.html.

13   'Australian Food Statistics 2005', Australian Bureau of Agriculture and Resource Economics, Department of Agriculture, Fisheries & Forestry, 2005; www.abareconomics.com/publicatons_html/economy/economy_05/foodstats05.pdf.

14   Domestic Markets—Retail and Foodservice, Meat and Livestock Australia, viewed 24 November 2007, www.mla.com.au/TopicHierarchy/MarketInformation/DomesticMarkets/Consumption/Retail.htm.

15   'Plastic Shopping Bags in Australia', Plastic Bags Working Group report to the National Packaging Covenant Council, Environment Protection and Heritage Council, 2002, p. 9.

16   'Policy Commission on the Future of Farming and Food', Advisory Committee on Consumer Products and the Environment, Department for Environment, Food & Rural Affairs, Canberra, 2002.

17   ibid, p. 1.

18   ibid, p. 3.

19   R Kendall, 'Greenpeace Tags "Bloody Poor" Companies', *Ethical Investor*, viewed 25 September 2002, www.ethicalinvestor.com.au.

20   CE Storer & FM Frost, 'Triple Bottom Line Reporting: Its Relevance and Application to Agricultural Production and Marketing', Curtin University of Technology, WA, 2002.

21   H Saddler, M Diesendorf & R Denniss, 'A Clean-Energy Future for Australia', WWF-Australia, Sydney, 2004.

22   The gazettal of these communities for assessment and listing was repealed by an amendment to the Act in December 2006.

23.   N Beynon, personal communication, October 2007.

24   N Beynon, M Kennedy & A Graham, 'Grumpy Old Greenies—Lament Waiting Lists, Wasted Opportunities and Wayward Pork-barreling in Australia's Biodiversity Programs', Humane Society International and Tasmanian Conservation Trust, 2006.

13 Heading in the Right Direction

1   US House of Representatives, cited in J Taylor & B Whelan, *An Introduction to Precision Agriculture*, Australian Centre for Precision Agriculture, University of Sydney, 1997.

2   'Precision Agriculture: Profiting from Variation', viewed 26 November 2007, CSIRO Sustainable Farming, www.csiro.au/science/PrecisionAgriculture.html.

3   P Andrews, *Back from the Brink: How Australia's Landscapes Can Be Saved*, ABC Books, Sydney, 2006.

4   ibid, p. 44.

5   ibid, p. 89.

6   ibid, p. 88.

7   'Passive Design' 'Passive Solar Heating', Factsheets, Australian Greenhouse Office, Canberra, 2005.

8   D Tabart, personal communication, November 2007.

9   D Hannah, 'Koala Beach Fauna Monitoring and Winter Fox Control Progress Report', Tweed Shire Council, New South Wales, 2007.

10   ibid.

11   Forest Stewardship Council, 'About FSC', viewed 21 November 2007, www.fsc.org.

12   Marine Stewardship Council, 2002, viewed 21 November 2007, www.msc.org/html/content_463.htm.

13   *Australia's Environment: Issues and Trends 2006* (cat. no. 4613.0), Australian Bureau of Statistics, Canberra, 2006.

14   See www.onearth.com.au/news1.htm for links and examples.

15   SK Pun, C Liu, C Langston, G Treloar and Y Itoh, 'Promoting the Reuse and Recycling of Building Demolition Materials', *World Transactions on Engineering and Technology Education*, vol. 5, no. 1, 2006.

16   J Pittman, 'Construction Industry Turning Green with Recycling Program', *Silicon Valley/San Jose Business Journal*, viewed 2 August 2002, www.bizjournals.com/sanjose/stories/2002/08/05/focus3.html?page=1.

17   ibid.

14 Ten Ways to Make a Difference

1 M Gladwell, *The Tipping Point: How Little Things Can Make a Big Difference*, Abacus, London, 2001.

2 General Assembly of the United Nations, Universal Declaration of Human Rights, adopted and proclaimed by United Nations General Assembly Resolution 217 A (III) of 10 December 1948.

3 Green Home—Eco-calculator, Australian Conservation Foundation, viewed November 2007, hwww.acfonline.org.au/custom_greenhome/calculator.asp?section_id=86.

ACKNOWLEDGEMENTS

This book could not have been written without the help of friends, former colleagues and experts in the many fields I have touched on, who also believed that this was a book worth writing. I am sincerely grateful to Peggy Eby, Averil Bones, Paul Gamblin, Richard Kingsford, Mike Weston, Andreas Glanznig, Damien Higgins, Hume Field, Hugh Possingham, Martin Denny, Peter Menkhorst, Lyndall Kennedy, Barry Traill, Richard McLellan, Chris Dickmann, Michael Kennedy, Graeme Gillespie, Graeme Saunders, Deborah Tabart, Linda Broome, Nicola Beynon, Christel Markus, Waminda Parker, Keith McDonald, Michael Mikov and my agent Pippa Masson, each of whom took the time to review and comment on specific sections of the text and to share their views, experiences and knowledge.

The thorough and critical scrutiny of specific chapters by Paul Sattler, Andrew Burbidge, Martin Schulz, Guy Fitzhardinge, Tony Trujillo and Greg Bourne led to lively and always useful discussions. Susanne Larson, Greg Bourne, Foong Ling Kong and Melanie Ostell provided constructive comments on the content, flow and readability of the text when I could no longer see the meaning for the words.

The opportunity to take a year out from other responsibilities to research and fully engage in a topic as complex as this one is precious and rare. My heartfelt thanks go to Greg Bourne and to the Purves Environmental Fund, both of whom provided financial support in the writing of this book and trusted me with its contents. It was written with one absolute conviction: that the world is run by those who show up.

INDEX

Aboriginal Australians, 18; culture, 128; land management practices, 29–30, 44, 46; Mirrar people, 158
Andrews, Peter, 184–6; *Back from the Brink*, 185
Australia: exploration, 67, 68; geological and climatic overview, 17–18, 20; (environmental) impact of European settlement, 18, 27, 60, 104, 134, 144–5; population growth and the environment, vii, 13, 18, 19, 20, 21, 87, 98, 180, 182; *see also* industry; pastoralism and agriculture
Australia Institute, 4
Australian Fisheries Management Authority, 110

Ban Ki-moon, 92
Bill and Ben (TV program), 60
biodiversity: Convention on Biodiversity, 154; and disease, 77, 79; and fire, 150; 'hotspots', 79, 82, 97–8, 148; impact of weeds and feral animals, 64; and land clearing, 22, 30–31; and protection, 101, 102, 117, 138, 165, 182, 186, 201
Brabben, Hilda, 60
Brown, Bob, 162
Burke, Robert O'Hara, 67

Campbell, Ian, 127
capitalist economy: impact of environmental damage, 138–9; placing a value on environmental 'products', 138, 139
climate change, 1, 91, 176; and environmental impact, vii, 12, 90–1, 94, 97, 101, 102, 109, 120, 168, 182, 187; and fossil-fuel consumption, 21, 90; impact on species, 9, 16, 48, 81, 89, 92–8, 100, 102, 154;

responses to, 90, 92, 102, 201; *see also* drought
conservation organisations, 1, 8, 102, 161, 170, 176–8; Australian Conservation Foundation, 21, 176, 197; Australian Koala Foundation, 188; Australian Network of Environmental Defenders Offices (ANEDO), 5, 6; Australian Wildlife Conservancy, 162, 163; Birds Australia, 49, 50, 51; Bush Heritage Australia, 162, 163, 164, 177; educational role, 163–4; expectations of, 179–80; Fitzgerald Biosphere Group, 164; Greening Australia, 164; Greenpeace, 176; Humane Society International (HSI), 5, 110, 177; The Nature Conservancy (USA), 164, 165; New South Wales Nature Conservation Council, 150; Pew Foundation (USA), 165; relations with government and industry, 176, 178–9, 181, 188–90, 199; Trust for Nature, 159, 160, 161, 177; (Tasmanian) Wilderness Society, 41, 105, 164, 176; WWF-Australia, 5, 20, 33, 114, 159, 176, 178, 181, 191; *see also* environmental campaigns
conservation and politics, 27, 71, 80, 105–6, 118, 127, 128, 129, 136, 141–2, 143, 145, 177, 180, 195; Australian Labor Party, 170; and challenges to decisions, 110; Hawke government, 106; Howard government, 1–2, 4, 5, 107, 117, 118–19, 165; Liberal Party, 15; political will and resources, 109, 112, 113, 116–17, 119, 123, 140, 143, 147, 149, 165–6, 168–9, 181, 201; and public opinion,